# The American Father Onscreen

The American father is constantly depicted by contemporary Hollywood as being under pressure and forever struggling, but why? By utilising an analytical psychological approach, this fascinating book reveals the depths, complexities and nuances of the depictions of the American father and his struggles with contemporary contextual challenges and offers a fresh and intellectually exciting set of perspectives and interpretations of this key masculine figure and his effect on cinematic masculinities.

Using a post-Jungian methodology and close textual analysis, the book seeks to explore the presence and impact of the American filmic father, and the effect his Shadow has on himself, his children and US society. It does this by examining the concept of 'father hunger', a term popularised by the mytho-poetic men's movement that holds fathers to be an essential link to the masculine continuum and masculinity in general. Analysing the role that Hollywood plays in depicting fathers and their relationships with their children and American society, *The American Father Onscreen* concludes that Hollywood presents the American paternal as crucial to the construction of US society and, consequently, American cultural myths, such as the American Dream.

Providing an alternative perspective into the fascinating, complex and under-researched figure of the American father, this book will be of great interest to academics and students of film, gender studies, American studies and post-Jungian psychology.

**Toby Reynolds** is an independent scholar working in the fields of post-Jungian cultural perspectives, film theory, gender studies and cult cinema. He is also a curator and podcaster and has a preference for vintage leather jackets.

# The American Father Onscreen

A Post-Jungian Perspective

Toby Reynolds

LONDON AND NEW YORK

First published 2022
by Routledge
2 Park Square, Milton Park, Abingdon, Oxon OX14 4RN

and by Routledge
605 Third Avenue, New York, NY 10158

*Routledge is an imprint of the Taylor & Francis Group, an informa business*

© 2022 Toby Reynolds

The right of Toby Reynolds to be identified as author of this work has been asserted in accordance with sections 77 and 78 of the Copyright, Designs and Patents Act 1988.

All rights reserved. No part of this book may be reprinted or reproduced or utilised in any form or by any electronic, mechanical, or other means, now known or hereafter invented, including photocopying and recording, or in any information storage or retrieval system, without permission in writing from the publishers.

*Trademark notice*: Product or corporate names may be trademarks or registered trademarks, and are used only for identification and explanation without intent to infringe.

*British Library Cataloguing-in-Publication Data*
A catalogue record for this book is available from the British Library

*Library of Congress Cataloging-in-Publication Data*
Names: Reynolds, Toby, author.
Title: The American father onscreen : a post-Jungian perspective / Toby Reynolds.
Description: New York, NY : Routledge, 2022. | Includes bibliographical references and index. | Summary: "Analysing the role that Hollywood plays in depicting fathers and their relationships with their children and American society, the American Father Onscreen concludes that Hollywood presents the American paternal as crucial to the construction of US society and consequently, American cultural myths, such as the American Dream"— Provided by publisher.
Identifiers: LCCN 2021041210 | ISBN 9780367189891 (paperback) | ISBN 9780367189884 (hardback) | ISBN 9780429199684 (ebook)
Subjects: LCSH: Fathers—United States—Psychology. | Fatherhood in motion pictures—United States.
Classification: LCC HQ756 .R479 2022 | DDC 306.874/20973—dc23
LC record available at https://lccn.loc.gov/2021041210

ISBN: 978-0-367-18988-4 (hbk)
ISBN: 978-0-367-18989-1 (pbk)
ISBN: 978-0-429-19968-4 (ebk)

DOI: 10.4324/9780429199684

Typeset in Times New Roman
by Apex CoVantage, LLC

# Contents

    Introduction – The American father on film: shadows
    and symbols         1

1   The American father and his contexts         7

2   Archetypes, symbols, cultural myths and cultural
     Shadows: psychological approaches to the screen         27

3   The father: shadows of the American Dream         59

4   The Child – living under the Shadow of the American Dream         102

    Conclusion – the future of the father         153

    *Filmography*         160
    *Bibliography*         163
    *Index*         173

# Introduction – The American father on film
## Shadows and symbols

Within contemporary Hollywood cinema, the visual, narrative and thematic articulation of fatherhood appears to have undergone a quiet revolution (Douglas and Michaels, 2004), with Bruzzi identifying that the cinematic father had been previously treated '"a bit like air" – omnipresent but rarely talked about' (2005, xi). It is now arguable that we are confronted at many turns with multiple images of the father and, concomitantly, of what has been termed 'father hunger',[1] contradicting the past perception of the father as a largely one-dimensional and under-analysed presence within films that involved masculinities. This development is arguably indicative of both cultural and artistic shifts that correspond to the perceived pluralisation of masculinities that is continuing within cinema. As Hamad states: 'Fatherhood has become the dominant paradigm of masculinity across the spectrum of mainstream U.S. cinema' (2014, p. 1). I will be arguing both that this foregrounding of the father and father hunger demonstrates the symbolic cultural importance of this hitherto under-analysed polysemous masculine presence and that it reflects how the figure of the father can be analysed in terms of the mediation of cinematic gender imagery. For example, the figure of Jack Horner (Burt Reynolds) in Paul Thomas Anderson's *Boogie Nights* (1997) highlights the complexity of these mediations of fatherhood and father hunger through an ambiguous representation of the father acting as both a benevolent and caring surrogate paternal whilst simultaneously sexually exploiting masculinities and femininities.

Before these arguments are engaged with more fully, however, there is a need to explore and outline the cinematic and cultural contexts and discourses in which the analyses take place and the theoretical perspectives and methodologies that I will be employing. I will be using two main theories, namely gender theory (in particular theories of masculinity) and post-Jungian theory as it relates to cinema and screen studies, combined with a methodology of textual analysis informed by post-Jungian paradigms and sensibilities.

## The post-war paternal

From post-war depictions of father-troubled teens (e.g. *Rebel Without a Cause*, Ray, 1955) to the fraught relationships with the paternal in the self-consciously

DOI: 10.4324/9780429199684-1

quirky and visually complex films of Wes Anderson (e.g. *The Royal Tenenbaums*, 2001), the presence of the father and examples of father hunger can be found throughout classical, post-classical and contemporary Hollywood (both mainstream and 'Indiewood') cinema. The hitherto largely unremarked-upon ubiquity and accompanying polyvalent nature of the cinematic paternal is strongly indicative of the importance of this key masculine figure. When we consider what men's movement writers (Bly, 1990; Biddulph, 1995; et al) term the 'masculine continuum', the father can be argued to represent the continuation of masculinity by virtue of his importance to both the son and daughter from a developmental perspective in terms of functioning both as a masculine progenitor and as an initiator of masculinity. Before we explore in more detail what this figure represents, we first need to contextualise any paternal analyses within the larger array of filmic gender discourses.

In terms of cinematic gender discourses, academic understanding of masculinity within film has been steadily moving from a largely binary understanding from the 1970s and 1980s (Mulvey, 1975, 1989; Neale, 1983) to a generally agreed-upon pluralisation of gender (Cohan and Hark, 1993) whereby, for the purposes of the thesis, 'masculinity' as a term has been supplanted by the more accurate plural 'masculinities'. This recognition of gender pluralism also coincided with broader cultural shifts in gender relations, namely, a declared crisis in masculinity,[2] held to be brought about by the triple impact of feminism, civil rights and gay liberation. Peberdy argues that 'it is impossible to deny the instability of the male image evident in the overwhelming permeation of a discourse of masculinity crisis during the 1990s and 2000s' (2011, p. 7). These shifts challenged notions of traditional societal gender norms with corresponding cultural imagery reflecting these undercurrents: 'The power of such images should not be underrated: the image of a 'true' gender is omnipotent. . . . Images of masculinity that go against the norm thus become all the more intriguing' (ibid, p. 28).

Reflecting the growing interest in this gender field, RW Connell (1995) formulated the key phrases 'hegemonic masculinities' and 'patriarchal dividends', explicit recognition of the pluralisation of male gender, and their concomitant rewards, with other theorists developing the idea to a point where there was a recognition that there were both supra-hegemonic and sub-hegemonic masculinities (Fouz-Hernandez, 2009, pp. 59–62). Fatherhood can therefore be said to both function and be performed (Butler, 1990; Pomerance and Gateward, 2005) in both spheres of this gender hegemony, with cinematic imagery reflecting these performances. Linking this with the men's movement theories of the critical central role that the father performs within the masculine continuum and cinema can be seen as accurately divining cultural perspectives in gender relationships. The mytho-poetic men's movement also supported the idea of a crisis in masculinity but held that father hunger was both a symptom and a cause of the crisis, with the perceived lack of father figures available to modern men causing masculinity itself to falter and fail. Consequently, the paternal has had attention focused upon it as both the cause of and solution to the crisis in masculinity, with both conservative (Blankenhorn, 1995) and progressive (Biddulph, 1995) elements identifying it as a key figure in the construction of masculinities. It would, therefore, be logical to focus upon and analyse the paternal as an originator of and contributor to masculinities. Having identified the importance of the father within cinema, it would now be prudent to explore why a particular psychological methodology and theoretical perspective was chosen with which to analyse representations of the father.

A post-Jungian methodology was selected primarily for an alternative psychological perspective on cinematic narratives, gender and the role of the auteur. Whilst film theory has traditionally, and successfully, utilised both psychoanalysis and cognitive theory to map out the psychological landscape of film phenomenology and provided valuable psychological insight into both film narratives and apparatus, there remains a danger in mistaking them for the only psychological approaches to cinema. A post-Jungian theoretical perspective (in the sense of theory developing after Jung's death in 1961, as well as classical Jungian concepts) includes both a revisionist slant on his main theories as well as outlining and exploring the central theoretical tenets of his work. Key to this set of what can more accurately be described as sensitivities (Bassil-Morozow and Hockley, 2017) is the importance that Jung assigned to the power of the image in terms of it engaging with the psyche and with the wider culture. Bassil-Morozow and Hockley argue: 'In Jungian theory the image exists somewhere in the space between the unconscious and consciousness' (ibid, p. 124), effectively existing simultaneously in a liminal and subliminal capacity. This emphasis on the prevalence, potency and importance of the image, and its consistent presence, both within (the spectator) and without (society), makes a post-Jungian methodology and theories highly attractive for analyses of visual cultural products such as cinema, as well as television and other digital media. However, this approach is not without its disadvantages:

> A Jungian-informed approach to cinema does not offer a prescription. Nor is it a set of tools for analysis. Rather, it is a set of sensitivities that offers a different framework within that which to go about the work of understanding how it is that meaning is made in, by and, crucially, with media artefacts.
> (ibid, p. 12)

Post-Jungian writers (Fredericksen, 1979; Izod, 2001, 2006) warn that in analysing cinematic symbols, a reductive approach (similar to psychoanalytical methodologies) can encourage ossification of meaning when analysing the text: 'Fredericksen also warns Jungian film studies against becoming a reductive approach only interested in decoding archetypal structures and individuation patterns instead of regarding moving images from a variety of perspectives' (ibid, p. 16). Or, to be more concise, 'Put simply, the meaning of an image is not fixed' (ibid, p. 7). Jung himself described the symbol as a 'corpus et anima' or body with spirit, something that resists easy categorisation.

In addition to rethinking the symbolic and imagistic approach to cinema, there are also other advantages. In terms of post-modernist theory and the collapse of totalising theories, a post-Jungian approach has the advantage of reacquainting the reader with a more open-ended interpretation of the symbol, thereby potentially enhancing interpretations of art, cinematic or otherwise (Potash, 2015, p. 145). This foregrounding and re-examination of the symbol and the archetype within visual cultural products are linked in with wider cultural and socio-political debates. Bassil-Morozow and Hockley identified Jung's claim that 'the psyche of the individual is inseparable from the psyche of his or her society, and that the process of individuation and spiritual progress are only as successful as society allows them to be' (2017, p. 17). This awareness and identification of what has been termed by post-Jungians as the *cultural complex* (Singer and Kimbles, 2004) also make post-Jungian thinking attractive when it comes to analysis of cinema and its effects on society, as well as reflecting societal issues. The gender issues described previously can therefore be analysed from a different aspect and potentially new interpretations considered, at both the individual level and the societal level. In addition to this, there is a need to distinguish between the universal father and the American father, given that metaphors of personal processes within individuation are inflected by specific cultural contexts, in this case, American cultural complexes such as the so-called American Dream with its emphasis on material success and social mobility (Winn, 2007, pp. 6–7).

Moving the focus to gender, we need to consider that Jung and post-Jungian theory also proposes that the psyche is archetypally bisexual (Izod, 2001; Singh, 2009). If we accept this, then there is scope to generate polysemous gender perspectives and their subsequent filmic representations. Susan Rowland reminds us that:

> Jung regarded psychic energy as essentially neutral and hence not privileging one gender. Where Freud (and Lacan after him) considers the Oedipus myth to possess an originating role in the structuring of the psyche, Jung makes room for many potential myths of being. Some of them can even emphasise the feminine!
>
> (Hauke and Hockley, 2011, pp. 148–149)

This recognition of the fluid nature of gender representation also enables a new perspective and approach to the producers of images, namely authors of films, whoever or whomever they are held to be.

In terms of more general post-Jungian gender theories, Tacey (1997) argues that both the political (pro-feminist) men's movement and the mytho-poetic (spiritual) men's movement have positive aspects to their differing ideologies, but that conversely, there is also a Shadow side to them. Identifying the tendency for reactive retrogression in many of the mytho-poetic writings of Bly (1990), Tacey argues that mytho-poetic writers are archetypally father-dominated. He conversely identifies the pro-feminist men's movement as archetypally mother-fixated and advocates a more balanced approach to analyses of masculinities. Related to this, other post-Jungian writers (Izod, 2001; Singh, 2009) have argued for recognition of both the anima and animus in both male and female psyches which allows for greater flexibility when analysing gender dynamics. As Tacey puts it: 'If we take away the patriarchal encrustations from around Jung's ideas, the androgynous and compensatory model of the psyche is still useful' (1997, p. 31). As ever with any theory, there are caveats to be aware of. When using post-Jungian theories, there also needs to be a recognition of what Charles identifies as the: 'conservatism inherent to the symbolism at the heart of Jung's psychological theory' (2013, p. 133). A man simultaneously both of his time and ahead of it, Jung, with his Jungian theory, has also faced accusations of dogma, sexism and racism, much of which has to do with overly rigid interpretations of archetypal theory, both by him and by others (Noll, 1994, 1997; Samuels, 1993). Nevertheless, as a set of theories and as a methodology, a post-Jungian approach has much to recommend and contains the potential for new perspectives on both cinema and gender.

The book is divided into four main chapters, each examining a facet of the paternal presence in American film and society. The first two chapters analyse the psychological, gender and cultural contexts of American culture as they pertain to the father, and especially his central role in the fulfilment of the American Dream, a cultural myth that resonates across American society and is open to critique and analysis. These chapters also act as an introduction to post-Jungian concepts and ideas to readers unfamiliar to these perspectives and outlines how we can view the paternal through a post-Jungian lens and perspective, which reveals a fresh series of aspects to this most important of archetypes. The third and fourth chapters analyse the figure of the father and the child in contemporary American cinema by virtue of close textual analysis of various films, both mainstream Hollywood (*Catch Me If You Can*, Spielberg, 2002) and so-called 'Indiewood' (*There Will Be Blood*, Anderson, 2007), a range of films that demonstrate the widespread presence of the paternal and his relationships with his issue across American cinema. Films were chosen as the main cultural and media text as cinema is one of the most consistent and revealing of mediums when it comes to acting as a cultural barometer. This is also reflected in television, with the father's presence within American television programming very similar to cinema and even mimics the struggle and engagement with the American Dream (e.g. *The Sopranos*, Chase, 1999–2007) to a large degree. The aesthetic and visual invention of cinema is not easily replicated, but at the time of writing, television and particularly so-called high-quality programming found on the emerging streaming sites (Netflix, Amazon, Hulu, etc.) are quickly catching up and in some cases expertly mimicking cinematic visual qualities and techniques (e.g. *Fargo,* Hawley, 2014–2020). Consequently, there is a strong case for a further analysis of television with regard to the presence of the father (e.g. *Sons of Anarchy*, Sutter, 2008–2014), but due to lack of space and a number of fundamental differences in television media theories, this will have to be for future research. Finally, the conclusion analyses where we are with the father within American culture and how the American Dream cultural complex both has been shaped by and still shapes the paternal archetype, with speculation as to the future cultural trajectory of this key psychological, societal and cultural presence.

## Notes

1  The term 'father hunger' was popularised by the mytho-poetic men's movement writer and poet Robert Bly in his 1990 book *Iron John*. Before this wider use, the term, and variations of it, had been used in psychological circles for a number of years including the classical post-Jungian writer Anthony Stevens (1994) and the psychoanalyst and psychoanalytical writer James Herzog (1983).
2  This was held to occur in the late 1980s and early 1990s and was perceived as a reactionary phenomenon to a number of gender challenges (Faludi, 1991, 2000, amongst other writers).

Chapter 1

# The American father and his contexts

At the risk of stating the obvious, the father has been a constant presence within cinema, yet curiously overlooked, with Stella Bruzzi highlighting this somewhat odd omission in her seminal discussion of the paternal *Bringing up Daddy* in which she identified that the cinematic father had been previously treated '"a bit like air" – omnipresent but rarely talked about' (2005, xi). From the brutal Battling Burrows (Donald Crisp) in D.W. Griffiths' *Broken Blossoms* (1919, USA) to the struggling Lester Burnham (Kevin Spacey) in *American Beauty* (Mendes, 1999, USA), the American father, in particular, has been a vital, yet under-discussed, onscreen presence. By exposing him and his presence within American society, along with his accompanying cultural myths, most importantly his place within the American Dream, we can provide important context to this figure and its impact on filmic discourses. This chapter, due to reasons of brevity and necessity, paints a broad picture in terms of reviewing the father. In particular, there is a vast, complex and ever-increasing body of work on film gender alone, with Kord and Krimmer accurately summarising this situation: 'Reading the vast literature on the subject is like walking into a hall of funhouse mirrors' (2011, p. 37). Given this situation, the chapter is structured around the father being contextualised within film studies, gender studies, and cultural studies, before we move on to analysing the paternal's presence from a post-Jungian perspective within cultural myths such as the American Dream in the next chapter.

## Masculinity and cinema

In terms of both film and cultural studies, what started to emerge from gender discourses around masculinity and men in cinema in the early 1990s was the key idea of pluralised masculinities that were to be located within cultural texts such as film. Since Mulvey's seminal work on gendering the male gaze and female subjectivity in her landmark 1975 essay 'Visual Pleasure and Narrative Cinema', the assumptions around masculinity was that of a monolithic cultural construct that was premised on the goal of patriarchal dominance of woman. Employing Freudian and Lacanian theories to support her critique of patriarchy within cinema, Mulvey sketched what Dix calls 'a pessimistic, even morbid account of

DOI: 10.4324/9780429199684-2

the female spectator's place as it is constructed by mainstream narrative' (2008, p. 234). Whilst invaluable in drawing critical attention to masculinity, and the undeniable power of the gaze, it was uncomfortably close to gender essentialism for many critics (Stacey, 1994; Peberdy, 2011), promoting, again in Dix's words 'a depressingly binary system' (ibid), with masculinity, and indeed femininity, still being identified as singular. Stacey echoes this, commenting how:

> Psychoanalytic theories of identification used within film criticism have led to very narrow conceptualisations of cinematic identification, which have ignored the broader meanings of spectator/star relations and indeed have led to some overly pessimistic conclusions about the pleasures of cinema.
>
> (Singh, 2009, p. 125)

Bruzzi concurs:

> For all its brilliance, *Visual Pleasure* has not only opened doors, but closed them, too . . . the overwhelming attraction of Mulvey's schema has, in turn, closed down alternative ways of interpreting gender operations in mainstream, principally Hollywood films.
>
> (2013, p. 7)

Continuing in a similar vein in the early 1980s, Steve Neale's 1983 essay 'Masculinity as Spectacle' applied psychoanalytical theories and continued the work that Mulvey started, with specific reference to men, rather than just women, being cast as an onscreen spectacle. It differed, however, with the influence of Ellis's work in *Visible Fictions* (1982), around the plurality of representations of men and masculinities. Whilst a useful and timely contribution to the debate, the psychoanalytical model it used was still subject to the restrictions inherent in a reductionist psychological paradigm. The emerging debates around masculinity were increasingly predicated on the growing realisation that there was now a plurality of cinematic masculinities that was on offer. This recognition of diverse male and female spectators, along with their corresponding diverse cultural, social and political perspectives, culminated in Cohen and Hark's seminal collection of critical writings: *Screening the Male: Exploring Masculinities in Hollywood Cinema*. Identifying the traditional view of onscreen manliness as an 'unperturbed monolithic masculinity produced by a de-contextualised psychoanalysis' (1993, p. 3), they provided a persuasive deconstruction of masculinity as cultural performances, performances that were subject to a spectrum of influences and discourses. *Screening the Male* was followed by Kirkham and Thumim's complementary collections of essays on masculinities, *You Tarzan* and *Me Jane*, (1993), both of which also addressed masculinities from a number of viewpoints (including psychoanalytical), although mainly from a cultural studies perspective. These two early collections provided inspiration for a rapidly increasing number of perspectives on masculinity and film, and as such, provided the basis for theories around masculinity being a wholly plural construct, firmly foregrounding these theories within debates on cinematic masculinities.

In addition to, and supporting the overall sense of, the debate widening, Kirkham and Thumim identified the following areas as being of primary concern with regard to depictions of masculinity, namely: the body, action, the external world and the internal world. These were, they argued, the main sites where male strengths, weaknesses, anxieties, pleasures, and pain reside:

> It is these sites that various traits of masculinity are signalled; these may be qualities either asserted or assumed in the construction and development of masculine characters, or they may be signifiers of themes quite consciously concerned with an interrogation of masculinity.
>
> (ibid, p. 11)

For example, Tasker's dissection of the first two *Die Hard* films in the long running franchise (McTiernan and Harlin, 1988–2013), in her in-depth study of male action films *Spectacular Bodies* (1993), makes a point around the transposition of male anxiety and the body:

> Anxieties to do with difference and sexuality increasingly seem to be worked out over the body of the hero. The male body (usually replete with muscles) is an arena where by contemporary anxieties are played out on screen.
>
> (ibid, p. 236)

This broad demarcation of where masculinities are enacted and played out within cultural products was a major step forward in establishing studies of masculinities and gender within film studies. Another noteworthy development within the literature was the emergence and adoption of the performative theories of gender theorists, such as Judith Butler (1990, 2004), RW Connell (1987, 1995, 2005) and, within film studies, (Pomerance, 2001; Pomerance and Gateward, 2005) amongst many others. Many of these essays and works argued persuasively that masculinity (also gender as a whole) is a performance, a masquerade, 'dramaturgical' in that it is, in effect, an exhibition for audiences and spectators that both reinforces and subverts cultural norms and discourses. Butler, quoted in Peberdy, stated that gender performances are 'ideological, created and fuelled by public and social discourse in order to normalise what is conceived to be 'masculine' and 'feminine'' (2011, p. 27). As such, filmic performances and onscreen representations therefore echo cultural and gender performances. This theory will be discussed further and in greater detail later on.

So far in this section, plurality still remains the over-arching concept when considering a cultural studies approach to masculinity and gender; the past idea of an essentialist single masculinity is expressly exposed as simplistic and restrictive when considering the polysemous cinematic depictions of masculinity. Simultaneously, there were a number of other aspects of filmic masculinities that were being explored. Masculine aspects of national cinema were starting to be analysed with French males and Gallic masculinity under scrutiny (Powrie, 1997), alongside later examples such as Russia (Goscilo and Hashamova, 2010) and Italy (Rigoletto, 2014; O'Rawe, 2014; Bini, 2015). Inspired by the development of the four main areas defined by Kirkham and Thumim, writers such as Holmlund (2001), Lehman (2001, 2007) and Fouz-Hernandez (2013) focused attention upon cinematic representations of the male body. There were also in-depth dissections and analyses of masculine representations within cultural, historical and social discourses (Cohan, 1997; Davies and Smith, 1998; Yates, 2007; Combe and Boyle, 2013), alongside overviews and analyses of males and masculinity within film and actorly performance (Bingham, 1994; Peberdy, 2011) and more generalised summaries and explorations of men and film (Baker, 2006, 2016; Benshoff and Griffin, 2003; Chopra-Gant, 2005; Gronstad, 2008; Burrill, 2014). Discussions of men within genre films (Grant, 2010) were joined by more specific inquiries, with horror (Greven, 2013, 2017) and war (Morag, 2009) being some of the genres under scrutiny. In terms of families and anxieties around the masculine, Harwood (1997) and Tincknell (1997) identified changing and responsive cinematic representations of the family under pressure; fathers being seen as still playing a key role within this social structure, albeit as figures also under a number of pressures. Filmic representations of the crisis in masculinity also came under questioning with Walsh (2010) and Fradley (2013) providing dissenting perspectives and trenchant critiques of this phenomenon. This recognition of the crisis that masculinity was facing in the late 1980s and early 1990s is echoed and explored further by, amongst others, Kord and Krimmer. They state:

> Upon entering the realm of cultural representation, a social diagnosis-the crisis in masculinity-metamorphoses into a crisis of *fatherhood*. In this new guise, it is propelled to prominence by a plethora of scholarly works, social movements, and cultural narratives, Hollywood cinema being amongst the most conspicuous among them.
>
> (2011, p. 37)

With these metamorphoses of crises in masculinity transforming into crises of fatherhood in mind, we are able to now turn to the main focus of this section of the chapter, that is to say, the mapping of the cultural discourses that deal directly with representations of fathers and fatherhood within film.

## Fathers in film

Film studies had a noticeable lack of emphasis on representations of the paternal figure until just before the millennium. This absence of discussion was reflected in the literature around the father and film. Susan Jeffords cogently analysed the depictions of father figures within *Terminator 2* (Cameron, 1991) in *Screening the Male* (1993), arguing that fatherhood within the 'new masculinity' is depicted as being a construct that 'transcends racial and class difference, but that the vehicle for that transformation is fathering, the link for men to 'discover' their new 'internalized' selves' (p. 254). This argument strongly echoes Robert Bly in that the paternal is the location of masculine self-discovery. Andy Medhurst provided a provocative analysis of the melodrama *The Spanish Gardener* (Leacock, 1956) within *You Tarzan* (Kirkham and Thumim, 1993), hinting strongly at a transgressive sexual aspect to the paternal relationships portrayed within, a point echoed by Bruzzi later. Fathers and fatherhood are either discussed in passing in (mainly) Freudian terms or present largely by their absence. It is not until Peter Lehman's *Masculinity: Bodies, Movies, Culture* (2001) that fathers and fatherhood receive more substantial attention in writings on men in cinema, although this is also treated as supplemental, rather than as a subject worthy of study in its own right. Beynon (*Masculinities and Culture*) also addresses the subject of fathers when he analyses them in his sub-chapter entitled 'Men Running Wild' (2002, p. 128). He quotes from Susan Faludi's seminal study of American men *Stiffed* (2000) when he outlines what Bly (1990) terms 'father hunger', around the situation 'having a father was supposed to mean "having an older man show you how the world worked and how to find your place in it"' (p. 130). This position of defining masculinity as a gender continuum will be analysed and argued for, albeit one that is inflected and shaped by both internal and external forces.

Bly and fatherhood are also mentioned in depth by Trice and Holland (2001) in *Heroes, Anti-heroes and Dolts*, an incisive analysis of portrayals of masculinity that manages to both celebrate and critique representations of the wide range of masculinities on offer in the twentieth century. The year 2004 saw the release of the collection *The Trouble with Men*, edited by Powrie, Davies and Babington that devoted a section purely to representation of fathers. The academic interest in fatherhood and film continued to gather pace, culminating in 2005 with Stella Bruzzi's *Bringing Up Daddy: Fatherhood and Masculinity in Post-War Hollywood*. This key text provided a trenchant and wide-ranging analysis and critique of the father figure in film as portrayed by Hollywood from World War II to the 1990s. Utilising a range of theoretical bases including psychoanalysis, gender studies and sociology, Bruzzi highlighted the range of onscreen fathers on offer within each decade and how they contextually related to the cultural battles being fought off-screen. While Bruzzi's work is invaluable in analysing the father figure and fatherhood, there is still heavy emphasis on the psychoanalytical psychological perspective, although there is occasional use of Jungian terms and concepts, albeit still in the minority, along with a brief mention of Robert Bly. Gerstner (2006) discusses at length early examples of cinematic masculinity in *Manly Arts* and in 2008, Reiter in *Fathers and Sons in Cinema* analysed father-son relationships using a Jungian framework, focusing upon what he terms 'filmmyths', and used Bly as a reference around the danger to men of experiencing father hunger, in particular using Alexander Mitscherlich's point about the hollow space left by an absent paternal as being filled by demons.

At the same time, Nicola Rehling's *Extra-Ordinary Men* (2009) manages to both use Bly when referencing the masculine wound, a key men's movement and Jungian concept, and critique his more controversial ideas, particularly around the role of male victimhood. Likewise, Peberdy analysed depictions and performances of males and masculine angst in *Masculinity and Film Performance* (2011). She also provides a critical discussion of Bly and *Iron John* that touches upon both fathers and the Wild Man, another key concept within men's movement gender theory. In 2011, Kord and Krimmer's *Contemporary Hollywood Masculinities* brought a focus on a number of filmic representations of men and masculinities. Similar to Bruzzi, Hamad delineates fatherhood as being a means to resolve masculine anxieties in her 2014 *Postfeminism and Paternity in Contemporary U.S. Film: Framing Fatherhood*. Also recently, *Millennial Masculinity*, edited by Timothy Shary in 2013, gathered together a collection of writings on a number of key areas of interest to the filmic masculine, namely representations of gay men, fathers, the 'man-child', and racial questions around men within film. Shary also summarises the ongoing attraction and academic necessity of analysing cinematic masculinities:

> Given the escalating developments within the gendered milieu of men in U.S. culture as well as the ongoing evolution of male roles (domestic, professional, performative) and the concerns that these vicissitudes presented to the patriarchal norm, a logical opportunity to re-examine masculinity at the turn of the millennium arises, especially since the positive advances in women's authority and men's humility over the past few decades have not created true gender equality. The comprehensive themes of cinema and its dependence on audience appeal to achieve success make movies the ideal medium through which we can better understand how men in contemporary culture have been changing and how our perceptions of men continue to change as well.
>
> (p. 4)

Bruzzi also returned to masculinity and cinema in 2013 with *Men's Cinema*, a study and exploration of masculine tropes and use of mise-en-scene within men's cinema (including mentions of fathers), along with a timely exploration of how men's cinema can be an *affective* experience as well as a cerebral or intellectual one. This question of affectivity is a potentially interesting area for further research; however, it will not, due to issues of space, feature within this book, although there is certainly scope for more research on this subject.

## Fatherhood as performance

The academic contexts established, we can now turn towards exploring what can be described as the performative paternal. Echoed by Kirkham and Thumim's arguments around masculinity being a plural construct (1993), the argument is that masculinity is a performance, a masquerade, 'dramaturgical' in that it is, in effect, an exhibition for audiences and spectators that can both reinforce and subvert cultural norms and discourses. For the purposes of the book, the question of gender, and more specifically, masculinity, is also a question of performance. Whilst there is much to be gained around Butlerian ideas of masquerade and dramaturgical performance, they can run the risk of becoming problematic when dismissing any identity or agency behind expressions of gender, very much like auteur theories that dismiss the idea of agency. Therefore, if Butler's metaphor of gender as a performance is to be continued, it can be posited that performances are invariably based on *something*, the gender vacuum that Butler seems to be asserting not necessarily being true. This effectively runs counter to Butler's assertion, quoted in Peberdy, that 'the notion of a true or original gender is a myth or "imitation without an origin"' (2011, p. 32). When it is considered that any dramaturgical performance, such as film or theatre for example, is invariably based on some memory or imaginative construct (an actor's performance will be informed by internal and external factors), Butler's argument becomes effectively untenable, especially when applied to gender, given its personal, biological, social and cultural factors. Advancing this argument further and assuming gender *is* a performance, it is a performance that is nuanced, influenced and shaped by a large number of factors including, but not restricted to, biology (Segal, 1990, p. 67), psychology, family dynamics, social forces, cultural pressures and political power structures.

Furthermore, and echoing a post-Jungian perspective, it can further be argued that gender can be both an *unconscious* and *conscious* performance (using these terms within a post-Jungian context) with regard to the individual psyche. An unconscious gender performance, for example, would be replaying or performing a gender role according to societal and personal factors, regardless of the consequences. A conscious gender performance, by contrast, would be a performance that is informed, but not dominated or dictated, by the performer's cultural and personal factors and one that is conscious of the consequences of the performances. In addition to this, it is arguable that archetypes and archetypal images can and do inform gender performances in both unconscious and conscious ways. When the collective and cultural unconscious is also factored in, gender performance in effect transforms into a complex and rewarding phenomenon for analysis. This multiplicity of influences would go some way to explain why there is such a pluralistic, diverse and complex range of masculinities that is reflected within cinema and why there is such a correspondingly diverse range of spectator and audience reactions to individual filmic texts.

Having established masculine performances as a fundamental part of cinematic masculinities, we can now focus on what has been said about the specific cinematic masculine performance that is of interest here: the father. The definition of the father as an essential link within the masculine continuum, albeit a continuum that is inflected and shaped by both internal and external forces, is a persuasive one and one that has strong echoes of Bly and other men's movement writers, both mytho-poetic and pro-feminist, with Chopra-Gant identifying 'the intergenerational reproduction of patriarchy' (2005, p. 144) via the father. It can therefore be posited that fatherhood is a site that constellates many differing discourses, both masculine and feminine, and as such needs to be considered in light of these. Hamad's definition of fatherhood is a salient one:

> a universalizing discourse of masculinity (notwithstanding the variety of modes through which it is articulated), with a high degree of cultural purchase that enables hegemonic commonality across a plurality of postfeminist masculinities.
>
> (2014, p. 1)

Yet fatherhood is, at the same time, often far from a means to resolve masculine anxieties; rather, it is, more often than not, depicted as an often unstable construct and one that is under pressure from a variety of different fronts. In other words, fatherhood can be part of the problem (or at least depicted as one) within the construction of masculinities, as well as being depicted as a solution. Leading on from this identification of fatherhood as multi-faceted and problematic is the desire for fatherhood, both *to be a* father and *for a* father: father hunger.

## Father hunger and film

In her analysis of the traditional Hollywood view of father-son films, Bruzzi summarises it thus: 'Over the decades, recurrent motifs and tendencies have emerged. Father-son movies vastly outnumber father-daughter movies and it is usually through a turbulent relationship with his son that a father's role is scrutinised' (2005, xv). In other words, it is the initial conflict between a father and his son that provides the narrative drive and sets up the subsequent portrayal and exploration of masculinity. Whilst dramas are routinely narratively driven by conflict of some kind, the assumption of the inevitability of paternal conflict is an interesting supposition (and one of the key theoretical ideas underpinning Freudian thought). It is, however, an assumption that leads to an important question regarding gender construction, namely: why does masculinity have to be born out of difficulty and, in particular, be born out of *conflict* with the father? An answer that appears to be favoured by classical Jungians such as Stevens (1994)[1] and the majority of mythopoetic men's movement writers (Biddulph, 1995, 1997; Lee, 1991; Bly, 1990; et al) is that a male (due to profound biological differences) has to make the journey to separate initially from his mother and bond with the father. Whilst the father bonding is held to be of crucial importance (the lack of which being identified by the aforementioned men's movement writers as the source of 'father hunger'), the son also has to make the final journey to mature masculinity and, in effect, outgrow and transcend his father (whether surrogate or biological). This effort for the son to, using the Jungian term, individuate seems to always involve an archetypal conflict with the father; by fighting the father (physically, emotionally or mentally), the son separates and moves away from both the paternal protection and the paternal Shadow. The son becomes a mature man, effectively, by dint of a conflicted separation. Peberdy comments on this at some length in relation to Bly's interpretation:

> For Bly, fatherhood is a central masculine signifier that has been usurped by the mother figure in the contemporary period. Bly repeatedly returns to this idea of father lack or loss as a significant explanation for the softening of men. The father or father figure, as Bly's pseudo-Freudian reading suggests is central to the process of initiating boys into manhood thus the rejection of the mother is a necessary step in reclaiming masculinity.
>
> (2011, 100)

This assertion of the usurpation of contemporary fatherhood by the mother within the male psyche is understandable but at the same time questionable when we consider the supposed masculine journey that males take, according to the previous argument. Rather than the mother usurping the father, males are seemingly stuck under the mother's influence to a degree past a normative developmental stage, in part due to the *absence* of the paternal. Rejecting the mother is not the same as transcending the mother, just as the father is also transcended, rather than destroyed, if we accept the assumed post-Jungian teleological psychic journey. This is fundamentally different to the Freudian infantile Oedipal dynamic, where the father is to be overcome in a struggle to possess the mother. The paternal is viewed by classic psychoanalysis as largely hostile and inimical to the child, rather than part of the child's individuative journey that is to be joined with, transcended and absorbed into the psyche. This alternative to classic psychoanalytical theory is attractive, in that it allows for much greater flexibility when examining cultural products from a psychological perspective.

Related to this is the foregrounding of the father at the expense of the feminine presence. As Hamad points out, the marginalisation (or removal) of motherhood allows the father to be foregrounded (2014, pp. 18–19). In particular, she highlights the role of the widowed father as a figure of 'an entrenched, culturally apposite and affectively charged paradigm of masculinity, whose appeals to empathy and victim status negotiate the attendant marginalisation of mothers germane to his narratives and to postfeminist culture' (ibid, p. 21). This father-widower status also has an added melancholic narrative effect, making the narrative conflict potentially all the more poignant due to the missing feminine. She goes on to link this to the location of the paternal within historical settings, 'Fatherhood is dualistically configured to signify ideals of both the past and present' (ibid, p. 28). Kord and Krimmer largely agree:

> As the last of the he-men around, the father is an ideal vehicle for national myths. Hollywood films strictly distinguish between "actual" fathers, who are often diminished or inept, and symbolic fathers, who start out that way

but in the end represent the unassailable ideal. As a national symbol, only the awesome primal father will do.

(2011, p. 52)

Michael Sullivan (Tom Hanks) in *Road to Perdition* is a prime example of this foregrounded melancholic father as a national symbol. The act of being widowed both acts as a catalyst to him in his relationship with his oldest son and sets him on a deadly road of retributive violence against his surrogate father, Irish Mob boss John Rooney (Paul Newman). The power of 'the awesome primal father' is unleashed in his quest for justice and redemption, his last act of violence in killing the assassin Maguire (Jude Law), an act intended to stop his son (Tyler Hoechlin) from committing murder. With regard to the masculine psychological journey, both Hollywood and Freud (for the most part) recognise the first stage that is outlined earlier but perhaps only partially recognise the need for the son to separate from the father and, in effect, outgrow or transcend his father. Freud's pioneering psychoanalytical work partially recognised this journey in his writings on the primal father and the Oedipus complex, but, as hinted at earlier, arguably became overly mired in the struggle with infantile sexuality and possessing the mother. For its part, Hollywood follows the Freudian arc but often leaves the story only partially complete with the son occasionally reconciled with the father, but not always transcending him. As Bruzzi argues at length, this is more often than not indicative of a basic confusion about the father's role in film:

[T]here remains a fundamental ambivalence towards what to do with the authoritarian, traditional father. Much of 1990s' Hollywood dispenses with him, but ultimately it seems to protest that the traditional father is what we want. Contemporary American cinema acknowledges the validity of alternative parental models, nevertheless it still feels – often quite urgently – the lack of a strong, conventional father. This conservatism continues to manifest itself in films as diverse as *Far From Heaven, Catch Me If you Can* and *Road To Perdition* (all 2002), all of which bind the father's failure to their unconventionality.

(2005, p. 191)

Contextually, Peberdy expands this argument further and outlines the need to provide a wider arena for the paternal to be performed:

1990s fatherhood is arguable even more of a performance; without breadwinning to define his masculinity and identity as a father, he must confirm his fatherhood and masculinity in other ways. The implication is that with contemporary changes to the family structure, it has become increasingly necessary to devise new cultural scripts for fatherhood and to redefine the parameters of masculinity.

(2011, p. 128)

This perceived and portrayed need for a conventional/unconventional father, and the corresponding new cultural scripts, and how he is both the cause and source of father hunger is strongly indicative of new attitudes towards both the father and his role, and an explicit recognition of multiple masculinities that are available. Hollywood, for the most part, recognises and depicts father hunger but, due to its deeply ambivalent attitude towards the paternal, does not always resolve it fully. This shortfall in understanding is also indicative of deeper cultural complexes around the father, which are discussed in more depth later.

## Men, society, politics and gender studies

The arena of gender studies is where the mytho-poetic (or 'spiritual') men's movement can be found. By necessity, the overall context has to be broad in range when being discussed due to the previously mentioned vast literature on the subject. What can be affirmed is that the men's movement first became visible with early writers such as Herb Goldberg (1977, 1991, and 2007) being inspired by the rapidly burgeoning women's movement into re-thinking traditional gender roles for men. This included the role (or lack) of fathers, with Gloria Steinem quoted in 1970 in the *Washington Post*: 'The truth is that most American children seem to be suffering from too much mother and too little father' (Hamad, 2014, p. 8). This perceived lack of father presence gathered pace throughout the 1970s and involved other writers such as Warren Farrell (1974, 1986, 1993, 2001), who attempted to highlight the negative gender roles and performances that men were also often held to be socially conditioned into enacting. As the 1980s progressed, various differentiated strains of the men's movement began to emerge, eventually coalescing into two main strands.[2] These were the pro-feminist, academic and socio-political men's movement, and the mytho-poetic, or 'spiritual' men's movement, the most famous exponent being the poet and cultural commentator, Robert Bly.

## Bly and the mytho-poetic movement

Based on a decade of seminars that he led involving story-telling sessions using myths and fairy tales,[3] Bly published his seminal text *Iron John* (1990) and popularised the term 'father hunger' although this phrase had been used previously to his work by Herzog (1980) in a clinical journal, and later was the title of a collection of clinical cases (1983). Variants of this term were commonly in use (the post-Jungian writer Anthony Stevens uses the term 'parent hunger' in print in 1994) in other settings, both clinically and culturally, and in all likelihood the term was not particularly new. The publication of *Iron John* also coincided with (indeed, was inspired by) the widening and gradual perception that there was, within the Western world at least, a burgeoning social, cultural, sociological and political crisis within masculinity in the late 1980s and early 1990s. Numerous writers and commentators, both academic and non-academic (Modleski, 1991; Horrocks,

1994; Connell, 1995; Faludi, 1991, 2000; Robinson, 2000 to name but a very few) broadly agreed that there was, at the very least, a *perceived* crisis within masculinity[4] itself (although there was passionate debate as to how real this crisis was), brought about largely by the triple impact upon masculinities of civil rights, feminism and gay liberation. These three social and cultural movements were held to put normative notions of masculinity and masculine gender performance under pressure, in terms of how men and their behaviour were perceived and, perhaps more importantly, how men perceived themselves and their behaviour.

Bly's answer to this crisis in masculinity (of which he held that father hunger in both men and women was the strongest symptom) was, unsurprisingly, more father. However, he held that father hunger in both men and women was for the missing (and idealised) *caring* masculine, a masculine energy that was (like idealised notions of feminine energy) also nurturing, protective, initiating and safe. By utilising Jungian, Freudian and mythic theories, Bly succeeded in challenging and provoking the debate around gender and masculinity, an approach that is not unproblematic, to put it mildly, given the subsequent critiques and rejections of his work as cloaked essentialism that sought a return to patriarchal dominance (Bruzzi, 2005; Rehling, 2009; Peberdy, 2011, amongst others). Picking up on this criticism, Bly cannot be construed or treated as a separate theorist in his own right partly due to his over-reliance and arguably mis-interpretation of existing and past theories. The post-Jungian writers Andrew Samuels (1993, p. 184) and David Tacey (1997) both recognise that Bly, in Tacey's incisive quote:

> has a habit of being half right and three quarters wrong. He correctly identifies a real and pressing problem of the time, and then puts forward a 'solution' that is wildly reactionary and not of the time.
>
> (p. 92)

Both writers subject Bly[5] and the mytho-poetic men's movement to sustained criticism of their positions, more detailed analysis of which will be in the next chapter. In academic film circles Bruzzi, in particular, analyses Bly incisively (2005, pp. 139–141) arguing both the strengths and weaknesses of his perspective and over-emphasis on the father. Conversely, many readings of Bly often manage to ignore much of his work when using mytho-poetic theories in critical dissections (Hall, 2005, pp. 43–52). As mentioned previously, both Peberdy (2011) and Rehling (2009) have critiqued Bly's writing, although their examples of his supposed misogyny leave out large parts of his work that contradict many of their arguments, particularly around discussion of the Fifties Man and the concept of the Wild Man (Peberdy, 2011).[6] Bly's work, as well as the phrase 'father hunger', is a large part of the contextual analysis for the book, mainly for the alternative nature of the text; with its questioning regarding existing masculinities, both 'soft' and 'hard', and its strong emphasis on the importance of the father, as both a real and symbolic figure to the construction of masculine gender performance.

Turning attention to wider effects of *Iron John*, one of the main effects was the placing of the father at the centre of debates around masculinities. Post-*Iron John*, as it were, a huge number of Bly and Jung-influenced texts, both academic and non-academic, were released throughout the decade (publishers quickly realising the potential profits to be made out of gender studies[7]) that focused attention on father hunger and healing the 'father wound' amongst men and women. Amongst these writers were Lee, 1991; Corneau, 1991; Moore and Gillette, 1990, 1992; Keen, 1991; Pittman, 1994; Schwalbe, 1996; Van Leeuwen et al., 2003, etc. Many of these writers (although not all) produced work that was, in effect, male pain confessionals. This tendency towards masochistic male soul-baring was critiqued by Tacey:

> [T]hese authors have decided that they will write from the gut and their emotions, and will not bother about 'head stuff' concerning feminism, rupture, history, alienation. In writing from the gut, we get blasted with an emotional longing that is alarmingly primal, fierce and unschooled.
>
> (1997, p. 54)

Whilst these confessionals highlight long repressed and unexpressed masculine emotional longing and pain, they are, as Tacey accurately points out, often unbalanced in their focus on the subjective and the personal, effectively deliberately ignoring historical gender contexts. However, not all writing on masculinities at the time indulged in this. Biddulph (1995, 1997, 2013), Clare (2000), Shwalb et al., 2012, and Seidler (1989, 1997, 2005) – amongst others – sought to maintain a more balanced view of where masculinity was located in various cultural, psychological and sociological contexts. Jungian and post-Jungian inspired writings will be analysed further on in this chapter, but suffice to say, many established Jungians and post-Jungians scholars (Samuels, 1993; Tacey, 1997, and others) were correctly suspicious of this sudden archetypally informed output. Another, more problematic from some perspectives, aspect of the literature was the emergence of a quasi-regressive style of cultural commentary (e.g. Thomas, 1993; Moir and Moir, 1998), where men were increasingly viewing themselves as victims, paradoxically both of patriarchy, and of feminism in the broader sense. Counter to these perspectives, and holding largely oppositional views, were the socio-political men's movement, the aims and origins of which will now be explored.

## Socio-political men's studies

Beginning initially as a companion movement to second-wave feminism (Goldberg, 1977; Farrell, 1974) in the 1970s, the socio-political men's movement was inspired by feminist thought and sought to apply similar theories to society in order to effect change in attitudes towards gender biases within culture and society, this time with men changing men. Largely based in academia, and generally left-wing in its sociological approach, by the time of *Iron John*'s publication, the socio-political men's movement had developed into a wide-ranging set of beliefs, ranging from more moderate voices (Seidler, 1989, 1997, 2005; Chapman and Rutherford, 1987) through to more uncompromising perspectives (Connell, 1987, 1995; Mac an Ghaill, 1994; Pfeil, 1997; Kimmel, 1995, 2000, 2009, 2015). Arguing in the main that patriarchy and patriarchal social structures needed to be destroyed, they tended to dominate academic discourses and attacked writers such as Bly (Samuels, 1993, p. 184), whom they viewed (not without good reason) as essentialist, retrogressive and neo-patriarchal. Connell (2005), for example, correctly identifies the mytho-poetic men's movement as a form of protest masculinity, and also, more importantly, identified the concepts of 'hegemonic masculinity' and the 'patriarchal dividend', concepts that were, perhaps, conveniently overlooked by mytho-poetic men's movement writers. However, there were also problems inherent in their own positions that were either overlooked or ignored. In *Remaking Men* (1997), David Tacey warned against the dangers of solely adopting a socio-political men's movement perspective towards questions of masculinity:

> Progressive discourses must oppose the father but not kill him, and they must 'shrink the phallus' but not mutilate it. If our radical activity gets caught in the killing and mutilating mode, society will not move forward at all, because we become paralysed by negative archetypal forces.
>
> (p. 51)

He went on: 'Despite the idealism of political rebels, the dissolution of patriarchy will not bring on a new golden age, but will necessarily leave many men in an emotional and psychological quandary' (ibid, p. 52). In case Tacey is perceived as being biased towards the 'spiritual'/mytho-poetic men's movement, he poses these questions around their beliefs:

> What about the deathly and demonic face of the patriarchy? What about the feminine zeitgeist? What about the urgent need for a new, post-patriarchal consciousness? All too often the spiritual movement ends up in conservative politics, a more reactionary set of attitudes, and a restoration of 1950s values.
>
> (ibid, p. 54)

This explicit recognition by both Tacey and Samuels (1993) of both the shortcomings and strengths of both strands of men's movement is indicative of an attempt to strike a more balanced approach to perspectives around masculinity, something that this book will attempt to emulate. Writing about the future of masculine gender discourses, Tacey states: 'We have still to discover a public men's movement that honours both styles at once, that has the guts to oppose and the courage to embrace' (ibid, p. 47).

## Social sciences and masculinity

Turning attention initially to the anthropological view of fathers and fatherhood, there are (like gender studies) a large number of other voices on this subject. For the purposes of the thesis, the work of anthropologist and theorist David Gilmore (1991) around masculinity and fathers is a useful entry point. He proposed that there are two major areas that need to be explored. First, the role that men, and especially fathers, were expected to perform. He summarised three areas where men were expected to perform adequately, namely as an impregnator of women, as a provider, and finally as a protector. He goes on to advocate that men are nurturers but in a different way to women:

> Men nurture their society by shedding their blood, their sweat, and themselves, by bringing home food for both child and mother, by producing children and by dying if necessary in faraway places to provide a safe haven for their people. This, too, is nurturing.
> (Beynon, 2002, p. 63)

Fathers, at least competent and successful ones (if permitted to use the normative definition of competency and success), are therefore primarily nurturers, protectors and progenitors of life, themes that are also reflected within Bly and post-Bly writers. Gilmore goes on, '[T]he manhood ideal . . . is not simply a reflection of individual psychology, but part of public culture, a collective representation' (ibid, p. 64). This is an important point to consider, namely that while the psychological approach to analysing masculinities is a useful tool, the wider contextual situation cannot be ignored and, indeed, is a vital component when considering any debate. Beynon (ibid, p. 62) also sounds a note of caution into the debate on fathers and fatherhood around unconsciously adopting an ethnocentrist viewpoint, namely viewing Western (British and American) masculinity and masculine discourses from a Western (British and American) perspective. Beynon highlights the restrictions that we can unwittingly place on analysing masculinities, with a tendency to regard our own culture as normative: 'It is all too easily assumed that contemporary western masculinity is the universal norm' (ibid). For the purposes of the book, the texts under analysis are (mainly) located in contemporary American social and cultural settings, and so it assumed that contemporary Western masculinity *is* the normative context in this case, especially when considering the films under analysis and the cultural myth of the American Dream.

The second major anthropological aspect that is of interest here is the question and depiction of the recognised rite of passage of *initiation*, both personal and social, that is addressed within anthropological and post-Jungian perspectives. Due to (again) the vastness and complexity of this area of scholarship, the book will be mainly focused on the Jungian and post-Jungian perspectives on initiation. Jung wrote widely on the archetypal initiatory drive, but post-Jungian discussions of this area (certainly as it relates to film) are conspicuous by their absence. Discussion as this initiatory drive relates to film (both as a practice and as a depiction), therefore, is limited and a potentially exciting new area of debate albeit due to reasons of brevity, the book will only be dealing with this area briefly. The argument, linked in to the earlier position of masculinity as a mediated continuum, is that just as there is successful initiation into childhood to adulthood, there is also both misinitiation (a failure for whatever reason to complete the journey into the adult world) and disinitiation (a deliberate abuse of initiation for other purposes, usually to do power and manipulation). Furthermore, within the films that will be discussed later, *The Master* (Anderson, 2012) is a text that has both misinitiation and disinitiation as a key symbolic ritual at its heart. This culturally and societally endorsed passage into adulthood, whether negative or positive, is a reminder of the power of culture in that anthropologically, culture also has a key role in reinforcing social norms and mores; any images that are presented in a film are also mediated by the culture.

## Society and politics

Linked in with anthropology are the sociological and political perspectives on masculinity, an area that has drawn an increasingly large amount of attention through the 1990s and 2000s. Connell (1995) introduced the influential term 'hegemonic masculinity' that was picked up and developed further by, amongst others, Kimmel (2000, 2009). Beynon's *Masculinities and Culture* (2002), nuanced by what Dix calls 'a politically more alert vocabulary' (p. 241), explored the debate further. Beynon reminds us that:

> Masculinity is always interpolated by cultural, historical and geographical location and in our time the combined influence of feminism and the gay movement has exploded the concept of a uniform masculinity and even sexuality is no longer held to be fixed or innate.
>
> (p. 1)

He goes on to argue for an awareness of how hegemonic masculinity develops and which is itself defined by various 'subordinate variants'. As Dix puts it: 'Various screen masculinities may themselves contribute either to the reinforcement of culturally dominant models of how to be and look a man, or to their critique and subversion' (2008, p. 241). Beynon also sounds a note of caution when discussing men and masculinities, using the work of Kenneth Clatterbaugh and his term 'adjectival masculinities' (2002, p. 23) to describe specific masculine communities based around race, class and sexuality. Arguing that 'there are no ready criteria that allow me to identify masculinities . . . it may be the best kept secret of the literature on masculinity that we have an extremely ill-defined idea of what we are talking about' (1998, p. 27). Clatterbaugh rightly warns of tendencies of viewing masculinities as self-contained and autonomous, prompting Beynon to ask the interesting question: Are masculinities the same as varieties of masculinity? He takes this argument further when he draws a distinction between discussing males and male behaviour, and male images and masculine discourses. Whilst in some ways intellectually exciting, the debates around masculinity were in danger of perhaps becoming too dense and convoluted, leading to at times an overwhelming sense of complexity.

Elsewhere in the theoretical landscape, Lupton and Barclay (1997), Burgess (1997) Hobson (2002), Gavanas (2004), Dermott (2008) and Featherstone (2009) all contributed critical perspectives around the figure and social position of the father, both symbolic and actual. What emerged was the theme of masculinities and fathering as being a gendered political discourse that is essentially shaped by society, unsurprisingly given that sociology is, by its nature as an academic discipline focused on the external social forces that influence individuals. Hobson, in particular, argues, not without some veracity, that fatherhood is a familial discourse that is virtually wholly shaped by external pressures. Whilst it would be disingenuous to deny the existence and power of external social factors upon individuals and the roles that they are expected to play within society, it would be equally disingenuous to deny that internal psychological drives also play a key role within the construction of fathering discourses and families, hence the focus of the thesis on the psychological approach. Society, after all, is made up of individuals, who often have diverse and contestatory agendas within the realms of family, and so would resist or even subvert hegemonic models (Connell, 1995) of fatherhood imposed from society. Individuals are also either consciously or unconsciously resisting or embracing their own experiences of fathering, whether positive or negative, or more realistically a mixture of both kinds of experience. What was agreed upon from the plurality of sociological perspectives is that fatherhood has undergone a fundamental shift from a broadly agreed-upon post-war model to a pluralist model, prompted in part, at least, by the forces of feminism, civil rights and gay liberation (as outlined in the earlier section), a move reflected in the perception of masculinity itself and outlined by Chapman and Rutherford (1987). What is also evident is that fatherhood has been 'rediscovered' as a source of masculine power, or at the very least, presented as such, mediated by the changes wrought by feminism in terms of division of labour, both inside and outside the home. What else is worthy of attention is that the increasing involvement of fathers within the family is reported as being demonstrably beneficial, on both a familial and societal level (Blankenhorn, 1995; Burgess, 1997).

Coupled with this resurgence of interest around the figure of the father as a possible re-discovered 'solution' to many of society's ills, however, is also what Jungians would term the Shadow side of this social and political discourse. Gavanas (Hobson, 2002) has identified masculinities as becoming, in effect, domesticated to other forces. At the same time that paternal discourses are moving into a plural set of models, fatherhood and the father figure have been increasingly appropriated by right-wing and reactionary political ideologies, arguably leading to a resurgence of patriarchal power and social hegemony, or so many feminist theorists believe. Bly's work has also been appropriated by right-wing discourses to provide psychological and mythic 'proof' of the essentialist nature of masculinity being naturally dominant, a position that is at odds with many of his arguments, and all the more ironic, given Bly's steadfast opposition to right-wing policies, particularly around economics and aggressive foreign policies.[8] One example of the appropriation of masculinity – as-neopatriarchy is the phenomenon of the Promise Keepers – a right-wing Christian social movement whose tenets are in line with born-again evangelical views on gender relations, namely the male is the leader and head of the house in all matters. On the surface, this movement appears to be a prime example of Faludi's (1991) backlash, with men seeking to reinstate patriarchal dominance over social territory contested by feminism. Yet when Faludi interviewed a number of Promise Keepers in her later work *Stiffed* (2000), she found a wide range of views about their role as men, and, somewhat surprisingly, an overwhelming and deep confusion around what promises they were supposed to keep. Many saw their role as protectors, providers and what was termed *servant-leaders* to their families. It appeared that patriarchal dominance was not necessarily on the agenda for many of these men. Conversely, there were many Promise Keepers that welcomed the confirmation of their place as a dominating patriarch, most notably the founder of the movement, Bill McCartney. Hobson (2002) also found this divergence of views within the ranks, leading to the conclusion that as with any large social movement, pluralities within its ranks were almost inevitably guaranteed.

Relating this back to masculinities and film, the sociological and political impacts of masculinity and fatherhood are resonant within the texts studied, containing as they do, many examples of sociological discourses around fatherhood. It appears that the psychic resonance of the father archetype is being felt at a wider societal level, not surprising when we consider that this particular archetype is one of the most fundamental within the individual psyche. The father existing as what has been termed by post-Jungians as a cultural complex will be explored in the next chapter; the paternal social discourse can be argued to be felt at all levels of society and can be analysed accordingly.

Contemporising the debate, there has been a visible return and re-focus on the father, and on men and masculinity within the mainstream media in recent years. For example, the *Observer* newspaper published a Father special edition of its *Woman* magazine on 25 October 2009 covering, amongst other topics, how fatherhood supposedly came of age, gay dads and an alternative fertility guru. The *Independent on Sunday* newspaper ran a double-page spread entitled 'The Changing Face of Fatherhood on 17 June 2012, the *Guardian Weekend* ran an article on single fathers by choice on 2 November 2013, with *The Times* dedicating its magazine as 'The Men's Issue' on 30 November 2013. More recently was the *Observer Magazine* on 1 March 2015 entitled 'How to be a man in 2015'. On 8 May 2016, the *Sunday Times* carried an article entitled how to be a modern caveman, which echoed a number of masculine anxieties and concerns in terms of practical competencies and other gender performance issues. In recent popular culture, the artist Grayson Perry published *The Descent of Man* in 2016 that dealt with his own masculine journey and, by proxy, modern masculinity. In 2017, the actor and comedian Robert Webb published a childhood memoir *How Not to Be a Boy* that dealt with contemporary childhood and fatherhood issues. In the same year, comedian Chris Hemmings, published *Be a Man*, which questioned contemporary 'macho' cultures and discourses, and Jack Urwin wrote *Man Up*, which discussed the same discourses echoed by previous authors. It appears, judging by recent media, political and sociological discourses, that fatherhood and fathers are here to stay, men and masculinities being of seemingly perennial cultural concern.

To conclude this section, the sheer number of voices around the debate on masculinity and male gender performance can be overwhelming. Such deafening volumes of discourse inevitably generates paradoxical positions, contradictions and confusion. However, what can be stated is that the crisis in masculinity is largely held to be still continuing, but, paradoxically, it can also be viewed as an opportunity, in that patriarchy and patriarchal institutions have been, and continue to be, under pressure to change. Accordingly, I will be arguing that patriarchy and its products are inimical to men as well as women (albeit for different reasons), a view that Bly and many other men's movement writers (Goldberg, 1974; Keen, 1991; Biddulph, 1995, 1997; Magnuson, 2007) concur with. It will also be posited that patriarchy is but one aspect of masculinity, albeit an aspect that has dominated both masculine discourses and culture to detrimental effects for both women and men. With the main gender and film discourses discussed and their impacts analysed, we now turn to a deeper exploration of Jungian and post-Jungian concepts and theories, and how they relate to film and screen texts.

## Notes

1 Andrew Samuels is a notable exception to more classical Jungian thinkers in terms of his pioneering work on fathers and the archetype of the father (1985, 1989 and 1993). As referred to earlier, his definition of the paternal is a markedly more flexible definition than some other Jungian writers, including Stevens.
2 Samuels (1993, p. 181) claims that there were four main groups – experiential, socio-political, mytho-poetic and gay men's movement. Tacey (1997, p. x) puts the figure as high a dozen differentiated male movements.
3 The cultural, political and sociological context of fairy tales is comprehensively critiqued by Zipes (1979).
4 There is a tendency by some writers to put the phrase 'crisis in masculinity' in quote marks. It is my assertion that this subtle grammar action can have the effect of reducing the importance of this phenomenon. The book will therefore not be using quote marks for this phrase, any more than it would use the same grammar action for the word 'backlash'.
5 Bly produced other work, such as *The Sibling Society* (1996) and, *The Maiden King: The Reunion of Masculine and Feminine* (1998). The former text was a polemic about the immaturity of society, and the latter was an attempt to reconcile and transcend the traditional binary view of gender by using another Grimms fairy tale, this time analysed with the help of Marion Woodman, a Jungian analyst. Both works were nowhere

near as impactful as *Iron John*, reflected in diminished sales and subsequent cultural ignorance of their ideas.
6   These critiques are understandable, but, when compared to Bly's actual work, appear to be contrary to what is actually written, given what he states in the preface of *Iron John*: '[T]his book does not seek to turn men against women, nor to return men to the domineering mode that has led to repression of women and their values for centuries' (1990, viii–ix). He goes on further:

> The dark side of men is clear. Their mad exploitation of earth resources, devaluation and humiliation of women, and obsession with tribal warfare are undeniable. Genetic inheritance contributes to their obsessions, but also culture and environment (ibid).

7   *Iron John* had sold over half a million copies by the early part of the 1990s (Samuels, 1993 p. 184).
8   Bly first came to public attention in the 1960s as a vocal and outspoken critic of the Vietnam War and later denounced the first Gulf War in similar terms (Smith, 1992).

Chapter 2

# Archetypes, symbols, cultural myths and cultural Shadows

Psychological approaches to the screen

> *'The Jung no longer believe in the Freud!'*
> 
> attributed to Sandor Ferenczi

Having explored the cultural and academic landscape around the American father, we now turn our attention to cinema and psychology. When psychological approaches to screen studies, including film, are examined more closely, we discover that a recurrent theme within studies on masculinity and cinema has been the two-pronged nature of psychological debates within cinema and television. If we are to judge by the psychologically inflected readings encountered within the broad general scope of screen studies, and film in particular, it would fair to assume that psychological interpretations and theoretical discourses either fall under the auspices of cognitive theory, championed and developed by, amongst others, Bordwell (1989), Currie (1995) and Buckland (2000), or are usually psychoanalytical (Freudian or Lacanian) in perspective. Essentially, for the majority of the time that screen studies has been considered a serious academic discipline, readers and students are restricted to two models of psychological interpretation,[1] the first of which, cognitivism, we shall turn to first.

With cognitive film theory, theorists such as Currie and Bordwell sought to bypass both psychoanalysis and filmolinguistic theory (e.g. Metz), rejecting such approaches as essentially untestable and unverifiable, therefore unscientific. As Stam puts it: 'Cognitivism looks for more precise alternative answers to questions raised differently about film reception by semiotics and psychoanalytic theory' (2000, p. 235). This theoretical approach dealt with film features such as narrative (Bordwell, 1985, 1989) and affect (Grodal, 1999, 2009), arguing for a: 'stance which "seeks to understand human thought, emotion and action by appeal to processes of mental representation, naturalistic processes, and (some sense of) rational agency"' (Bordwell and Carroll, 1996, p. xvi) (ibid, p. 236). Cognitivism favoured an emphasis on what Bordwell termed 'contingent universals' (ibid, 236) that were to be found in all humans (hard-wired cognitive and physiological systems). Compared to psychoanalytical approaches, cognitivism had an appeal

DOI: 10.4324/9780429199684-3

in terms of a concrete, 'provable' theoretical basis, but, as Stam summarises it, a less appealing aspect in that:

> Cognitive theory allows little room for the politics of location or for the socially shaped investments, ideologies, narcissisms, and desires of the spectator, all of which seem too irrational and messy for the theory to deal with.
> (ibid, 241)

Compared to psychoanalysis and *analytical psychology* (Jungian and post-Jungian approaches), with their foregrounding of theories concerned with the messily irrational and unconscious psyche, cognitivist approaches treated aspects of film theory more as pragmatic problem solving, conveniently leaving out important questions around the personal, the contradictory, the subjective and the emotional.

For insights into these, less quantifiable, areas of film theory, a psychoanalysis approach was, more often than not utilised, one of the benchmark texts in the 1970s being Mulvey's classic essay 'Visual Pleasures and Narrative Cinema' (1975) mentioned previously. As the decade progressed, an intimidatingly large and complex body of theory emerged, using both Freudian and Lacanian concepts (Lacan's concept of the psyche operating as a language neatly complementing the semiotic approach). However, psychoanalytical discourses threatened to dominate psychological approaches to film, with little room for competing or dissenting theoretical frameworks. Criticisms of the psychoanalytical approach to gender, for example, include the not unreasonable accusation that it is essentially a patriarchal and phallocentric approach that seeks to pathologise the psyche, focusing as it does on issues such as sadism, masochism, castration, fetishes and voyeurism. While it is undeniable that cinema does contain these themes, it would be a mistake to view this as all encompassing. The dogmatic psychoanalytical insistence around the supposed universality of the Oedipus complex (itself based on a male child's supposed development, biased against by its nature, female child development) is one example of psychoanalytical reductionism and pushes any debates around gender towards more rigidly essentialist thinking, something that is inappropriate when the performative and fluid aspects of gender are considered. Added to this, the contextual considerations that should be applied to psychoanalytical approaches, both Freudian and Jungian, and any psychological perspectives on the screen would appear to need a certain dose of healthy scepticism in terms of theoretical considerations.

## Jungian and post-Jungian concepts

Whilst unarguably of enormous value in terms of analysing screen texts, psychoanalytical and cognitive film theories have often been perceived or at least presented as the *only* psychological approaches to film, an emphasis that has often marginalised analytical psychological approaches. These approaches have not been considered, until relatively recently, as an appropriate psychological lens with which to analyse film. As Bassil-Morozow states: 'Jung had been an unwelcome name at film and media conferences, short of unmentionable. Seen as conservative, apolitical, antiscientific, bizarre and obscure, Jungian theory has been ignored by cultural studies for decades' (2015, p. 132). It must be noted at this point that post-Jungian tools are similar to psychoanalytical tools, in that they cannot be taken as absolutes. Similar to biology, psychological methodologies work best when interpreted as *tendencies*, rather than prescriptive diktats. Hockley quotes Terrie Waddell to this effect:

> The body of work left to us by Jung . . . might be better understood as a 'tool' that we can use to help us with meaning. In the academic world, the ideas of theorists are rarely taken to be absolutes.
>
> (2007, p. 7)

Setting aside, then, the regrettably often hostile differences between Jungian and Freudian adherents (dogma not being restricted to only Freudians), Jungian and post-Jungian film theory can be said to posit a number of new concepts and tools with which to interpret cinema and the screen as both a cultural text and a cultural process and practice. With analytical psychology, there is a marked difference in approach to the structure of the psyche from a psychoanalytical perspective. Jung was primarily concerned with the individual's psychic[2] approach to, and interaction with, his/her environment and culture, and how this impacted on the teleological[3] psychic journey towards what Jung termed 'individuation', or, to put it more simplistically, a state of self-conscious, aware wholeness.[4] Compared to the broadly reductionist psychoanalytical model of a psyche consistently seeking to reconcile and/or repress conflicting tensions and drives based wholly around sex and death (materialistic and mechanistic forces), there is an immediate and fundamental shift in emphasis on how psychic forces operate both within the individual and in the wider society. This is not to deny that Jungian and post-Jungian theory is unproblematic. Bassil-Morozow and Hockley highlight the potential problems around using an analytical psychological approach to screen studies:

> Jungian film theory seems diffuse and unfocused – a miasma that floats alongside the more concrete and structural presence of psychoanalysis. It is enormously difficult to get any purchase on the subject and the answer to the dreadfully penetrating and simple question: 'what *is* Jungian screen theory?'
>
> (2017, p. 2)

They argue that Jungian screen studies should be viewed as 'a school of thought rather than a diffused set of ideas' (ibid). Whilst some Jungians (and indeed post-Jungians) have also exhibited tendencies towards dogmatic insistence upon their particular creed, they may well have missed a crucial point of Jung's philosophy, which is to be the individual that you are born to be (Waddell, 2006), namely a conscious and fully balanced whole, which may well run counter to following any dogma or belief system too rigidly. This insistence upon individuality, individuation[5] and the uniqueness of the individual psyche runs counter to many of Freud's assumptions about the mind. Consequently, this individualistic approach is attractive in film analysis terms, in that it begins to explain the widely differing impact that cinema can, for example, have on individual spectators viewing the same film, rather than forcing the contents of texts and the cultural, industrial and social contexts that produce them into potentially restrictive theoretical frameworks. Another example is the role that symbolism plays within Jungian and post-Jungian writings, with the symbol being a signpost, rather than a symptom, of the state of the psyche. This issue will be explored later in more depth, challenging the Freudian view of symbols as essentially reductive phenomena that seek to obscure, rather than clarify psychic communications.

Similarly, a post-Jungian methodology and perspective is valuable when we consider the role of onscreen gender, as covered by the last chapter. By employing Jungian and post-Jungian film theories, new gender perspectives on masculinities and fatherhood in cinema begin to emerge. Linked in with this is Jung's treatment of the arts as a general area of psychological interest. Jung utilised many aspects of the arts when describing and illustrating his theories, although this was limited in the main to classical forms of art (painting, poetry, music), and, indeed, often citing classical motifs, myths and legends (Greek and Roman mythologies being especially favoured). In *Modern Man in Search of a Soul*, Jung also divided art and artistic creations into what he termed *psychological* art and *visionary* art. He gives vivid descriptions of both:

> Whatever its particular form may be, the psychological work of art always takes its materials from the vast realm of conscious human experience-from the vivid foreground of life we might say. I have called this mode of artistic creation psychological because in its activity it nowhere transcends the bounds of psychological intelligibility.
>
> (1933, p. 159)

Similarly, he then goes onto define visionary art in his usual colourful style:

> It is a strange something that derives its existence from the hinterland of man's mind-that suggests the abyss of time separating us from pre-human ages, or evokes a super-human world of contrasting light and darkness. It is a primordial experience which surpasses man's understanding, and to which he is therefore in danger of succumbing.
>
> (ibid, p. 160)

These two distinct terms can be used when analysing the various chosen films; indeed, in a general sense, a number of films can be accurately described as being both visionary and psychological. A note of caution needs to be sounded, however, due to any misapprehensions that films are in any way binary in terms of this dichotomy.[6] Realistically, most films will be comprised of psychological elements, but this does not preclude them from having some visionary elements; similarly, many visionary films have a strong psychological component to them. In a more generalised context, there have been a number of critical evaluations around Jungian and post-Jungian perspectives on art and culture from, amongst others, Charles (2013), Colman (2017), Gardner (2015), Hauke (2000, 2005, 2014), Homans (1979), Potash (2015) and Rowland (2008, 2013). Charles, for example, identifies Jung and his psychology, particularly around symbolism, as being innately conservative:

> Whilst some post-Jungians have associated Jung's concept of the symbol with a post-modern critique of modernity, such a move risks deflating the historical, material and metaphysical dimensions necessary to engage critically with the conservatism inherent to Jung's account of symbolic 'conjuration'.
> (2013, p. 120)

Gardner agrees and adds that:

> Art that seemed fragmented or overly sophisticated or modernist, which demands intellectual combined with aesthetic appreciation, was not compatible to Jung's theories, and so he did not find them appealing.
> (2013, p. 256)

This said, Jungian and post-Jungian critical theories have at their heart capacity to accommodate contradiction, ambiguity and ambivalence within art forms and artistic phenomena; a valuable feature when analysing cinema. As Bassil-Morozow and Hockley state:

> The Jungian approach to images and films in particular, seeks to preserve such unstable and shifting qualities – it is polysemic in orientation and regards meaning as a process in which the film itself, its viewers and film theorists are together engaged in a hermeneutic activity through which meaning is constellated and brought into being.
> (2017, p. 7)

Taking these perspectives into account, we can now examine how some of Jung's main theories and concepts can be applied to cinema and the screen.

## The importance of the image

Jung's foregrounding within his psychology of the importance of the *image* has to be of interest to any student of cinema, one of the most powerful generators of communicative symbols, with Jung emphasising on how important this was and still is 'image alone is the immediate object of knowledge' (1967, CW7, para 201). Bassil-Morozow and Hockley outline two fundamental questions in the Jungian approach to films: where is the image, and where is the meaning? They state: 'Ostensibly both (image and meaning) reside on the screen, yet the interplay of the unconscious with a film results in the creation of a new image' (2017, p. 75). This said, however: 'The film's imagery belongs to its internal world, while the reception of the film gives the film a life off screen created by the life of the viewer' (ibid). Where Jung differs from Freud is his emphasis on the image as a vital clue as to the psyche's attempts at psychic rebalancing via structural mechanisms (persona, personal unconscious, etc.) rather than Freud's insistence of images and symbols as being essentially deceptive phenomena whose purpose it is to mask the repressed desires that live in the unconscious. Analysing the matter of *archetypal images*, we can immediately see the appeal of post-Jungian theories to cinema theorists, dealing as they do, with an art form that consists of a constant stream of signs, symbols and (potentially) archetypal images. With the Jungian model of the unconscious consisting largely of archetypes, the potential application of this theory to the generation of art is described well by Oliver Davis:

> Whereas the Lacanian unconscious is composed of potentially word-forming linguistic structures, the Jungian (collective) unconscious is made up of structures with a potential for image formation. According to Jung, it is the presence of images formed by these "archetypes", or "archetypal patterns" that characterizes the true work of art.
>
> (Baumlin et al., 2004, pp. 66–67)

These are reductive words, assuming that 'true' works of art by this measure must contain archetypes. If we are to follow this argument through, there is an implication that works of art that do not contain archetypal images are somehow 'false'. Perhaps a better term to use here is to *succeed* (a definition of successful art being its ability to engage with the viewer, reader, or, in these post-modern times, consumer). By this measure, art that does succeed must contain archetypal images. Assuming this to be true, what are archetypal images, and how do they relate to cinema, the most visual of artistic mediums? Moreover, what is their purpose in being placed in art? A shallow reading of Jung in relation to cinema seems to be content to identify characters as being archetypal and largely content to leave it there (Iaccino, 1994, 1998). Which begs the question: so what? What value is there knowing that, using *Star Wars* (Lucas, 1977, USA) as an example, Obi Wan Kenobi is the archetypal image of a Wise Old Man? Or that Luke Skywalker is the archetypal image of a callow Youthful Hero? Whilst we can congratulate ourselves for having applied and identified Jungian archetypes within a filmic text, the role and purpose that archetypal images play is not explored nor explained using this reading. As mentioned previously, Fredericksen identifies this archetype-spotting as 'archetypal literalism' (Hauke and Hockley, 2011, p. 102). Whilst it functions as a diverting psychological parlour game of sorts, this kind of reading does not advance post-Jungian film theory. Samuels goes on to explain further the role and function of archetypal images within art:

> In post-Jungian analytical psychology, the view is gaining ground that what is archetypal is not to be found in any particular image or list of images that can be tagged as anima, trickster, hero, Shadow, and so on. Rather, it is in the *intensity of affective response* to any given image or situation that what we find is archetypal.
>
> (Baumlin et al., 2004, xiv)

A post-Jungian view of successful art, then, can be measured by the audience's archetypal *affective* response, both individually and collectively, to a film. This emotional response is triggered, or catalysed, within the psyche of the viewer or audience by the archetypal images contained within the film and how they are articulated, Samuels reminding us that '[t]he archetypal can therefore be *relative, contextual and personal*' (ibid). To this, we can also add cultural, echoing the post-Jungian idea of the cultural unconscious. Taking this idea further, we can introduce the theory of psychic resonance; archetypal images contained within art resonating to the same psychic frequency within the psyche of the viewer or consumer. This resonance, or identification, is what triggers the affective/emotional response, or charge, within the psyche, and therefore affects (and in some cases) changes and develops the psyche (Izod, 2006; Hauke, 2014; Singh, 2014; Bassil-Morozow and Hockley, 2017; Hockley, 2018). Singh expands upon this debate:

> The act of viewing film engages our subjectivity (and sense of subjectivity) in much less discreet ways. It is a sensuous and affective act, connecting as it does the intimacy of perception-expression and our experience of it. In other words, what we see and hear *out there* is very difficult to separate from what we feel *in here* in any meaningful sense.
>
> (2009, p. 177, italics in the original)

If the archetypes are largely unconscious, then we know them through the images that are generated by them. These psychic features are also encountered within dreams, which are similar, although not the same, as films.

It is the archetypal image that alerts us to the presence of an archetype within a film, the archetypal image that engages with the audience's collective and individual psyche to generate an affective response, if we are to accept Samuels' explanation of affect above. Hockley puts it thus: '[T]he archetype is better conceived as a way of understanding, in the form of an image, how an individual is engaging with both inner and outer worlds' (2007, p. 10). The image is, therefore, the key to understanding an archetype and the role in which it plays in engaging with the psyche. Hockley continues, 'Jung suggests that the images associated with a given archetypal pattern may be broadly similar even though they will vary over time and will respond to the influences of different cultures and different family experiences' (ibid). Jung himself has defined the archetypal image as 'essentially an unconscious that is altered by becoming conscious and by being perceived, and it takes its colour from the individual consciousness in which it happens to appear' (Hauke and Hockley, 2011, p. 187). Izod provides more detail in that 'these are not ordinary images in terms of their impact. Jung referred to figures that have this kind of power as being pitched from 'the treasure-house of primordial images; into the arena of consciousness' (2001, p. 35). Going back to the theory of psychic resonance, archetypal images that are identified with by the audience or viewer can only resonate if they have power to so. Archetypal images are also mutable and evolutionary, reflecting changing eras, cultures and environments. Izod again: 'Archetypal or primordial images, however, are more exposed to the erosions of time and culture than the forms that they can only fill out provisionally' (ibid). He quotes Jung in a classic explanation of the archetypal image:

> The primordial images undergo ceaseless transformation and yet remain ever the same, but only in a new form can they be understood anew. Always they require a new interpretation if, as each formulation becomes obsolete, they are not to lose their spellbinding power.
>
> (ibid)

Archetypal images are not restricted to religious (or filmic) imagery; rather they are activated and generated by the unconscious power of the archetype that lies behind them and that seeks expression within the culture of the individual and the individual themselves. Relating this to cinema, John Beebe makes a crucial and similar point when he differentiates between stage acting and screen acting: 'The actors are not up on screen, their images are; and this translation of person into image is crucially important psychologically, because it moves film past the personal and into the archetypal realm of psychological experience' (Hauke and Alister, 2001, p. 216). We are also reminded by Jean-Luc Goddard's maxim, 'Cinema is truth at twenty-four frames a second'. It is this power of the archetypal image that is explored further in the shape of the archetypal image of the father and how it interacts and changes in the different films it is contained within. To help explain further how the archetypal image works, and what it contains, we need now to examine the post-Jungian concepts of the sign and the symbol.

## Signs and symbols

With regard to signs and symbols, post-Jungian film theory differs sharply from Freudian, Lacanian and Marxist film semiotics. Perhaps the biggest difference is that Jung's psychology is one of amplification and expansion, rather than reduction, an approach that holds both the (archetypal) symbol and the sign as equally important, although with arguably a greater value and emphasis placed on the symbolic. In essence, post-Jungian theory values the symbol (by its nature, an unknown), rather than reduce it to a sign, a known, as the semiotic approach would have us do. Fredericksen's seminal 1979 essay *Jung/sign/symbol/film*, revised and updated for *Jung and Film* outlines why:

> Semiotic approaches are limited to psychic expressions that are in fact signs, and to that subset of symbolic expressions for which one can attempt semiotic interpretations . . . the semiotic attitude is ultimately limiting because it either denies the existence of the symbolic realm by definition, or denies its existence in practice by attempting to explain symbolic expressions semiotically.
>
> (2001, p. 27)

He goes on to identify the weaknesses of the semiotic approach towards symbols as resulting from what Edward Edinger calls the 'reductive fallacy':

> The reductive fallacy is based on the rationalistic attitude which assumes that it can see behind symbols to their "real" meaning. This approach reduces all symbolic imagery to elementary known factors. It operates on the assumption that no true mystery, no essential unknown transcending the ego's capacity for comprehension exists. . . . This attitude does violence to the autonomous reality of the psyche.
>
> (ibid, p. 28)

Fredericksen goes on to warn of the dangers of such an approach, echoing Jung's own warning of rationalistic hubris towards the unknowable:

> The limiting character of the semiotic attitude involves a clear hubris of – and often a fear of – the rational and the conscious toward the irrational and the unconscious mind. Throughout his life, Jung warned against this hubris, without ever denying the absolute necessity of reason and consciousness in one's striving for self-realisation. For Jung, *the point is not to identify with either the conscious or the unconscious mind, but to forge and keep a living tie between them.*
>
> (ibid – italics in the original)

This approach is pertinent to film studies if only to explain the affective nature of film that semiotics, or, indeed, cognitive film theory, does not always engage with successfully. Where Fredericksen goes awry somewhat is the arbitrary way in which films he identifies as being symbolic, value judgments creeping in as to what films are judged as being symbolic and which are 'merely' semiotic. There is a clear implication in his writing that popular cinema is largely semiotic and therefore 'known' and easily analysed, and art cinema that is somehow more symbolic, 'unknown' and therefore of greater value. Singh takes issue with this reasoning:

> It is apparent that Fredericksen is employing a hierarchical structure that presupposes a poverty of meaning in semiotic films, and a pregnancy or richness

in symbolic ones . . . troublesome in the assumption that the majority of films are 'predominantly semiotic in character', an assumption that tars mainstream and popular cinema with symbolic poverty. It risks placing many films *en masse* in this bracket before analysis has even begun.

(2009, p. 92)

Singh also identifies that Fredericksen does not keep in mind Jung's exhortation to forge a 'living tie' between the conscious and the unconscious when choosing a film to analyse in order to flesh out his theory, focusing as he does on the symbols within Wright's *Song of Ceylon* (1935), an example of his own post-Jungian film analysis.

Taking Fredericksen and Singh's positions further, it can be proposed that films are potentially both semiotic *and* symbolic, the (unknowable) symbols birthing the (known) signs that are shown as images. Successful films, that is to say films that possess psychic resonance, would consequently have a strong tie, less successful films a weaker tie. It is also worth noting that successful films (in post-Jungian terms) can also be popular in an industrial and commercial sense, just as unsuccessful films can be seen as art or 'worthy'. Bassil-Morozow and Hockley agree:

> Further, the psychological worth of an image does not necessarily stem from its aesthetic and intellectual qualities – it is quite possible, even normal, to find something of psychological worth in images that lack cultural sophistication.
>
> (2017, p. 8)

Tying this back to the definitions earlier of archetypes and archetypal images, it is also proposed that symbols and signs are, in effect, differing and co-existing forms of archetypal images, active and activating within the psyche of the spectator, forging, as Jung and Fredericksen would have it, a living tie between the conscious and unconscious. This said, Bassil-Morozow and Hockley issue a caveat around the analysis of symbols and signs:

> While the Jungian view of images appears to be flexible, intuitive and non-rational, in fact it is highly codified, constrained and structured . . . in this respect, Freudian and Jungian views of the image and the symbol are actually much closer than they first appear, and much closer than Jung himself allows for.
>
> (ibid, p. 65)

This recognition of post-Jungian film analysis being in danger of becoming symbolically reductive is both useful and challenging, given that the book will be engaging with close textual analysis. That said, filmic symbols and signs can and should be identified and their meanings interpreted, albeit with an awareness and appreciation of their innate polysemous nature and polyvalence (ibid, p. 63). It is arguable that the filmic context of any symbol or sign can change the meaning significantly, reflecting its essential plurality of meaning.

## The archetype

As Jung developed within his analytical psychological theoretical discourse, the concept of the archetype quickly began to gain currency and usage, both within psychoanalytical circles and, later on, within the humanities as Jung's ideas began to make their presence felt. Before my own definition of this key term is offered, it is worth examining other attempts by both Jungians and post-Jungians to define what this concept is, and isn't. First, we can examine Jung's own definition of the archetype, albeit a definition that avoids precise parameters to say the least:

> The concept of the archetype . . . is derived from the repeated observation that, for instance, everywhere . . . these typical images and associations are what I call archetypal ideas. . . . They have the myths and fairy tales of world literature contain definite motifs which crop up their origin in the archetype, which itself is an irrepresentable, unconscious, pre-existent form that seems to be part of the inherited structure of the psyche and can therefore manifest itself spontaneously anywhere, at any time.
>
> (1967, CW7, para 847)

This lengthy opening description of what an archetype is sets out some of the ideas, and problems, with this concept. First, an archetype is, by its nature, largely undefinable in and of itself; it is the archetype that gives shape to an archetypal idea and image. Second, archetypes are also present in the collective, cultural and personal unconscious, and therefore cannot be conscious. Rather, that the corresponding archetypal *images* and ideas can be made conscious and visible, the phenomenon that gives rise to them cannot. Thus, the archetype is not known directly, rather it is known by the *images* it is held as producing. Third, they appear to be evolutionary and universal, in that archetypal images reflect the culture that produces them. Jung also warns of the danger of attempting too rigid a definition of this term: 'It is necessary to point out once more that archetypes are not determined as regards their content, but only as regards their form and then only to a very limited degree' (ibid, para 155). The concept of the archetype, therefore, is itself seemingly undermined by the nature of the archetype, being widely perceived as a vague and largely undefinable concept. The popular, but often mistaken, usage of the term is of a phenomenon that is more concrete, a pre-cursor or cousin to a stereotype, in effect a clearly defined, differentiated example of the psychological landscape, such as the parent, mentor, sibling, child, enemy, friend, etc. This misuse of the term 'archetype' is something that both Jungians and post-Jungians have attempted to combat, albeit with differing degrees of success. Part of the problem is that there is considerable debate within analytical psychological circles about how an archetype is defined and whether or not an agreed-upon definition is even worth attempting. If we are to proceed with a Jungian analysis of film, then it would seem both timely and circumspect to at least attempt one as discussion of the father archetype in the book would demand this. Before this can be attempted, however, it would be circumspect to review the definitions of archetypes offered by both Jungians and post-Jungians.

Samuels (1985a) has streamed post-Jungians into three broad schools as summarised by Waddell from Samuels' work: 'The *Classical* School, largely uncritical of Jung's theories; the *Developmental* School, privileging personal development and links with psychoanalysis; and the *Archetypal* School, interested in the primary nature of the archetypal image' (2006, p. 12). Starting with Jung's successors from the classical Jungian school, we can examine the different definitions of archetypes. Anthony Stevens, a practising Jungian analyst, scientist, and writer, describes and defines the archetype thus: 'Innate neuropsychic centres possessing the capacity to initiate, control, and mediate the common behavioural characteristics and typical experiences of all human beings' (1994, p. 48). As mentioned previously, Stevens goes on further to propose that archetypes have a virtually biological basis in the psychological life of an individual by cross-referencing ethology with psychology. For Stevens, the archetype is a definite concrete psychological structure that not only produces archetypal images but also controls and influences psychic behaviour. Waddell also highlights this point in her discussions around the philosophical background to Jung's development of the psyche 'he [Jung] saw the mind as matter; a biological structure like the body, genetically determined and programmed, yet open to variation through cultural and environmental factors' (2006, p. 13). This definition is at odds with later post-Jungians, particularly in the field of film. Samuels et al define, or rather summarise, what an archetype could be, and what it contains, as follows:

> (a) Archetypal structures and patterns are the crystallisation of experiences over time (b) They constellate experience in accordance with innate schemata and act as imprimatur of subsequent experience (c) Images deriving from archetypal structures involve us in a search for correspondence in the environment.
> (1986, p. 27)

This collection of points around what an archetype's features are, and more importantly, what its function is, is a step further towards a deeper understanding of the archetype, a point perhaps missed by some Jungians. For their part, post-Jungians' definitions also differ widely. Izod offers this definition, echoing Jung's own writings:

> The contents of the collective unconscious. They are not inherited ideas, but inherited modes of psychic functioning. Until activated, they are forms without content; when activated they control patterns of behaviour. The centres of energy around which ideas, images, affects and myths cohere.
> (2001, p. 215)

It is, perhaps, this last sentence that is of particular interest to film and cultural scholars, drawing, as it does, attention to the cultural and filmic impact archetypes can have. Izod offers a further commentary around classical Jungian theories on archetypes: '[A]n archetype is a theoretical concept that not capable of proof precisely because it is a component of the unconscious' (2006, p. 25), a view that is reflected in my earlier introduction to the term. What needs to be borne in mind is that Jung's ideas progressed over a considerable length of time, with some of his theories contradicting others and varying greatly in their definitions, hence the clear divergence in interpreters and students of Jung's work. Returning to post-Jungian film theory, Hockley defines the archetype as:

> The deep structure(s) of the unconscious. . . . These are the patterns which influence our psychological development and growth. They are also the patterns that interact with our culture, our personal experiences and family lives to bring shape and form to an individual psyche. The archetypes are the mechanism through which the psyche maintains its sense of balance and health.
>
> (2007, p. 25)

Hauke, another leading post-Jungian writer on film, defines the archetype as 'the unconscious structuring principles of the psyche which make our experience, perception and behaviour distinctly human' (2001, p. 244). Singh's discussion and definition of the archetype are directly quoted from Roger Brooke:

> A hypothetical construct, used to account for the similarity in the images that cluster around typically human themes and situations . . . anything said about the meaning of an archetypal image, or *symbol*, is only ever an approximation to this core.
>
> (2009, p. 121)

This definition is clearly at odds with the more classical view of Stevens, refusing, as it does, to propose the archetype as a solid feature, more a theoretical reaction to existing human behaviour. This divergence of opinion is one of the problems facing anyone attempting to define the archetype as it excites and inspires so many differing views. For my own part, I disagree with Singh and Brooke's cautious labelling of the archetype as theoretical in that whilst it is an unconscious phenomenon, it can be known, at the very least, by the archetypal images that it produces and the behaviours it generates. Clearly *something* is present; the fact that it is essentially unknowable apart from the images it creates does not necessarily make it a hypothetical construct. Similar to the Freudian unconscious, it is discernible via the traces it leaves within culture and language. For the purposes of our discussion here, the archetype can be defined as an unconscious but distinct nexus of dynamically essential psychic energy that is located within the collective unconscious. This energy both influences and is influenced by the individual's exterior and interior environment and generates archetypal images and behaviour, depending on the particularities of an individual's culture and surroundings.

## The archetype of the father

Having defined what an archetype may be, we can now examine the archetypal figure of the father. As such, the father has been the subject of a considerable amount of attention from both Jungian and post-Jungian writers. Jung himself in *Aspects of the Masculine* (1989) discussed at length the gender archetypes (specifically the anima and animus) and fathers, linking his thinking with analyses of various myths and mythic journeys. He held that the *animus* was the male contrasexual archetype, brother to the *anima* as it were, that existed in all women but not in men. He also confessed in a lecture that the animus intimidated him: 'But we had better not talk of the animus now. It just scares me, it is much more difficult to deal with. The anima is definite, and the animus is indefinite' (1989, p. 151). Consequently, much more has been written on the anima by Jung than the animus, an interesting psychological asymmetry that in a way, betrays his own gender bias as a man. He did define both archetypes' function, 'the animus and the anima should function as a bridge, or a door, leading to the images of the collective unconscious, as the persona should be a sort of a bridge into the world' (Storr, 1983, p. 415). *A Critical Dictionary of Jungian Analysis* defined it 'as the figure of man at work in a woman's psyche . . . a configuration arising from a basic archetypal structure . . . the 'masculine' aspects of a woman' (1986, p. 23). Hauke and Alister concur: '[T]he corresponding masculine principle at work in a woman's psyche' (2001, p. 244). For Hockley it is the archetype of 'traditional masculine behaviours and attitudes [that] represent themselves in the image of the *animus*' (2007, p. 130). Samuels not only echoes these definitions but also reminds us that anima and animus are not necessarily male and female, 'animus and anima images are not of men and women because animus and anima qualities are "masculine" and "feminine"' (1989, p. 103). This point around flexibility of definition needs to be borne in mind when analysing this key archetype. Samuels has this definition to offer us:

> This (archetypal) structure functions as a blueprint or expectation of certain features in the environment; it is a predisposition which leads us to experience life in a patterned way, the psychological equivalent of an instinct. Whatever the salient features of fatherhood may be, and whether or not a male figure has to be their executor, those features are not the result of accident or coincidence. The perception of our personal father is an end product resting on an archetypal substructure.
>
> (1985b, p. 23)

This definition is useful because it hints strongly at the possibility that fatherhood does not always need to be carried out by a male figure, an interesting proposition, running, as it does, contrary to many of the views held by the men's movement. The performativity of fatherhood, it seems, does not always have to be carried out by a man, a point echoed in both *Frozen River* (Hunt, 2008) and *Winter's Bone* (Granik, 2010) with their female protagonists being forced into acting within traditionally defined paternal gender roles. Barbara Greenfield provides another useful definition of the archetypal masculine:

> [W]e may characterise the archetypal masculine as an *intrusive, active* principle that pushes the development of consciousness out of primal undifferentiation and unity with the mother. Unlike the anima, this male principle is *mental* rather than material, pertaining to activated spirit, intellect and will. In short, those aspects of the psyche that we characterise as ego are traditionally identified with the masculine.
>
> (ibid, p. 189, italics in the original)

This particular definition is useful in that it echoes the developmental progression that the mytho-poetic men's movement also focuses on with regard to the idea of masculinity as a continuum. Whether or not it has to be a man that performs this intrusive, disruptive function is debatable. When discussing the animus, and by proxy, the paternal, post-Jungian writers such as Izod (2001, 2006), Samuels (1989) and Singh (2009) have contradicted traditional notions of the animus, arguing that both *animus* and *anima* exist within a person's psyche. Singh, in particular, attempts to establish the concept of the psyche possessing both contrasexual archetypes. He sounds a note of caution around the concept of contrasexuality itself, with 'the common mistake in dealing with contrasexuality is that it sometimes suggests polarisation of gender, as well as a naturalized notion of equivalence between gender, sex and sexuality' (2009, p. 126). It needs to be stated that any polarisation needs to be avoided, lest there occurs a slippage from archetypes into stereotypes. What can be termed a gender syzygy (dynamic union of opposites) was what Bly was attempting to highlight and popularise with *The Maiden King* (1998), albeit with little success. In terms of his earlier work, as mentioned previously, after the publication of *Iron John*, there was a literary glut of Jungian-influenced texts that sought to emulate the success of Bly's work. As mentioned previously, both Samuels and Tacey sounded a strong note of caution. In *The Political Psyche* Samuels argued: 'The way in which Jungian psychology has been hijacked by the mythopoetic movement is a disaster that stifles its progressive potentials' (1993, p. 188). He recognised the same danger that Tacey warned against four years later, namely that the conflation of the father figure runs the risk of warping the view of this archetype. As Tacey points out: 'Jung spent much of his intellectual energy warning against an unconscious or infantile return to an identification with the archetypal figures' (1997, p. 19). He went further, warning specifically against mixing the energies of an archetype with the individuative and archetypal energies of the self/Self:

> [T]he popular fusion of archetype and gender is, at bottom, a symptom of the nervousness of our time, an attempt to create a fixed world order amid the chaos of contemporary experience. It is also a fundamental and determined resistance to the bisexuality or androgyneity of the soul.
>
> (ibid, p. 23)

He goes on to issue another warning, one which is perhaps more relevant than ever in contemporary times: 'Moreover, a real danger inherent in the mythologisation of one's own gender is that there is a natural tendency to demonise the opposite gender' (ibid, p. 24). This mythologisation of the father can lead to the Shadow; a dark aspect to the men's movement that Bly unwittingly denies by his idealisation of the Father archetype and the attractive simplicity of prescribing it as a panacea to current gender issues. As we will analyse later, the Shadow Father is a ubiquitous figure in American cinema, threatening to, at times, edge out other representations of the paternal. It is the importance of this figure, on an archetypal level, both personally and culturally, that leads us to consider what has termed the need for a father figure, and the need to be a father: father hunger.

## Father hunger: an archetypal need?

The term 'father hunger' itself implies some kind of masculine parental need that a child (adult or otherwise) needs and consciously (or, more often than not, unconsciously) seeks out, successfully or unsuccessfully. This need manifests itself in different ways and on different levels and in different arenas, psychologically, politically, socially, and culturally. Broadly speaking, the term can be defined in two ways: first, on an individual level by examining the psychological aspect and origin of the term, and second on a wider collective level by examining the cinematic, cultural and political impact of father hunger as a cultural presence. Both these definitions feed into cinematic analysis and the overall impact of father hunger on contemporary American film. When considering these definitions, the impact and influence of the external must be taken into account in terms of defining the role of the father and consequently, of father hunger. Archetypal images of the father, as presented to us by film, are of equal importance as internal (introverted) drives when considering how father hunger arises. Jungian psychology has previously been viewed as essentialist and introverted, as it appears to focus on the individual and side-line the external. Hockley disagrees, pointing out that:

> Jungian psychology has at its very centre the importance of social and cultural factors in shaping our sense of self. In part this is implicit in Jung's constant use of literature, philosophy, science, and mythology as sources from which to shed light on contemporary psychological situations, both culturally and

personally. More dramatically, Jung remarks: 'Individuation does not shut one out from the world, but gathers the world to oneself.'

(2007, p. 9)

The external psychic environment (as previously mentioned, psychic being concerned with matters of the psyche, rather than occult phenomena) is therefore of fundamental importance in consideration of gender-based issues, particularly when analysing specific cultural complexes. The universal father needs to be differentiated from the American father, as discussed later in more detail. American fathers are also products of their culture, with the father occupying a crucial position within American cultural complexes such as the American Dream. When the cultural complex falls into Shadow, the father falls into Shadow as well. Consequently, contextual factors, in this case received mediated images, both reflect and inform definitions of father hunger. As outlined in the previous section, the term 'father hunger' was first clinically identified and defined in a paper in 1980 by Herzog. His definition of father hunger is complex and rooted in Freudian psychoanalytical terminology but has similarities with the Jungian interpretation (see later) of a father-figure's role:

> The recognition of sameness with the father, the need to manage a mutual concern, and the need to be shown how is common. I have come to consider this need to be "shown how" a hallmark of the pre-oedipal boy's relationship with his father. Of course, girls need their fathers too. It may be, however, that either they need them more when they reach oedipal age or they can make out better without them before that time.
>
> (p. 34)

Another aspect of his investigations included studying men who have a compulsive need to *be* a father-figure to other men. In most cases, this was linked in with their relationship with their own fathers (most often absent, either physically or emotionally). In both child and adult arenas, father hunger emerges as a psychological response to inadequate or incomplete male parental input during a child's developmental stage. This carries over into adult life with potentially profound consequences for the future psychological health of a person, both male and female. The psychoanalytical explanation, however, assumes that the son will, in effect, transform into his father, the masculine continuum continuing largely unchanged, the best outcome being an acceptance of an instinctive psychological pattern. Having found a brief psychoanalytical definition of the term, attention can now be turned to the Jungian explanation of this phenomenon.

From a Jungian (analytical psychological) perspective, the father is a fundamental archetype within the human psyche and Self. Jung proposed that the human psyche and Self was, in essence, a self-balancing, psychically homoeostatic structure that strived to adapt to its environment and maintain a sense of itself, gradually developing to the point of what Jung termed individuation or complete wholeness: 'The Self, therefore, possesses a teleological function, in that it has the innate characteristic of seeking its own fulfilment in life' (Stevens, 1990a, p. 41). Psychic Self-actualisation is the goal of the Self; an attainment of fully conscious awareness. This quest for wholeness utilises the rest of the psychic structure (ego, persona, Shadow, animus/anima); all these parts develop from this matrix and are under the guidance of the Self. Archetypes (in a clinical sense), therefore, are also part of this structure and can take many forms, such as mother, father, son, daughter, child, hero, villain, initiate, trickster, etc. Archetypes, however, also fulfil what Hockley describes as 'a mediating role between the collective unconscious and the conscious' (2007, p. 11), a bridge between our inner psychic life and the wider environment around us. This assertion echoes with Jung's conviction that 'through psychological images . . . it is possible to come to an understanding of ourselves and of our relationship to the world . . . the individual and his or her cultural location are inseparable' (ibid, p. 7). The archetypal image, therefore, of the parent or father that is received, and the archetype that is animated and activated by the biological father or surrogate father are held as one of the most important and fundamental parts of the Self and psyche. Without the activation and bringing to life of this parental archetype by actual biological parents, the developing child or teenager will tend to unconsciously seek out phantasy, substitute or surrogate father figures within the family or without, in the wider world, with greater or lesser degrees of success. This seeking out of substitution is closely linked with the previously mentioned teleological function of the psyche; where there is a gap, it will seek to close or fill it.

When we focus on males, developmentally speaking, a male child's identification with a father-figure (not necessarily the biological father) is held to be crucial to his sense of himself as a male and as a man, experiencing as he grows and develops, a fundamental identity difference between himself and his mother. Stevens 'At this point, the presence of a father-figure can prove crucial, enabling the boy to move from a self-concept based on mother identity to one based on identification-with-the-father' (1994, p. 69). The male child then begins to identify himself as profoundly different to his mother, not least because of his biology and his sexual organs. At some point he realises that he has to know, learn and absorb from his father, not necessarily as an enemy and rival as Freud proposed, but as a bridge into the world of men and masculinity that his own, slowly activated father archetype is directing him towards. The teleological journey of the son towards manhood is to ultimately transcend the father (both the father archetype and the biological father), a major difference from a psychoanalytical perspective. This is a somewhat more optimistic outlook with both the father's individuation and the child's development psychologically potentialised. As a bridge/evolution of the male child's increasing sense of himself, the presence of the father, or father figure, is perceived and viewed as a crucial one. If, for whatever reason (absence, weakness, deficiency, or even over-involvement), the father is not available for the male child to learn from, then Stevens holds that the archetype of the father within a child's emerging Self and ego will not be fully activated, leading to psychic distortion and subsequent neuroses which will affect the future health of the child:

> Thus the boy whose father was inadequate or absent may fail to actualize his masculine potential sufficiently to establish the social or vocational his talents equip him for, or he may be unable to sustain a relationship with a member of the opposite sex long enough for him to become an adequate husband or father himself.
>
> (1994, p. 75)

Or, to put it another way: 'The less adequate the parents, the greater the unfulfilled potential, the more ravenous the parent hunger and the more obsessive the Flying Dutchman quest' (Stevens, 1990b, p. 122). Stevens goes on to describe what he envisages the likely fate of such children to be:

> [T]hey are more likely to embark on an unconsciously motivated quest, like Flying Dutchmen seeking to redeem themselves from a bitter fate: they pass from one dependent relationship to another – employers, teachers, older companions and lovers – people perceived as being able to make good the deficiencies of the parents. The pangs of such *parent hunger* can be powerful indeed and may gnaw away in the unconscious for the rest of life.
>
> (ibid, p. 121, italics in the original)

This colourful description of parental hunger, and by extension, father hunger, is problematic for a number of reasons. There are urgent questions about what constitutes adequacy within a parent here that Stevens does not directly address within the passage, implying earlier on that a degree of responsibility, maturity and ability in the giving of care is what makes an adequate parent, quoting D.W Winnicott's pithy phrase 'good enough', 'that is to say, whether they are capable of discharging the basic obligations of parenthood' (ibid, p. 119). There is also a strong assumption around heterosocial and heterosexual familial discourses that has a notably biological[7] bias to it, assumptions that come with all the attendant baggage that this view brings. Part of the problem is that Stevens views the archetype as being as solid as the composition of a biological entity, 'archetypes are as fixed as the genetic structure of our species' (ibid, p. 120). This is a rigid definition of an archetype, and one that is disagreed with by several post-Jungians, Hockley among them:

> Jung also refers to the presence of the structures, which he names 'archetypes' and the role they play, as a hypothesis . . . there is a tendency in some branches of Jungian theory to over-literalize the archetypes. This results in treating them as either actual biological structures or as concrete psychological forms.
>
> (2007, p. 10)

This over-simplification of the archetype of the parent can also lead to over-simplified and fixed notions of what the lack of 'adequate' parenting will result in. What must also be borne in mind is that a classical Jungian position is generally from a therapeutic perspective. Subsequently, any approach to cinema studies from a pathological perspective needs to be treated with appropriate caution. Samuels strongly hints that a father need not be a masculine figure: 'Whatever the salient features of fatherhood may be, and whether or not a male figure has to be their executor, those features are not the result of accident or coincidence' (1985b, p. 23). This is echoed by his statement later: '[T]he fluidity of the psyche means that anyone can stand in for a symbol for anyone else' (ibid, p. 37), including, for example, a woman standing in for a father figure within lesbian couples. These assertions run counter to many of the men's movement's more rigid ideas around gender roles and will be examined later on when we examine specific depictions of the father. Both Paul Thomas Anderson and Wes Anderson subject the family unit to close analysis and often finds it wanting (*Boogie Nights*, *Magnolia*, *The Royal Tenenbaums*, *The Life Aquatic*, in particular), with the nuclear family being deconstructed and new families being substituted. As so much of the family disruption is concerned with the father, it behoves us now to examine this figure through the contextual basis of the men's movement.

## Continuing the masculine

According to the men's movement, the father figure has been afforded an increasingly important role since the early 1990s. This importance attached to the figure of the father is also largely reflective of the crisis in masculinity that was identified as occurring in various guises in the late 1980s and early 1990s. As outlined earlier, the crisis in masculinity was held as coming about due to the triple impact of civil rights, feminism and gay liberation, the crisis focusing attention on the construction of masculinities, with the father being thrust into the spotlight as both a problem and a solution to this crisis, certainly by the mytho-poetic men's movement. Since the early 1990s, the men's movement has been largely perceived as a 'reactive masculinity' (Connell, 1995). Bruzzi (2005), Rehling (2009), Peberdy (2011) and Kord and Krimmer (2011) all make the point that masculine crises have been occurring in various guises since post-war times, with the 1980/1990s crisis being one in a long string of crises. For Biddulph, a popular psychologist and cultural commentator on men and masculinities, the crisis is mainly due to father hunger, manifesting as a 'hidden grief' (1995, p. 31) within men. He went on to provide a fuller description: 'Father hunger is the deep biological need for strong, humorous, hairy, wild, tender, sweaty, caring, intelligent masculine input' (ibid). From this description, father hunger appears to also be an experiential and affective phenomenon, rather than just a psychological one. From a mytho-poetic men's movement perspective, both the main cause and effect of father hunger is the discontinuation, or the interruption, of masculinity which itself is the failure of a father figure to fully initiate and guide his son into adulthood. This viewing of masculinity as a continuum (as detailed earlier) is a fundamental part of men's movement ideology and was first proposed by Bly in *Iron John* (1990) and consequently developed by Biddulph and other writers (Lee, 1991, Moore and Gillette, 1992, etc.). Detractors of this approach, including Bruzzi (2005) Samuels (1993) and Tacey (1997), argue that the obsession with the father as the *sole* source of masculinity both effectively ignores the role of the mother and the role that social forces and institutions play in shaping ideas around masculinities, points that need to be considered. Samuels also argues, for example, that Bly's use of Jung for men's movement ideological purposes is deeply problematic due to his sharp delineation of gender roles masquerading as 'archetypally drawn' (1993, p. 186). Tacey (1997) also argues that Bly mistakenly conflates the father archetype with the idea of the self/Self and does not recognise the Shadow that is archetypally omnipresent.

We would argue that filmic depictions of father hunger indicate an *innate*, rather than *essential*, archetypal need in men for a father figure, as well as the need to act as a father figure to younger men. Going further, this perceived and depicted initiatory need is not, however, the end of the masculine journey. Rather that, whilst the cinematic portrayal of the father figure as an initiator into and mediator of masculinity has veracity, the journey of gender construction continues past this stage, with the adult male interacting with both feminine and masculine social constructs and institutions as part of a dynamic masculine continuum. A number of films, *Jarhead* and *The Road to Perdition* in particular, portray patriarchy and patriarchal institutions as mostly inimical to men, and to fathers and fatherhood. There is also the question, touched upon by Bruzzi, around the position of the father within the psyche. She gives *American Beauty* alongside *Happiness* (Solondz, 1998) and *Affliction* (Schrader, 1997) as examples to illustrate that the father in 1990s films is more often than not portrayed as being, to use the appropriate Jungian term, a Shadow father in that the paternal is used to display and channel the darker side of masculinity. This Shadow is where the father is potentially sexually dangerous (*American Beauty* and *Boogie Nights*), physically dangerous, (*There Will be Blood*) and spiritually dangerous (*Magnolia, The Master*). Where there is disagreement with Bruzzi and her analysis of the dark father is that fathers are also shown by Anderson and Mendes to have redemptive qualities (*Road to Perdition*) and are also shown to be redeemed (*American Beauty* again), a position that is barely acknowledged. Moreover, the seeds of what can be termed masculine numinosity lie with the dark father and effectively co-exist with the Shadow, the films showing the masculine journey that is made within them, both successful (*Road to Perdition* and *Jarhead*) and unsuccessful (*There Will be Blood*). It is the journey made by the father, either driven by a psychic hunger for the paternal or to be a parent, which ultimately constructs the masculinities within these films.

## The archetype of the child

By the nature of its existence, a father *is* a father because they have been instrumental in creating new life, giving rise to the child. This figure operates linguistically, effectively, as a noun, verb and an adjective. The child, by contrast, is in the position of having been created but yet is to be a creator of life, the creation of new life a key rite of passage and arguably an archetypal and initiatory stage within a psychic journey. The archetype of the child, therefore, differs considerably from that of a parent, representing, as it does, a symbol of innocence, renewal and change. Chevalier and Gheerbrant summarise this particular symbol: 'Childhood symbolizes innocence, which is the state anterior to Original Sin and hence a paradisal state. . . . Children are spontaneous, unaggressive, self-contained, without forethought or afterthought' (1994, pp. 189–190). Cooper largely agrees: 'The embodiment of potentialities; possibilities of the future; simplicity; innocence. The child, or son, also symbolises a higher transformation of the individuality, the self-transmuted and reborn into perfection' (1978, p. 35). Where the figure of the child is mediated in American cinema is interesting as the child both benefits from and suffers from the presence of the father, a contradictory position that a post-Jungian position can illuminate. For an example, we can briefly examine Daniel Plainview (Daniel Day-Lewis) and his adopted son, H.W. (Dillon Freasier). Within the text, there are a number of complex and conflicting images and themes at work here. Initially, Plainview is an example of a solitary cipher of a man, with no past or family, who is depicted as being wholly venal and materially driven. His narrative and psychological journey starts to develop when he adopts HW, the orphaned son of an employee after a fatal accident early on in the film.

This conscious act of fathering (father hunger here being portrayed as the hunger *to be* a father), in effect, the masculine continuum being continued, is initially signalled as a potential source of redemption for Plainview. However, when HW is deafened after an oil-well blowout, Plainview sends him away, unable to deal with his son's disability, having admitted that he despises human weakness. This rejection of his son signals his descent into madness and soul-darkness, Anderson showing Plainview's dark patriarch becoming lost within his Shadow and specifically referenced within the mise-en-scene and colour palette of the film.

Anderson portrays fatherhood here as a symbolically potentially redemptive act, an act that Plainview fails to perform, a failure which is shown to eventually damn him. It is the figure of the child that allows this potential redemption to happen, the child being a carrier, or vessel, of the numinous. It is this potential numinosity that can redeem Plainview from his Shadow, a redemptive opportunity that is wasted due to Plainview's Shadow being too strong for him to deal with and so effectively damns him.

## The archetype of the Shadow

The Shadow is one of the best known of Jungian concepts and one of the most misunderstood. Jung defined the Shadow in 1945 thus: 'The thing a person does not want to be' (Samuels et al., 1986, p. 138). Samuels et al. defined it as 'the negative side of the personality, the sum of all the unpleasant qualities one wants to hide, the inferior, worthless and primitive side of man's nature, the 'other person' in one, one's own dark side' (ibid). Hauke and Alister define it as:

> The part of the personality that one does not identify with or wishes to disown; it usually refers to negative aspects, but may also include positive aspects that – due to family or social beliefs – have remained rejected and unavailable to the individual.
>
> (2001, p. 246)

They go on to outline a more nuanced view of the Shadow in that there are benefits to it due to this archetype containing a tremendous amount of psychic energy:

> It is an archetype whose powerful aspects – obsessional, possessive, autonomous – are capable of startling and overwhelming the well-ordered ego, and it often takes the form of a projection on to others.
>
> (ibid)

Bassil-Morozow and Hockley define it as:

> the Shadow is the 'dark brother' in whom all the negative aspects of human nature are stored. It is home to greed, aggression, envy, jealousy, fear and hatred. Humans' relationship with the Shadow has always been a key *leitmotif* of art and literature.
>
> (2017, p. 39)

Many other archetypes dwell within the Shadow, such as the Trickster, the vampire, the psychopath, the zombie, werewolf, alien, in other words, familiar tropes and figures from horror and sci-fi films, as well as dramas and even romance films. Other archetypes such as the mother, the father, etc., can be influenced, or even dominated, by the Shadow and temporarily transcend it, a dynamic psychic dance of sorts where the unacknowledged aspects of the psyche are in an interplay with the personal unconscious, as well as the cultural and collective unconscious. For the purposes of this book, we will focus on the Shadow and the Father's relationship with it, a complex and nuanced interaction which takes in aspects of cultural myths, specifically the American Dream and how Hollywood has more often than not depicted the Father as being an integral part of this particular national narrative, putting the paternal, in effect, at the centre of a pressured cultural space where, more often than not, the father fails in some way, both materially and spiritually. As Lydia Lennihan cogently states in her analysis of *Pulp Fiction* (Tarantino, 1994): 'The idea is intriguing that our collective Shadow is symbolized by underworld criminals having a spiritual awakening, for this suggests an unsuspected spiritual energy in the Shadow' (Hauke and Alister, 2001, p. 58). Criminals are not supposed to have spontaneous spiritual awakenings; an explicit recognition by filmmakers of the subtlety and polyvalent nature of this particular Archetype. Similarly, the more nuanced films from this period recognise that the Shadow is intimately connected with not only individual redemption and individuation but also the wider cultural complexes that both affect and afflict individuals and American societies.

## The cultural unconscious and the cultural complex

Before we can examine the specifically American cultural myth of the American Dream in post-Jungian terms, we need to become aware of the cultural context, and by implication, the post-Jungian perspective on what has been termed the *cultural unconscious* and the *cultural complex*. Examining first the cultural unconscious, it would, perhaps, be wise to give a Jungian and post-Jungian definition of culture in the first instance. Samuels et al. state: 'From a psychological point of view, he [Jung] suggests that culture carries the connotation of a group which has developed its own identity and consciousness, together with a sense of continuity and purpose or meaning' (1986, p. 38). This reference to a *group* consciousness that is indicative of a separate entity from an individual's (or personal) consciousness is fundamental to a deeper understanding of the cultural unconscious. Izod expands this further:

> A term first used by Joseph Henderson (1984) is helpful because it points to an intermediate zone from which unconscious or semi-conscious arousals disturb and sway consciousness but without the potentially cataclysmic consequences which can occur when contents irrupt from the collective unconscious.
>
> (2006, p. 18)

This intermediate psychic zone is a useful development in post-Jungian thought, in that it provides a link between the personal unconscious of the individual and the deeper collective unconscious, or, to use a more recent phrase, *the objective psyche*. It also allows for the effect and influence of specific and localised cultural symbols and energies upon the individual psyche, something that Jung managed to avoid fully engaging with (despite his emphasis on locating the individual within their particular culture), mainly preferring to posit that archetypal symbolic energy came directly from the objective psyche/collective unconscious. Izod again points out: 'symbols found in screen texts (like other cultural forms) must indeed, to conform to Jung's meaning of the word, have a dimension that receives energy from the unconscious' (ibid). He goes on:

> The concept of the cultural unconscious . . . extends post-Jungian theories of the psyche, positing a less deeply buried level of unconsciousness based on the recognition that social and cultural pressures conjoin their considerable influence with many other factors in forming all but those images generated by the most profoundly hermetic psychological forces.
>
> (ibid, p. 146)

This concept of a cultural psychic buffer zone is crucial when we also consider the different effects generated by cultural or onscreen symbols within a cultural product, the meaning and message varying enormously to different audiences within different cultures. When the concept of the cultural unconscious is coupled with symbols and symbolic energies, differences emerge between cultural symbols and natural symbols:

> Jung's notion of natural and cultural symbolism denotes a crucial differentiation between the realm of the natural, which should be regarded as an eternally evolving source of images wholly deriving from embedded forms of the collective unconscious, and that of culture.
>
> (Singh, 2009, p. 55)

He more problematically claims that when discussing global shifts in late-capital culture:

> These cultural shifts, in the most general sense, therefore tend to be naturalized and internalized through very similar hegemonic processes of consensus and consent . . . and tend to (if not negate, then) render symbolic signifying systems redundant in the everyday sense.
>
> (ibid)

This point of view is interesting but arguably goes too far in dismissing symbolic signifier systems as redundant. Whilst it would be folly to claim that deeper symbolic signifiers consistently trump cultural pressures and movements, in this case within American culture, symbols are still socially and culturally potent phenomenon and can still be analysed as such, especially in cultural products, film being a prime example. Related to Singh's arguments, Hockley reminds us that:

> The notion of a cultural unconscious is indeed a controversial one. It seems to perpetuate some of the problems that come from use of the term 'collective unconscious'. . . . The very notion of some sort of unconscious psychological agency is something to which there appears to be an almost instinctive resistance.
>
> (2007, p. 16)

This resistance is understandable when the individual, or personal, unconscious is threatened by the idea of their environment exerting a stronger influence over them than is comfortable to admit. In addition to this resistance, Samuels also reminds us that:

> the cultural unconscious as an idea, needs further thought. For example, is the cultural unconscious a kind of repository of cultural experience – a storehouse of difference? Or is it the means, already existing as a potential, by which the human psyche gives birth to cultural difference? Or both?
> (1993, p. 328)

More recently, Bassil-Morozow and Hockley offer this insight into the collective unconscious, part – progenitor of the cultural unconscious:

> By itself, the collective unconscious is speechless. It is dark, passionate and confused, and needs a language to make itself clear and understood. Its free-floating impulses can be turned into narratives with the help of symbols. . . . The personal layer of the unconscious is structured by culture and by language. The amorphous contents of the collective unconscious transform into 'words' and 'phrases' of particular cultural constructs.
> (2017, p. 54)

With so many questions around the nature of the structure and function of the cultural unconscious yet to be answered, it would be unwise to make too many claims for it. However, there are strong arguments that individuals are also products of their social and cultural surroundings as well as individual families and genetics. Following on from these definitions and considerations of the cultural unconscious is the concept of the *cultural complex*. At this juncture, it would be judicious to revisit the definitions of what a complex is. Samuels et al. state that:

> Jung asserted that 'complexes behave like independent beings' (CW 8 para.253). He also argued that 'there is no difference in principle between a fragmentary personality and a complex . . . complexes are splinter psyches'.
> (CW 8, para. 202) (1986, p. 34)

They define a complex as 'a collection of images and ideas, clustered around a core derived from one or more archetypes and characterised by a common emotional tone'. Hauke and Alister state that:

> A complex is a collection of images, ideas and behaviours which have a common emotional tone; it derives its force ultimately from a corresponding archetype. Complexes contribute to behavioural patterns and are marked by their powerful emotional tone.
> (2001, p. 244)

If we extrapolate these definitions to the American cultural unconscious, where we can presume American cultural complexes to reside, then potentially useful insights can be generated. As a culture also includes numerous subcultures, then cultural complexes can also be refracted through different cultural lenses, so to speak. For example, any cultural complexes concerned with social organs of the state (such as local government, police) and how they function across a society is almost certainly refracted by individual societal, racial, cultural, economic and gender positions. For more than fifty years, cultural and subcultural studies scholars have asserted that structural relations to power influence groups and individual's experience of the state and its various organs (Hoggart, 1957; Williams, 1961; Cohen, 1972; Hall and Jefferson, 1976; etc.). Based on these theoretical principles, it could be argued that an American white, middle-class suburban nuclear family, for example, is more likely to have a trusting and less-conflicted perspective and experience of the state and its various organs, than, perhaps, an economically deprived, ethnic minority one-parent family, who have had previously negative or socially disadvantaged encounters. This situation is further refracted when we consider the *individual* positions of each member of the family, or social unit, and what other social or gender groups they belong to.

Singer and Kimbles develop this further: 'Cultural complexes are not the same as cultural identity or what has sometimes been called "national character", although there are times when cultural complexes, cultural identity and national character can seem impossibly entwined' (2004, p. 5). This entwining can complicate analysis of cultural movements and features, yet there can be detected certain commonalities to a cultural complex that also impact and constellate cultural and national identities. We can analyse the commonalities that cluster around the figure of the American father; cinematically speaking, a societal archetypal presence can be analysed and examined. When an archetype such as the father, can, in effect, be argued to catalyse cultural complexes within the cultural unconscious, new cultural forms and identities can emerge. Singer and Kimbles provide an interesting post-Jungian analysis of oppressed cultural identities:

> [T]hose groups emerging out of long periods of oppression through political and economic struggle must define new identities for themselves which are often based on long submerged traditions. This struggle for a new group, identity can get mixed up with underlying potent cultural complexes which have accrued historical experience and memory over centuries and trauma and lie slumbering in the cultural unconscious, waiting to be awakened by the trigger of new trauma.
>
> (ibid)

When the prevailing cultural and social energies in the twentieth and twenty-first centuries within American society regarding the positions of gender, race and sexuality are considered, the quote just cited clarifies and partially explains the pluralistic social and cultural positions that we are currently engaged with. American fathers are arguably asked to carry the Shadow aspects of American society and the American Dream, with its emphasis on material success and social mobility. This success 'by any means necessary' exacts a price. As mentioned previously, the American father is tasked with the role of provider, often at the expense of other, equally important, roles. With regard to the social and cultural position of the masculine, as theorised earlier in the thesis, the triple challenge of feminism, gay rights and civil rights has prompted, in effect, the eruption of a masculine cultural complex. Added to these economic challenges, and echoing Connell's (1995) work on hegemonic and subaltern masculinities, the masculine has arguably pluralised and reacted to these challenges in various ways. As Singer and Kimbles identify:

> Intense collective emotion is the hallmark of an activated cultural complex at the core of which is an archetypal pattern. Cultural complexes structure emotional experience and operate in the personal and collective psyche in much the same way as individual complexes, although their content might be quite different.
>
> (2004, p. 6)

The father as a cultural and cinematic presence in American society can therefore be arguably located in the cultural Shadow, as Bruzzi (2005) correctly identifies, and if we are to judge by the filmic representations and depictions in the films discussed later. Going further, the father is portrayed as a highly nuanced and complex cultural symbol of American masculinity, as well as functioning as a cultural complex in itself, with a degree of capacity for redemptive behaviour which is sometimes, but not always, depicted as embracing.

## American fathers, American Dreams

When we consider the paternal cultural complex, there is an obligation, imposed by the recognition of cultural differences, to be culturally specific. Considering that all of the case study films pertain to American society and culture, it is contingent that our analysis addresses the specificities of American culture and how they are specifically depicted within the said films. What can be termed the universal father is not necessarily the American father; the American archetypal father has distinct features that are discussed in more detail later. Before we begin a deeper critical analysis of the films, it is necessary to explore the myths and cultural narratives that are present within American society that impact on the father archetype, and, in particular, the so-called American Dream. It is this cultural construct that provides contextualisation of the American paternal.

## Dreams, fantasies and film

The American Dream is a near-constant presence within both mainstream and fringe-American culture and originated within the American Constitution, specifically in the famous statement ' that among these [rights] are Life, Liberty and the pursuit of Happiness'. This founding statement of egalitarianism, individualism, and with strong hints for both social and financial improvement, developed into what has been termed the 'American Dream', a cultural myth that promoted the illusion of meritocratic fairness and equality of opportunity within American society. This myth was further promulgated by, amongst others, the nineteenth-century works of writers such as Horatio Alger, in whose stories the main protagonists were able to socially and fiscally advance by hard work, thrift and honesty. By the twentieth century, the American Dream was arguably well established as a national narrative that echoed the material and social benefits of the puritan work ethic but simultaneously contained a deep denial of other factors (social class, race and economic inequality) that contradicted the idea that happiness and freedom were available to all who, crucially, were prepared to work for it.

When applied to film and cinematic portrayals, there have been a large number of analyses of the American Dream. Writers such as Arnold (2013), Duncan (2015), Narloch (2008), Ortner (2013), Osteen (2012), Rosen (1973), Sands (2017) and Winn (2007) have all argued that the American Dream (refracted via different genres and narratives) has proved to be a largely illusionary affair. This is in spite of Hollywood producing numerous films that doggedly depict that the American Dream is both alive and achievable – e.g. *The Pursuit of Happyness* (Muccino, 2006, USA), or, with a rare mainstream nod to feminist sensibilities, *Baby Boom* (Shyer, 1987, USA). Winn argues, 'The American Dream assures that no class system hampers an individual's advancement, even though many Americans experience structural class limitations daily' (2007, 6). He quotes Fisher (1973) to reiterate that the American Dream consists of two myths, 'the materialistic success myth and the moralistic myth of brotherhood' (ibid). Financial, career and social improvements are held to be achievable to anyone who is prepared to work hard, and there exists a supposedly supportive egalitarian society in which this advancement takes place with opportunities available to all who seek them. These myths extend throughout American society but are, at their heart, a contradictory discourse in that they simultaneously celebrate, reinforce, challenge, subvert and openly disbelieve the American Dream, if we are to judge by recent cultural products such as film. It is these contrasting symptoms that indicate that the American Dream operates not only as a national narrative but also as a cultural complex with the American father at its heart.

The previous example of *The Pursuit of Happyness* demonstrates the filmic American father as a key player within the American Dream. In the film, Chris Gardner (Will Smith) is beset by setback after setback in his quest to advance his career and provide for his son (Jaden Smith). In this film, it is crucially the father who assumes both paternal and maternal roles; the mother (Thandie Newton) is represented as giving up on improving her situation and abandons her family. After a stereotypical Hollywood uplifting narrative journey involving struggle, sacrifice and hard work, Gardner is successful at gaining well-paid employment with a stockbroking firm (both material success and social mobility being presented here as the rewards for all of his efforts), ensuring a twenty-first-century version of the American Dream is achieved.

Whilst based on real events and people, the social and cultural contexts of the characters are largely marginalised. The overall focus of the film is concerned with a virulently Darwinian version of subjective self-help and pathologically asserts that the American Dream is still shown to be achievable and, more importantly for our purposes, has the father at its core. The film depicts the paternal as the source and producer of familial and financial power and simultaneously implies that poverty is more often than not a matter of laziness and poor choices, rather than socially endemic, or economically engendered. When compared to films that sharply critique the American Dream and the paternal within them, e.g. *Wall Street* (Stone, 1987, USA) or *Happiness* (Solondz, 1998, USA), contemporary mainstream Hollywood is arguably still generating celebratory myths of the American Dream.

Focusing on the films and fathers within the case study films, the American Dream and its effect on the American father are refracted in complex and interesting ways. The elements of success and failure with regard to the American Dream are acutely observed, for example, in both *American Beauty* and *Revolutionary Road*. Lester Burnham is aware that he is supposed to be chasing the American Dream and be successful, but he is also aware that somehow he fell asleep along the way. This is to the chagrin of his wife, Caroline (Annette Bening), who is still very much in thrall to this aspect of the American cultural complex. She is landed with carrying this energy but at the cost of their marriage. Frank Wheeler (Leonardo di Caprio) is portrayed as a victim of the American Dream, sacrificing his wife and soul in the name of suburban security and success. By sharp contrast in *There Will Be Blood*, Daniel Plainview is driven to slow madness and murder by being consumed by the idea of success; the American Dream effectively becomes an American nightmare for him. With the film showing how America's cultural complex developed and eventually became located in the collective Shadow, his role as father holds out the hope of redemption, but this chance is rejected by him. In Anderson's *Magnolia* and *Boogie Nights*, the American Dream can still be achieved, not by hard work, but by shortcuts, as mentioned earlier. In *Hard Eight*, Sydney (Philip Baker Hall) mentors his surrogate son through the shadowy world of professional gambling and low-level crime, a big win or a big score being the easy route to material success. Similarly, in Spielberg's *Catch Me If You Can* (2002), Frank Abalone (Leonardo Di Caprio) takes the self-invention aspect of the American Dream to extremes when he performs skilful confidence tricks. In *Magnolia*, TV quiz shows promise instant success and riches to ordinary people, most significantly children, who seek to minimise or circumvent the hard work ordinarily required to succeed. These faster routes to success and material wealth are, in effect, short-circuiting the American Dream, with the Puritan work ethic being subsumed into other, shadowy areas. The fathers in these films are still mediating the American Dream but from within the Shadow, confounding normative expectations of American society.

Elsewhere, fathers are present by their absence, e.g. *Fight Club* (Fincher, 1999) and are specifically referenced in the dialogue as being irresponsible and worthy of contempt. Tyler Durden (Brad Pitt), the film's narrator's (Edward Norton) Shadow driven alter ego, coldly states, with a distinct vicious flatness to his voice, that he'd 'like to fight his dad!'. The father has effectively become the Shadow in this film, with Fincher brutally satirising the emptiness of late capitalist America material wealth, and by proxy, the American Dream. In *Winter's Bone* (Granik, 2010), the father is absent and yet still negatively affecting his family from beyond his watery grave, as his heroic daughter, Ree Dolley (Jennifer Lawrence), struggles to both fulfil his traditional role as caregiver and provider, and at the same time, prevent their home from being seized due to his failure to make his court appearance. In addition to these symbolic journeys, the symbol of the gun also emerges as being a key part of the American father's symbolic portfolio, with, for example, *Road to Perdition* explicitly showing that the father is an armed presence, a throwback in some ways to early frontier fathers. Guns are also the necessary tools of the trade for the criminal gangs in the film, crime essentially being one of the main Shadow sides of capitalism and another Shadow response to the American Dream. In *American Beauty*, the enlightened father (Lester) is killed by the Shadow father, Colonel Fitts (Chris Cooper) by gun, and in *Jarhead*, guns are explicitly signalled both as masculine symbols and, more significantly, as paternal symbols, Staff Sergeant Sykes (Jamie Foxx) firing a noticeably bigger machine gun than his men at the end of the conflict. As discussed in more detail in later chapters, guns are an integral tool of both the father and part of the wider American cultural complex.

In summary, the American father is a key part of the American Dream and of American culture. The personal processes and masculine individuative journeys depicted are strongly coloured by their cultural context. When the American Dream becomes part of the American Shadow cultural complex, then the father falls within this complex and Shadow as well. When the American Dream becomes a cultural complex and an obstacle to masculine individuation, the father archetype can also become an obstacle to American men seeking to transcend the American cultural complex. In these cases, the father carries the cultural Shadow, which in American society can also represent competitive capitalism. With the child archetype (both sexes) also arguably suffering the effects of Shadow capitalism and the American cultural complex, father hunger takes on a transcendent function in that the child archetype points the way towards a more balanced American culture, transcending the American cultural complex and its preoccupations with material success, power and social mobility. With this borne in mind, we can now turn to deeper analyses of the films and the various father figures within them.

## Notes

1 (Bassil-Morozow, 2015; Stam, 2000) – 'In a way, using Jung to analyse film narratives is an equivalent to thinking outside the box – to challenge the established norm'.
2 It needs to be stated that 'psychic' here is used in a very specific way in analytical psychology, in that it relates primarily to matters both of the psyche and anything arising from it. It does not relate to any supernatural or occult phenomena.
3 Teleological explanations are concerned more with an understanding in terms of purpose and the end result, rather than the more reductionist view that involves known and identifiable prior causes.
4 This journey of the Self includes compensating for imbalances in the self-regulating psyche which can manifest as complexes, neuroses and psychoses.
5 Individuation is the name Jung gave to the process of the human psyche becoming a fully realised, self-sustaining and self-reliant whole.
6 Don Fredericksen in his classic 1979 essay *Jung/sign/symbol/film* falls into this trap when discussing signs and symbols in relation to films.
7 The role that the father in the formation of the daughter's psyche is covered later within another chapter and has distinctly different developmental features compared to that of the father-son relationship.

# Chapter 3

# The father

## Shadows of the American Dream

The father, both symbolically and imaginary, is fundamentally an ambivalent figure. Within American cinema, he represents both liberty and restriction, danger and safety, asexuality and eroticism, nurturing and neglect. As such, he is perfectly suited to be a locus point of the American Dream with its fundamental ambiguities and contradictions. In Levinson's *The American Success Myth on Film* (2012), she argues that the American Dream is successful *precisely* because of these contradictions around the search for success and their high price for the searcher:

> We embrace the bromides of the success myth, all the while harbouring doubts about its promises. Both perspectives are strands in a densely woven, if not always logically coherent, narrative about success and American identity. This bifurcated stance toward success runs side-by-side throughout the history of Hollywood, sometimes within a single telling of the tale.
>
> (p. 174)

The American Dream, in other words, is a classic cultural complex, embracing cultural neuroses and psychoses about the American nation and society. Cinema acts as a symptomatic barometer of this complex; Levinson again summarising the role that films play:

> They tap into the essential duality at the heart of the cultural rhetoric about the American idea of success; the exhilarating sense of freedom to craft our own destinies co-exists with anxiety, bafflement, and disappointment about the limitations of personal agency in fulfilling our ambitions and balancing our material and spiritual desires.
>
> (ibid)

Bearing these contradictions in mind, we can now start to analyse the American father in terms of the roles he is put in by filmmakers and how he contributes to father hunger, either his own or his children's. At the same time, his role within the American Dream needs to be scrutinised and to what extent he is a puppet of his society's cultural complexes, as well as his contributions to the cultural

DOI: 10.4324/9780429199684-4

complexes. Accordingly, this chapter is divided up into a number of archetypal roles that the father is often cast in; these roles are deeply symptomatic of the differing ambiguities of both father hunger and the American Dream. The American family and the American father are depicted in the chosen films as social constructs that are primarily located within the American cultural complex and are, more often than not, dominated by the patriarch. Redemption is depicted within these films as a main narrative driver; the father is essentially portrayed as fallen in a spiritual sense and shown to need to redeem themselves in order to connect to the numinous. This numinosity is not a feature of the American Dream within the texts; indeed, the films show the American Dream as more of an obstacle to achieving a spiritual awareness than a channel towards the same. Levinson argues that hard work used to have spiritual connotations, but that this belief is now under pressure:

> Careerism has generally replaced the notion of a calling, and work is often seen simply as the route to riches and recognition that are the emblems of success. . . . Characters in success stories frequently find themselves in a double bind: success is gained through one's work, but work doesn't seem to yield contentment. The ambiguity and anxiety at the core of these movies are part of an ongoing American discourse about the vexed relationship between work and self-worth, as well as between material and spiritual fulfilment.
>
> (2012, p. 66)

In addition to this awareness of the cultural complexes and symbolic energies at work, there is also a need for methodological alertness. As we will be analysing the films from a symbolic perspective, we need to be aware of the potential limits of Jungian symbolism, outlined in the previous chapter; these need to be made explicit. Bassil-Morozow and Hockley argue that:

> While the Jungian view of images appears to be flexible, intuitive and non-rational, in fact it is highly codified, constrained and structured . . . in this respect, Freudian and Jungian views of the image and the symbol are actually much closer than they first appear, and much closer than Jung himself allows for.
>
> (2017, p. 65)

Consequently, whilst Jungian symbol interpretation will be followed, paradoxically there needs to be maintained a healthy scepticism of the meanings assigned to the symbols, in effect building on the work carried out by previous scholars, but being mindful of differing interpretations. Bassil-Morozow and Hockley comment further:

> Looking for a definitive meaning in a film is not a mature attitude because it gives an illusion of safety and control. True meaning is unpredictable,

exciting or even dangerous, and is linked to that moment in space and time when the film is being watched by this particular audience.

(ibid, pp. 20–21)

The danger is that by over-literalising the symbols, analysis can lead to what is termed by Bassil-Morozow and Hockley 'reverse alchemy' which can 'transmute[s] the affect-laden symbolic quality of the image into a leaden literal description' (ibid, p. 74). Clearly, this is inimical to deeper understanding of the symbolic power of film and is similar to the caution urged by Fredericksen when regarding semiotic interpretation; we need to bear in mind that the classical semiotic approach is intent on eliminating mystery from a cultural product; to make the unknown known. This can also lead to 'reverse alchemy'. Whereas a psychoanalytical approach thrives on making the unknown known, in effect decoding symbols (the image and symbol functioning as an obstacle); a post-Jungian approach is to restore the unknown as a method or gateway to experiencing other aspects of the psyche. As Fredericksen puts it:

> The semiotic attitude is ultimately limiting because it either denies the existence of the symbolic realm by definition or denies its existence in practice by attempting to explain symbolic expressions semiotically. Frequently it does both simultaneously since the two denials implicate one another. The limiting character of the semiotic attitude involves a clear hubris of – and often a fear by – the rational and the conscious mind toward the irrational and unconscious mind.

(2001, pp. 27–28)

With these caveats borne in mind, attention can now be turned to a closer engagement with the symbology and semiotics of the films.

## The redeemed father – *American Beauty, Hard Eight, The Road to Perdition*

### *Redeemed by rebellion: Lester Burnham in* **American Beauty**

*American Beauty* (Mendes, 1999) is located in contemporary American suburbia, a symbolically significant location. David Coon (2014) provides a pithy description of this liminal space:

> Suburbia is a concrete spatial arrangement that shapes the everyday lives of the majority of Americans and expresses many of the hopes and fears embedded within American society. Although it may be a far cry from reality, the idea of a perfect suburban life still exists in the collective imaginations of millions of Americans.

(p. 3)

Similar to *Revolutionary Road* (Mendes, 2008), analysed later and set in 1950s Connecticut, little is changed in terms of the American cultural unconscious and its various cultural complexes lurking within its cultural Shadow. In the film, Mendes depicts the wider American society and environment, including the modern workplace, as ultimately damaging to the figure of the father, albeit with the focus on an older father who slowly realises the danger he is in and rebels accordingly. Alongside this emphasis on the dangers of symbolic urban space for masculinities and for fathers, the father is highlighted as symbolically rebelling by reclaiming a sexual presence. Before we analyse this further, it is worth examining the American father, in this case, Lester Burnham, and his space in terms of home and workplace as they reveal key symbolic details for consideration.

Lester is portrayed in the early scenes as symbolically, socially and economically castrated, with his dull, life-sapping job that threatens to redeploy him, and his false, image-of-success position within the Burnham's social circle, a view that his wife wholeheartedly subscribes to, much to Lester's distaste, but one that he reluctantly goes along with, not having the courage, at least in the beginning, to say no. Mendes refracts the clichéd view of the American Dream and the idealised American home with a white picket fence specifically referenced within the opening sequence of the film. When Lester is making his family late for work, the camera places Lester directly at the centre of the shot, balanced by the carefully controlled and clipped garden (naturally adorned with American Beauty roses). The palette is carefully chosen to reflect the thematic concerns, with the red, white and blue of this particular scene specifically symbolically referencing the American flag's colours, leaving the spectator in no doubt as to where we are, both geographically, symbolically, and societally. Lester's neighbourhood is, like Frank and April Wheeler's in *Revolutionary Road*, white, middle-class and defiantly aspirational; all the more jarring when we consider Lester's voiceover at the beginning of the film: 'My family think I'm this giant loser. And, in a way, they're right. I have lost something . . . but it's never too late to get it back'.

The shot of a grey-clad Lester dozing in the back of his wife's SUV on the commute to work is also carefully symptomatic of another one of the film's main themes: that of soul unconsciousness. By deliberately choosing a grey palette and placing Lester in the back of the car, while his wife is driving, Lester's apathy and timidity about his role as a husband and father is subtly emphasised. Lester and Frank Wheeler are kindred spirits in that they have unconsciously allowed their individual identity to be subsumed; greyness is depicted as the symbolic uniform of the working American male. Similar to Frank, Lester is positioned in an anonymous cubicle within a much larger (and grey) office, his worker-drone status (or as Leonard puts it, a 'semi-conscious cubicle worker' [2010, p. 828]) reinforced by a striking image in the opening scene at his work of his reflection on his computer screen, held captive behind meaningless columns of numbers reminiscent of prison bars, as he deals with a fruitless phone call. The scene with his efficiency expert boss Brad is shot deliberately to emphasise Lester's lack of power within his working realm, traditionally viewed as a source of male power and privilege.

It is clear from the camera angles on Brad (shot from below eye line and composed so that Brad fills the screen) contrasted with the camera line on Lester (shot from above and composed so that Lester only fills half the screen) that Lester is not a male with any real power or agency within his workplace, a common complaint with contemporary capitalist corporations (Faludi, 2000). Within the workplace depicted here, there is the illusion of being part of a team working towards a goal, but workers within this type of structure are under no illusions that they are expendable, redundant and ultimately powerless. Warren Farrell identifies this as part of the greater attitude to males that they are often perceived as both 'success objects' and disposable if they do not achieve enough success (1988, p. 134). As Lester puts it in the second meeting with his boss, after he has begun his rebellion: 'I've been a whore for the advertising industry for fourteen years'. He views his job as little more than economic prostitution for a corporate paymaster; an explicit critique of the American Dream and its overweening emphasis on material success as the source of happiness. Levinson identifies Lester as one of the

> work-averse refusenik(s) crop[ing] up in other guises in the age of commodity capitalism . . . a middle-aged malcontent who opts for underemployment rather than unemployment, as he knowingly bails out of his career in order to search for what he hopes are more authentic satisfactions.
> 
> (2012, p. 170)

This scene of successful rebellion is almost the reverse of the first in terms of mise-en-scene, with Lester framed by the camera in much more equal terms to Brad. Lester's triumphant march out of his corporate prison is composed of a long tracking shot, with partially opaque glass partitions between us and Lester, until he emerges, openly celebrating his victory over his corporate oppressors, a victory that came about through threatened financial and sexual workplace blackmail.

Lester's largely unconsciously handover of his power to his corporate employer is left deliberately ambiguous and vague; we are not informed within the film itself whether he embraced the corporate role or reluctantly took the job. The net result, fourteen years later, is the same, Lester is depicted as essentially powerless. His supposed source of economic power, his job (and the privileges that are assumed to accompany it) is depicted as a male privilege that exacts a high price, similar to *Revolutionary Road*. Lester's growing recognition of the symbolic and actual restrictions that the American cultural unconscious and American society, with its overt emphasis on material success (usually at the expense of, or substitute for, inner psychic development) impose on both masculinities and femininities, is what gives the film a large part of its narrative drive and power. Symbolically (and ironically), as Lester rebels and rescues his masculinity from his workplace and society, he becomes sexually more potent, re-discovering his wife as sexually attractive, and flirting with his daughter's best friend Angela (Mena Suvari). In terms of redeeming himself, a part of Lester's redemption is achieved by rebelling against his invisible prison; another part is his decision *not* to have sex with his daughter's best friend, discussed in more detail later.

The father in *American Beauty* is initially located as needing redemption; he has symbolically sinned by allowing himself to be controlled by the cultural complexes within the American cultural unconscious; the symbolic depiction of the paternal shows the father as trapped by normative American societal expectations, the figure of the suburban father is effectively shorthand for a strain of conformist subaltern masculinity. The paternal is signed as not being free (in a Jungian sense) to pursue individuative psychic desires. Heteronormative American society is, therefore, arguably portrayed as actively repressing the numinous; the heart of *American Beauty* is the encounter with the numinous that Lester experiences, courtesy of his anima. This is explicitly shown as being counter to what American society is shown to demand (conformity and obedience to normative mores). When we further consider the depicted repressed sexual desires and drives of both Lester Burnham and Colonel Frank Fitts, the figure of the father within wider American society is also signalled as a site of repressed emotions, both personally and culturally, despite the fundamental act of fathering being a sexual act; there is an open questioning of normative, conformist, heterosexual and heterosocial familial masculinity, with Lester Burnham (and Frank Wheeler in *Revolutionary Road*) as father figures who are undergoing similar crises of masculine identity. Yet with both texts, there is a sense that each of the films is in love with the very thing it is criticising; *American Beauty* with the incest motif, and *Revolutionary Road* with the conformity it purports to despise, despite there being only white, middle-class pain on offer to melodramatically denounce. There is, consequently, an ambivalent attitude depicted towards fathers and men within American society (similar to the ambivalence within the American Dream) within these films, despite signalling how patriarchal social structures are depicted as being damaging to fathers, sons and men.

## *Hard Eight*: The redemption of the replacement father

Paul Thomas Anderson's first film, *Hard Eight* (1996), like *American Beauty*, has emphasis on father hunger from the point of view of the father himself, Sydney Brown (Anderson regular, Philip Baker Hall). Sydney is the main focus of the film, his presence both reassuring and at the same time, ambivalent, another thematic consistency of the director that can be found across his output. King notes that the film:

> opens with a strong narrative enigma, setting up firm expectations . . . Central narrative enigma remains important, and is subject to strategies of retardation and partial answer that might be found in Hollywood, but there is also a degree of sustained delay and displacement that would not usually be expected in the mainstream.
>
> (2005, pp. 77–78)

Here, the father is shown as driven by a need for redemption in seeking out a surrogate son, in this case a failed amateur gambler, John Finnegan (John C Reilly). Here, the filmic context is the shades-of-grey world of American gambling capitals Las Vegas and Reno and their inhabitants, another fringe social group that have their own rules and culture, very similar to the porn industry explored within Anderson's second film, *Boogie Nights* (1997). The film, a psychological crime drama, examines the mystery around the motivations of Sydney in choosing to look after and mentor John and his girlfriend, later wife, Clementine (Gwyneth Paltrow). Similar to *American Beauty*, the film nails its thematic colours to the mast within the first few scenes as Sydney and John Finnegan meet, seemingly by accident, and Sydney quietly and efficiently teaching John how to survive in his newly adopted subculture. This teaching is deliberately reminiscent of paternal instruction and is arguably indicative of the masculine transfer of worldly knowledge as referenced previously (a grey-area *logos* energy, as it were). This archetypal masculine transfer of knowledge is set amidst the shadowy atmosphere of the American gambling subculture and associated dangers and traps, a world which it is presumed that the spectator is unfamiliar with. Here, the American Dream has transmogrified into how to win at gambling, an inversion of the puritan work ethic, and a shortcut to material success, in effect, short-circuiting the American Dream. The father figure here is, in effect, indirectly teaching the audience tips on how to survive and thrive in this world, a form of subtle paternalistic mentoring. This assumption of surrogate father to John by Sydney is also consistent with the major theme of what Goss observes being within 'the Andersonian world: the implosion of family life and the longing to restore it' (2002, p. 180). This implosion and subsequent need for restoration is a dominant theme within the film; Sydney's surrogate parental role is notable as it establishes him as John's protector and father to the point where he manipulates Clementine and John into becoming a couple. John is portrayed as being under Sydney's influence to such a degree that he has to establish permission to sleep with her by confirming that Sydney has *not* slept with her. As Goss comments: 'She functions within the film as a "gift" bequeathed by the guilt-laden father figure to the surrogate son' (ibid).

Sydney's surrogate relationship with John is both noticed and commented on first by Clementine. His self-appointed role as surrogate father to John is obliquely critiqued by her when she asks Sydney in a scene in a diner whether or not he has any 'real kids?' His affirmative answer, after a defensive pause, is both surprising and illuminating; he has not seen them in many years and does not know where they are. With this scene, we are presented with a partial explanation for Sydney's now acknowledged fatherly presence; he is missing his own biological children and seeks to replicate his missing relationship with them with his new relationship with John. It is not until later, when Jimmy (Samuel L Jackson), John's sinister new friend, who has prior knowledge of Sydney and his past, does the truth emerge. Jimmy acts a Shadow truth-teller/Trickster[1] figure around the depth and veracity of Sydney and John's surrogate relationship when he points out to Sydney in a confrontation near the end of the film: 'No matter how hard you try, you will never be John's father'. This explicit refutation of Sydney's new parental role is devastating for Sydney and, coupled with Jimmy's attempted blackmail over the fact that Sydney himself shot dead John's biological father years before, results in Sydney shooting Jimmy dead to preserve his guilty secret. The symbolic family unit that Sydney has carefully and painstakingly built is protected by him by deadly means, such is the depth of his hunger to be a father, driven by guilt at his previous transgressions.

This key reveal for the audience of Sydney's guilty motivation for taking on the parental role to John solves the initial mystery set up at the beginning. By depriving him of a father, Sydney feels obliged to fulfil the role himself. The father hunger examined in *Hard Eight* is depicted as being generated by violence and guilt but is also motivated by the need for masculine redemption, later echoed in Anderson's *Magnolia* in particular. Father hunger is depicted here as a mutual, co-dependent emotion, with both John and Sydney being caught up in its affective grasp. The recognition of the truth by Sydney is reflected by his final phone call to John in one of the last scenes of the film: 'There's something I want you to know. This is very important. I want you to know that I love you. (Pause). *Like* a father loves his son' (my italics). Sydney has now faced up to the knowledge that he can never truly be John's father, and acknowledges that to John, all the while hiding past truths. Sydney is portrayed as a complex and ambivalent figure, his motivations initially unknown and murky, not surprisingly, considering the sub-culture he has chosen to make his career in. His chance at a symbolic form of masculine redemption via surrogacy is what gives the film its narrative drive and thematic impact and constructs the masculinities performed here as essentially hopeful in terms of guilt lifted and redemption partially achieved. Here, the American Dream, as well as the role of the father within it, is neatly inverted by Anderson into a narrative examining the price that is paid by subaltern cultures that American cultural complexes have forced into the collective cultural Shadow.

## *Road to Perdition*: redemption of the criminal father

Sam Mendes's second film, released in 2002, was, on the surface, a conventional gangster film, located in a specific time period and geography (the American Mid-West/Chicago area in the winter of 1931) and was based on a graphic novel by Max Allan Collins. Ostensibly the story of how an Irish mob hitman and enforcer (conveniently a First World War hero), Michael Sullivan (Tom Hanks), takes his revenge on his employers after they murder his wife and youngest son after the elder son witnesses a mob hit; the film also deals with strong redemptive themes and marks the individuative journey of both the father and the son. Whilst the film is comfortably located within the gangster genre (signalled by the use of signature motifs and tropes such as Thompson machine guns, black getaway cars, etc.), the main difference to other films in its genre is that it approaches the subject matter from a markedly different angle, namely examining the henchman and his family through the perspective of a twelve-year-old boy, Michael junior (Tyler Hoechlin) and the violence that they suffer when the familial and societal power structures that surround the family, and they are an integral part of, turn against them. This has echoes of an older, almost mythic like tale, a point picked up by Beck:

> *Road to Perdition* is such a tale, honoured for the strength of and depth of all its elements, especially the performances. . . . Here is a straightforward version of the old story of an honourable, loyal, and violent man whose family is destroyed and whose own life is threatened by the self-centred cruelty of those he served and who owed him good treatment.
>
> (2003, p. 25)

Oxoby concurs with this view when he points out the similarity to other, more classical narratives 'more than one film critic has compared *Road to Perdition* to Greek tragedy, in which, regardless of the choices the characters make, their fates are sealed' (2002, p. 111). This observation around the mythic quality of the film also is reminiscent of Joseph Campbell's arguments: 'Freud, Jung and their followers have demonstrated irrefutably that the logic, and the deeds of myth survive into modern times' (1949, p. 4). Added to the classic archetypal narrative foundations of the film is the emphasis on the father-son relationships that permeate throughout, from the dark patriarch Mr Rooney's (Paul Newman) sharply differentiated natural and surrogate sons, Connor Rooney (Daniel Craig) and Michael Sullivan respectively, and Michael Snr's relationship with Michael Jnr., Mendes demonstrates keen awareness of the mythical narrative logic within his film by virtue of his mediation of the imagery and awareness of masculine development and paternal relationships, with the story involving classical themes and motifs of violence, appeasement, and sacrifice, themes that are dealt with from different aspects by Freud and Jung. Alongside the mythic elements, the genre and historical setting echoes Hamad about historical locations being deliberately used to locate paternal post-feminist representations:

> [I]n films like these the past is configured as a safe space in which to locate and idealize archaic formations of masculinity, a scenario typically negotiated through a mediating discourse of post-feminist fatherhood. These masculinities thus appear divested of political charge as their cultural recidivism is naturalized by their displacement to historical settings.
>
> (2014, p. 28)

The fathers and sons depicted here are engaged in complex and tension-ridden patterns of relating, echoing the masculine journey, but fleshed out with telling details and skilled use of cinematic features, techniques, and most important of all for the purposes of the book, symbols. For example, when Michael Jnr is sent by his mother to the parental bedroom to call his father down for dinner, he spies his father emptying his pockets of keys, money, and finally a Colt .45 automatic pistol, explicitly signalling this particular dark father's power. Symbolically speaking, and individually, money, a gun and keys can possess any number of meanings; referencing the symbolic context, these symbols *together* portray the father's role as a symbolically and semiotically explicit figure of power at this juncture. The paternal is thus established in the film under what Jung described as *logos*, or the rule of the father,[2] and is signed as both provider and protector for the family in the material world. The son, for his part, can only watch from afar into this explicitly adult and masculine space that he is not yet ready or old enough to inhabit.

After his wife and youngest son are murdered by his surrogate brother, Connor Rooney, Michael Snr and his oldest son Michael Jnr embark on a Shadow-driven journey of redemption, which will involve violence and death. Spiritual redemption for Michael Snr is signalled throughout the film and culminates in his penultimate meeting with his surrogate father figure, John Rooney. Taking place in the basement of a church, this site resonates with a number of symbolic meanings. Traditionally in Jungian psychology, any underground spaces signify the unconscious, and the descent into the unconscious, very often meeting some archetypal aspect of the Shadow whilst located there. In this scene, the space is not only dark, cold, dank and uninhabited, but filled with broken and disused religious icons and statues (presumably Catholic, given the Irish ancestry of the gang), hinting strongly at the spiritual state of both men. This deliberate use of redundant religious imagery and the location is a potent reminder to the audience of the spiritual state of both men and reflected by the following angry exchange between surrogate father and surrogate son:

ROONEY: There are *only* murderers in this room. Michael, open your eyes! This is the life we chose. The life we lead. And there is only one guarantee – none of us will see heaven.
SULLIVAN: Michael could.
ROONEY: Then do everything that you can to see that that happens.

The use of this symbolism is obvious and overt, arguably even heavy-handed; both men are on their way to hell (beneath a church, place of redemption, and consequently unlikely to find any). As the crypt can be viewed as representing the unconscious, we can posit that Michael Snr is now confronted by Shadow aspects of his psyche and also by his own chosen surrogate paternal telling him a hard truth. This confrontation illuminates the chance of redemption that Michael Snr has before him. Despite being a murderer, he can still prevent his son from following him down a violent path. This redemption, however, comes at a heavy price; in order to get to Connor Rooney and complete his vengeance, Michael Snr must violently supplant his surrogate father, John Rooney. After Michael Snr's execution of Rooney and most of his gang, and his subsequent execution of Connor, the masculine spaces *appear* again to be safe for father and son. Father and son decide to go to their relative's house on the lake in the town Perdition, a seemingly safe space to recuperate and begin the next phase of their lives. However, the now-deformed assassin Maguire (Jude Law), who has been lying in wait for them, manages to mortally wound Michael Snr by shooting him in the back in a wordlessly composed, almost ghostly, scene, highly reminiscent of the opening sequence that introduces to the story. In turn, as he gloats over Michael Snr dying in front of him, Maguire is challenged by Michael Jnr threatening him with his own pistol. As this tense standoff proceeds to a potential dangerous climax, his father shoots Maguire from behind, thereby saving Michael from going down a road to violence and redeeming himself from his previous parricidal actions when he killed his own surrogate father. This act of sacrifice and redemption can be seen as highly symbolic in terms of Michael Jnr's spiritual development (in the graphic novel, he is narrating the story from his calling as priest).

The mythic qualities of violence and blood being shed are mediated here symbolically, with violence paying back violence to achieve narrative resolution. The space that Michael now inhabits is a liminal one with his spiritual safety ensured; from a post-Jungian perspective, the father has made a profound psychic transformation with his sacrifice for his son. The film ends as it begins at the lakeside, a masculine initiatory journey and cycle successfully embarked on and completed with Michael Jnr completing his original voiceover from the beginning describing his father in front of the lake, water being a constant motif that is used throughout the film. Water operates not only as a sign for death but also a symbol for spirit. Ronnberg and Martin highlight how lakes have carried an archetypal symbolic resonance:

> The lake, for many peoples, has been a symbol of the land of the dead, of life gone missing into the fluid substance and darkness of another world.... Standing at water's edge and gazing out over the surface, we pause and give way to dream, reflection, imagination and illusion: to other worlds below and beyond in ourselves, making lake symbolically the entry, for good or ill, into psyche's unconscious dimensions.
>
> (ibid, p. 44)

This act of reflection by Michael Jnr is referenced directly in the final shot, a circularity achieved as Michael Jnr narrates the end of his story, looking out over the lake and gazing into his past as he remembers his violent but redeeming father who saved both himself and his son by his sacrificial death. It is strongly implied that the son has transcended the father here, rather than become like him, a key difference between Freudian and Jungian psychological approaches.

## The unredeemed father – *There Will Be Blood, Magnolia, Revolutionary Road*

### *There Will Be Blood* – black oil and a dark soul

With *There Will Be Blood*, the father is portrayed in much darker tones, both in mise-en-scene and thematically. The story of Daniel Plainview (Daniel Day-Lewis) and his descent into greed-fuelled paranoia and madness, the film is set in the early days of the Californian oilfields, an apt metaphor for patriarchal American capitalistic urges, successes and excesses. Here, a determined and unflinching portrait of what can be termed 'Shadow American patriarchy' is depicted, with a much darker view of fatherhood and the consequences of father hunger, refracted primarily through the character of Plainview. The masculine journey is effectively depicted as a symbolic journey into a psychic void where the father and his *Logos* law may eventually rule supreme but, in doing so, costs the male protagonist his soul. The film is essentially the journey of a dark father, a violent and rapacious patriarch, described by Heyraud as 'a demonic force of nature, the incarnation of evil. His character embodies the underside of the American success story, stunningly illustrating how greed so tragically ignites violence' (2008, p. 180). In terms of the filmic techniques that Anderson uses, there is a marked difference between the two films. Compared to the director's previous film (*Magnolia*) with its telling and intimate close-ups of the main characters and hyperkinetic camerawork and editing to reflect the inner turmoil of the relationships on show, *There Will Be Blood* is a much more sombre affair in terms of mise-en-scene with Anderson directing the camera in a series of tableaus and slow pans, enabled by supportive editing. This is also a film without much dialogue; what there is, is often biblical in flavour and starkly delivered, reflecting both the historical milieu and the discourses under examination. In a similar vein, there are a number of symbolic images within the film, including memorably epic scenes of oil as a metaphor for the earth's blood (a direct reference to the film's title), gushing out of the ground similar to the bleeding from a huge wound. As Bassil-Morozow and Hockley remind us, 'Importantly, symbols should be respected and not over-interpreted; they are not signs with a fixed meaning but have multiple meanings' (2017, 52). Accordingly, oil is signalled as functioning within the film as power *and* money, but it also carries a dark spiritual charge. Early in the film, and in a deliberately ritualistic manner reminiscent of the Christian baptism ceremony, H.W.'s biological father symbolically anoints him on the forehead with a smudge of oil taken from a jet-black pond, looking like a huge and crude baptismal font. This short scene is arguably deeply symbolic and numinous in that in consciously substituting holy water for oil, this powerful initiation rite is both used and subverted. Fontana states: 'Baptism is a symbolic cleansing of sin – rebirth in the life-sustaining fluid of the earth-mother's womb' (1993, p. 70). Stevens agrees: 'Baptismal initiation, for example, proceeds through the stages of baptism, chrism and communion; and these correspond to the three degrees of mystic life: purification, illumination, and union' (1998, p. 216). Ronnberg and Martin also echo this potentially numinous act of rebirth:

> Christian baptism, with its commitment to the life of the spirit over that of the flesh, was in itself a bathlike immersion, originally meant to symbolize drowning and representing death to the old life and one's rebirth as a new being.
>
> (2010, p. 604)

This ritualistic rebirth is symbolically subverted by depicting H.W. as being baptised into a much harsher realm, as well as into the care of a dark father figure. What is worshipped in this film, namely power, greed and money, are all represented here by oil, the economic and material lifeblood of the twentieth century, and a quintessentially American industry, in that it contains all the ingredients of the American Dream.

Plainview's subsequent adoption of H.W. briefly offers the chance of humanising him, as he cares for what Heyraud calls 'a son-partner who carries the thread of conscience and reflection, symbolising the "divine child" that Daniel cannot integrate' (2008, p. 179). This act of fathering affords Plainview a brief hope of redemption until the child suffers deafness due to an accidental well blowout. Now crippled and consequently useless in his adoptive father's eyes, he is promptly packed off to school and away from Plainview's sight, another sly pun on his name, thereby causing Plainview to 'lose the only link to his already shattered sanity' (ibid). This slim chance at redemption for Plainview, in spite of his avowed dislike of humanity, is wasted by him as he continues to carve out his own empire in the style of his contemporary American robber-barons. To emphasise his character's outlook on life, the usually taciturn Plainview outlines his philosophy in an exchange with his possible half-brother as a simple hatred of humanity and an ability only to see the failings in others. McQuillan and McQuillan link this deep-seated misanthropy to the prevailing social and cultural ideas that were circulating in American society at the time: 'Plainview's ideology is reminiscent of the social Darwinistic theories prominent at the time that purported the benefits of the culling of the weak from society' (2008, p. 273). As Karlyn comments on the film in Hamad, 'the epic [film] celebrates nationhood, war, racial purity, and the "law of the father", offering spectacles of national violence and mythmaking in worlds peopled primarily by men' (2014, p. 29). This assertion is questionable in that *There Will be Blood* has epic qualities (cinematography, etc.) but in effect shows Plainview and his philosophical outlook as deeply flawed and destructive, the worst kind of chauvinistic American masculinity. The dark father in this film is depicted as both beyond redemption, and more importantly, not interested in its possibility. The hunger to be a father, had he allowed it (and explicitly exposed by his enemy, Eli Sunday (Paul Dano) in a deeply telling confessional scene), may have redeemed Plainview, but the narrative is steered towards dysfunctional patriarchalism, madness and violence. Many years later, when Plainview is semi-retired but still in control of his businesses, H.W. returns to him asking him to dissolve their business partnership so he can start out for himself. As H.W. has had the temerity to marry the sister of Plainview's arch-enemy Eli Sunday, Plainview refuses and deliberately and cruelly taunts him about his ancestry, deafness and character. This is archetypal dark father behaviour, mocking and destroying any masculinity other than his own, including his own family, and his own masculine line, ultimately proving to be self-destructive and self-devouring. Heyraud describes this encounter in more detail:

> His barbaric behaviour is alienating. A shred of redemptive possibility is expressed through the separation of H.W. from Daniel. If this were a dream or fairy tale, H.W.'s deafness could suggest a quiet inner connection that enables him to finally leave Daniel's house – a separation from the archetype of the "old King" presenting the possibility of new life. This is quite a heroic and hopeful stance – a very small spark of light in the midst of an atmosphere of darkness.
>
> (2008, p. 180)

The son (Child archetype) makes the first steps in transcending the American capitalist father, in this example, an enforced separation and determination to be never like him, expressed by H.W. with heartfelt feeling. When Plainview clubs to death Eli Sunday (the man who earlier forced him to admit that he had treated his son badly) in his bowling alley and utters the final lines of the film: 'I'm finished' it can be read as both an explicit recognition that he is finished as a man and a damned soul. All his efforts and material riches essentially count for nothing: he is alone in the world and will end his life as a murderer.

## *Magnolia*: Jimmy Gator: the unredeemed incestuous father

Unlike Sydney in *Hard Eight*, who achieves a partial redemption of sorts by the end of the film, Jimmy Gator (Philip Baker Hall) in *Magnolia* does not. One of a number of complex dysfunctional familial relationships that the film uses to weave its narrative, Jimmy and Claudia Gator (Melora Walters)'s relationship is presented as a troubled one from the start. Our first encounter with them takes place in Claudia's apartment, where the seemingly kindly and concerned Jimmy enters Claudia's domestic space to discover her casual lover from the previous night. Her violent language when he gently challenges her about her promiscuous behaviour is all the more shocking when contrasted to his own puzzled and ostensibly caring demeanour. Anderson uses the tight space in more subtle ways, the camera unflinching as it focuses on Claudia as she slumps to the ground, defeated by the visit of her father and the implied shame that he brings to her.

His seemingly genuine concern for her contrasts sharply with her swearing, and we are left with the impression that she is emotionally unstable (she is also shown snorting cocaine) and selfish. Anderson, however, paints a more subtle picture than at first appears. Writing about the puella aeternas (sister to the puer aeternas[3]), Schwartz describes Claudia's internal world accurately:

> [T]he emotional distress of the Puella, which remains hidden behind a persona that disguises the psychological tensions experienced by a woman in the Western world. . . . She feels essentially unlovable and experiences shame, vulnerability and fear, all based on a conviction of not being enough. When these feelings descend into the Shadow, they become internal persecutory figures that feel overwhelming.
>
> (2009, p. 112)

Through her tentative relationship with sensitive police officer Jim Kurring (John C Reilly), it is gradually revealed that Claudia *is* damaged, but damaged by her relationship with her father who, it is strongly implied, sexually abused her. Schwartz identifies the critical role that the father plays with the puella in a daughter's psyche:

> Fathers provide a doorway to the world and his interaction with her forms part of the foundation upon which a daughter builds her sense of self. He is integral to her identity formation as a woman and the unencumbered expression of her truth. The father complex is healthy or ill depending on how its energy has been internalized. A negative father complex adversely affects a daughter's intellectual confidence; promotes idealization of others, especially males; and destroys initiative. It feeds an internalized cycle of self-hatred, oppression and revenge.
>
> (2009, p. 115)

Claudia's troubled relationship with her ostensibly normal and, by the standards of the American Dream, highly successful father (he is well-known and popular TV host for a children's quiz show) is a classic case of this negative father complex, feeding her self-loathing (symbolically marked with her drug abuse and foul language) and hesitant and fumbled emotional encounters with Kurring. The sexual abuse revelations come after a verbal and emotional showdown with Jimmy's wife, Rose Gator (Melinda Dillon), in a tightly framed and claustrophobically filmed scene, powered by hesitant, but compelling dialogue:

JIMMY I think that she thinks I may have molested her.
(Pause). She thinks terrible things that somehow got in her head . . . that I might have done something. She said that to me last time . . . when it was . . . ten years ago she walked out the door, "You touched me wrong . . . I know that." Some crazy thought in her, in her head. . .
ROSE Did you ever touch her?
JIMMY No.

ROSE  Jimmy, did you touch her?
JIMMY  I don't know.

His transgressive secret uncovered, Rose declares flatly: 'You deserve to die alone for what you've done' and leaves him to be with her daughter. After this exchange, all hope extinguished by his abandonment by his family, and also suffering from terminal cancer, Jimmy attempts suicide on his own using a revolver.

Unbeknown to him, fate appears to have another plan with the *deus ex machina* narrative device of a rain of frogs spoiling his plans for suicide and instead condemn him to the grisly fate of burning to death via electrical fire. This scene is an uneasy mix of pathos and laughter with the plague of frogs acting as catalysing the climax to the multiplicity of narratives. The use of the frog is not only deliberate (referencing the Old Testament plague, hinted at by the relevant Bible reference in a blink-and-you-miss-it piece of graffiti on a wall) but on a symbolic level, more than a little significant. In *Ariadne's Clue*, Stevens reminds us that the frog represents:

> [A]n obvious symbol of transformation for not only does it change from tadpole to frog but it is a much at home in the water as it is on the land. It is a borderline or liminal case, hopping about on the threshold between consciousness and unconsciousness.
>
> (1998, p. 338)

Ronnberg and Martin also highlight its symbolic power of transformation:

> In dreams and fairy tales the frog arrives quite suddenly, out of water somewhere, just as an aspect (often princely) of self-substance emerges from the waters of the unconscious, but is not yet in fully conscious, recognizable form.
>
> (2010, p. 190)

Cooper states that the frog also represents:

> As arising from the waters it is renewal of life and resurrection, likewise as possessing the moist skin of life, as opposed the dryness of death . . . represents the dark and undifferentiated prima materia, the watery element and the primordial slime, the basis of created matter.
>
> (2016, p. 72)

In the film, Anderson mediates the frog symbolism as a highly effective pointer to the various psychic transformations that are taking place within the multiple narratives. In this particular case, the transformation is that of the dark American father in the form of Jimmy who cannot face his past actions towards his daughter, actions that are indicative of the erotic playback function (discussed in more detail later) in its negative form. The first scenes showing his initial bemusement about Claudia's reaction are all the more telling, and retroactively speaking, disturbing, when we consider his secret. The psychic transformation, hinted at by the rain of frogs, condemn him to a more painful and slower death than from his bullet, as is strongly hinted at by the fire that is inadvertently started. It appears that fate will punish Jimmy and that he will be transformed, if only to ashes, by the fire. Claudia and her mother are also shown as having re-connected, both of them tightly embracing each other as the frogs continue to fall, the maternal and daughter being joined as one feminine presence. Claudia's initial and obvious pain and father hunger displayed to us in her opening scenes is explained in these tragicomic final scenes and adds to the complex tableau of father-and-children relationships that is depicted throughout the film. Similar to Stanley, the quiz kid, however, the situation is far from hopeless. In a final coda, reminiscent of *American Beauty*, we see Claudia framed in close-up as Kurring stating positively that she can heal and that he will always be there for her. In a sense, the daughter's potential to transcend her father and the father-effect that he has had on her is very similar to the son's potential transcendence, discussed elsewhere. Claudia's tentative half-smile is a deliberately encouraging sign that daughters can yet survive both father hunger and the damage that dark American fathers inflict.

## *Revolutionary Road*: the trapped and unredeemed father

With *Revolutionary Road* (2008), Mendes depicts the figure of the American father as being trapped, and unredeemed, by two obstacles. The first is by another father (in this case a surrogate father), to the detriment of the younger man's psyche and maturation. Second, the American father's environment and social space also trap him, in both the domestic space and the work space. This state of what is, essentially, arrested masculinity is the journey of Frank Wheeler (Leonardo di Caprio) and is portrayed as a largely negative, tragic passage. Similar to *American Beauty*, the film also shares the same locale of suburbia as the principal setting for the narrative. By representing suburbia as a symbolically stifling and choking space for both the American masculine and the American feminine, fatherhood and masculinity are shown as being negatively affected by white, American middle-class, heterosocial society – suburbia being portrayed as its natural home (Coon, 2014) – with assumed male economic and social privileges accorded to the main protagonists either being scant consolation or being largely absent. Bruzzi identifies this situation:

> The strains, the repressive instincts, the disavowals and all the other attendant strategies deployed to hold up the 'normality' and hegemony of white, middle-class, heterosexual masculinity emerge furtively but frequently within classical Hollywood cinema, at a time when the explicit questioning of masculinity's status would have been more problematic.
>
> (2013, p. 38)

Heyraud also describes this situation: '*American Beauty* dramatically depicts how the psyche is lulled into a stupor by an illusional but seductive image of the "American Dream" in which real human connection is gravely sacrificed' (2000, p. 147). This assertion is equally applicable to *Revolutionary Road*, with its shared emphasis on keeping up clichéd white picket fence and barred windows appearances that are specifically referenced within the mise-en-scene of both films. Investigating this further, Richardson argues that the setting of the suburbs is more symptomatic of the deeper themes explored within *Revolutionary Road*: '[T]he deeper-lying problem . . . is the exposure of an empty self' (2010, p. 10). He then quotes Cushman for a more detailed summary of the landscape that has led to this situation:

> [T]his terrain has shaped 'a self that experiences these social absences and their consequences "interiorly" as a lack of personal conviction and worth, and it embodies the absences as a chronic, undifferentiated emotional hunger.'
> (ibid)

Mendes depicts the symbolic space of the American suburbs as masking this 'emotional hunger' that is expressed as father hunger by Frank within the film, an increasingly dark drive that ultimately leads to tragedy. *Revolutionary Road*'s subtext of the father's masculinity being under threat from the perceived restrictions and emptiness of mainstream heterosocial American society is also signalled by Mendes' deliberate use of the colour grey, similar to *American Beauty*. Ronnberg and Martin assert: 'Gray evokes saturnine "lead" and the moods that leadenness conveys: sadness, inertia, melancholy, indifference or boredom' (2010, p. 662). This is certainly echoed in Frank's job as an anonymous functionary in the catalogue/advertising department at Knox Business Machines, a middle class, white-collar position. The symbolic societal workspace that Frank occupies at Knox and travels from home to get to reflects this colourless landscape. Mendes portrays this anonymity of the father-worker through an extended and largely wordless sequence early in the film, where Frank goes through his morning routine of catching the commuter train to the city, where he is blended in the greyclad crowd of other workers through a subtle mix of cinematography, costume and mise-en-scene. The only way of identifying him is by virtue that he is centred within the framing. As Ronnberg and Martin describe it: 'There is indefiniteness about gray, embodied especially in gray clouds and fog, which add to its ambiguity' (2010, p. 662). This implied symbolic ambiguity perfectly describes Frank's position in both his internal psyche and his societal role. As Frank gets deeper into his paternal and personal crisis, he starts to challenge his routine actions (commuting to work, going through the motions within his marriage) and embarks on a brief affair with a new co-worker, Maureen (Zoe Kazan), as a thirtieth birthday gift to himself, despite his family providing a surprise party directly afterwards. What is instructive about the scene involving Maureen, and gives a strong clue as to his inner life, is, in effect, a confession when he describes the father-son talks he used to have with his father, Earl Wheeler, another Knox man who was employed for twenty years, now dead. He confesses that he never wanted to be like his father, 'yet here I am at thirty. A Knox man'. He has unconsciously repeated his father's career and life decisions, despite consciously not wishing to, in effect, repeating a negative masculine loop, rather than a developing along a masculine continuum.

The Wheelers are portrayed as being subject to what some aspects of the American cultural unconscious had decided is a successful life; April (Kate Winslet) and their neighbours' mentally troubled son John Givings Jnr (Michael Shannon) are shown to offer up a resistance or alternative to societal expectations. Inspired by April, Frank decides to rebel and travel to Paris in an individuative journey to discover his life, and himself, again. His archetypal journey as an emerging newly conscious father and man has begun; unfortunately, his subsequent actions and the forces within his external world (the American cultural unconscious and cultural complexes around the American workplace) conspire against him to stymie this journey. Ironically, it is what appears to be a piece of good fortune that derails Frank's would-be soul journey. Frank is faced with a dilemma: to take a new job at his employer and enjoy the security and extra money that it will bring, or to carry on with the Paris move, and an unknown future that may or may not involve personal self-discovery. Persuaded to stay by his wily boss, Bart Pollack (Jay O. Saunders) who, in a deliberately casual lunchtime meeting, cleverly uses Frank's dead father and Frank's unconscious father hunger to convince him that Wheeler senior would be proud of him if he took the job: 'It would be a fine memorial to your dad'. His words run directly counter to those of April: 'It takes backbone to lead the life you want'. Ultimately Frank is shown as being spineless in the face of Bart's manipulations and he submits to normative patriarchal masculine expectations, simultaneously destroying an opportunity for self-realisation. He is not yet strong enough to transcend his father, whether dead or a surrogate. His depicted role as a father, and as a man, suffers accordingly. Tacey concurs with this:

> [W]ork becomes the site of self-validation itself . . . instead of acting as 'elders' who put men at peace and provide a sense of affirmation, managers and supervisors will sometimes whip men into a frenzy of overachievement . . . bosses and employers assume the role of the negative senex or devouring father, leading men into a spiralic condition of performance anxiety, where the emotional rewards are very few.
> (1997, p. 124)

Frank's decision to stay at Knox has profoundly negative narrative consequences; April is furious at being betrayed by Frank's timidity at facing up to the truth and willing to be comfortably miserable. Frank's father hunger as starting to invert, eventually resulting in tragic consequences with April dying after a home abortion goes horribly wrong. Similarly to Lester Burnham, Mendes shows that it's what Frank Wheeler *doesn't* do that decides his fate within the film; his refusal to go to Paris but stay at Knox (justified by the pay rise and potential for advancement) means that his journey into fatherhood stagnates and eventually crushes his soul. Frank's lack of paternal backbone and action damns him and his family, despite both his wife and the repeated warnings from their neighbour's son John when discussing the hidden dangers of living a bland, conventional, suburban life: 'It takes real guts to see the hopelessness'. In many ways, Frank Wheeler embodies the ambivalent nature of the 1950s father as described by Bruzzi:

> A yearning for the strong authoritarian patriarch synchronous with the Freudian model was manifested in the films of the 1950s as a fascination with the domineering father who is frequently out of control. Alongside this father resided the paternal image most readily associated with the 1950s – the nine-to-five 'man in the grey flannel suit'.
>
> (2005, p. 38)

Mendes depicts Frank as attempting to perform *both* these paternal roles; his attempts at performing the role of patriarchal American father-and-husband within his family, combined with his role as faceless, anonymous office drone within Knox Business Machines, is something that Mendes portrays as an impossible task that he cannot hope to fulfil. The narrative bears this out as his frustrations at being unequal to the task eventually destroy his family, and by proxy, himself. This is both similar to, and dissimilar from, actual 1950s films (Biskind, 1983) that dealt with the same subject matter, such as *The Man in the Gray Flannel Suit* (Johnson, 1956) and *Executive Suite* (Wise, 1954), where the fathers in the films (Gregory Peck and William Holden) both managed to have their binary-role masculine privileges, balancing both corporate and family lives, and achieving some kind of domestic and familial harmony. Mendes shows that this does not happen to Frank Wheeler. What Frank and Lester Burnham discover to their cost is that the world of white-collar work, especially corporate work, exacts an unbargained-for price on the worker, as described by Biddulph:

> Many men have long discovered too late that rising in the class hierarchy does not make you freer – in fact the reverse. If you are a blue-collar worker, the company wants your body but your soul is your own. A white-collar worker is supposed to hand over his spirit as well.
>
> (1995, p. 154)

This symbolic possession of both Frank Wheeler's body and soul by Knox, and by implication the wider American society that Frank is part of, is a large part of what Frank chafes against; he is depicted as being anonymised by his work to the point where he is virtually indistinguishable from all the other commuters. Richardson also identifies a key anxiety of Frank around his vaguely defined position at Knox: 'Instead of producing anything tangible, Frank's job is to perform – his product *is* his performance' (2010, p. 11). As the father in the film, Frank is depicted as a largely conflicted and disempowered figure, unsure of himself, where he is going in life, and what he is supposed to do. Compared to Lester Burnham (Kevin Spacey) in *American Beauty*, it is Frank's failure to successfully rebel and move to Paris that ultimately damns him and eventually leads to the destruction of his marriage and family. Conversely, *American Beauty* shows the father's journey as becoming conscious from a state of unconsciousness (despite opposition from his family and society); *Revolutionary Road* is a depiction of a father who effectively performs the opposite of this awakening by running away from the chance of self-knowledge to pursue an illusionary ideal of fatherhood that is societally approved of, yet is shown to destroy the family.

Frank has regressed into acting as what he believes the societally approved role and image of a contemporaneous father should be like: responsible, unemotional, rational, authoritarian, patriarchal even. Or, as Biddulph would have it 'man as block of wood!' (1995, p. 27). It is the conflict between the heterosocial role that Frank has found himself forced to play, against his confused inner longings that provide the pain which is depicted as forcing Frank to act the way he does. Alongside his boss and cynical co-workers, the Wheelers' neighbours, Shep (David Harbour) and Milly (Kathryn Hahn), also play their part in ensuring that Frank is encouraged to stay, their private reaction (crucially seen by the audience, but not the Wheelers) to the news that a move to Paris is imminent, one of horror and disgust: 'A man sits around all day picking his nose in his bathrobe while his wife goes out to work!' Here Mendes depicts the conservative and reactionary heterosocial American society and its cultural complexes at their restrictive worst, stifling the freedoms and desires of both the father and the mother. Forces from the American cultural unconscious rear up; aspects of which are shown as dictatorial and restrictive. If the chance of career and material success is offered, American society seems to dictate that the father should accept unquestioningly. Conversely, April Wheeler articulates it thus: 'We're just like everybody else. We bought into the same ridiculous delusion that you have to resign from life and settle down the moment you have children'. Their attempt at transcending the comfortable prison in which they find themselves in is doomed to fail, however, due to Frank's failure to break free. This is due to his increasingly dogged insistence on the illusionary American suburban ideal of marriage and children, an image generated by the cultural unconscious. Herb Goldberg, quoted in *Manhood*, also identifies other reasons why Frank is struggling:

> The traditional male harness has meant the early and often premature establishment of career, marriage and family, which gave the man the appearance of maturity but actually made genuine self-development very difficult, because he was constantly struggling to deal with external pressures.
>
> (1995, p. 137)

Frank is depicted as being increasingly lost because he is simply not ready for the responsibilities that he has taken on. His refusal to commit to the Paris move (and potential individuation) shows that Frank is ultimately afraid of feeling alive, a tragedy that ends up blighting his life and destroying his wife and family. By the end of the film, after the tragedy of April's death that has overcome him, Frank is still depicted in his work clothes (tie now askew and his clothes shabbier), his body hidden away by his stifling uniform of a grey and anonymous suit as he watches his children at play, with a hopeless sense of fatherly devotion. Mendes still uses colour to indicate the paternal mood: 'Gray is (also) associated with the sackcloth and ashes of penitence and with the symbolism of ashes in general' (Ronnberg and Martin, 2010, p. 662). As Ryan Gilbey observes of DiCaprio's performance in his *New Statesman* review: 'He wears defeat well' (2009, p. 47), Mendes emphasising his end position, a trap that he fell into, courtesy of a dark surrogate father figure and a powerfully restrictive father-hostile American cultural unconscious.

## The absent father – *Fight Club, Winter's Bone, Frozen River*

Fathers do not have to be present to do damage: their mere absence can be harmful to a child. As a cultural trope, the absent father was recognised to such a degree that Bill Clinton used the phrase 'deadbeat dads' in a political address in 1992 and later signed into law the 1998 Deadbeat Parent Punishment Act, which made it a felony offence to miss child support payments, thus making absent or uncaring fathers into, quite literally, criminals. On a psychological level, the lack of paternal has been identified by Biddulph (1995) and Bly (1990) in the mytho-poetic movement, and by Anthony Stevens (1994) within the post-Jungian movement, as just as damaging as an involved and present but abusive father. Gershon Reiter in *Fathers and Sons in Cinema* quotes Bly, who quotes Alexander Mitscherlich to demonstrate what happens when the father is absent:

> A hole appears in the son's psyche. When the son does not see his father's workplace or what he produces, does he imagine his father to be a hero, a fighter for good, a saint, or a white knight? Mitscherlich's answer is sad: demons move into that empty place – demons of suspicion.
>
> (1990, p. 95)

This fatherly absence can have profound consequences for the lives of men, this masculine absence arguably being the main cause of father hunger. When we examine and analyse David Fincher's *Fight Club* (1999), we can expand this psychic hole to include not just demons of suspicion but a range of dark psychic eruptions, including destruction, both personal and societal.

## Generational betrayal: Tyler Durden and *Fight Club*

In Fincher's fourth feature, the paternal can be argued to be present by his absence, with consequences for the masculine performances and masculinities within the film. As Gronstad puts it: 'In FIGHT CLUB, masculinity itself is a crisis scene, society "an urban nightmare labyrinth disrupted by the seething, denatured and corralled male ego it was built to control"' (Whitehouse 46) (2008, p. 175). The unnamed narrator (Edward Norton) and his Shadow Trickster alter-ego Tyler Durden (Brad Pitt) are shown to be bereft of the paternal and of any guiding older men. Norton's automobile recall specialist is quietly unhappy in his fruitless attempts at using consumerism as a route to happiness (an explicit critique of the materialistic aspects of the American Dream), until his repressed psyche generates Tyler to express his Shadow-driven dissatisfaction: 'The things you own, they end up owning you'. In an early exchange between them about they'd most like to fight, Tyler quietly responds: 'My dad. No question'. The Narrator responds with his own story of how his father left him at age six and married another woman to have another child, and then repeated this behaviour. 'Every six years or so he'd do it again; new city, new family'. Tyler responds in turn: 'He was setting up franchises . . . a generation of men raised by women'. This exchange goes to the core of the film; namely that it is the lack of father that has given rise to a generation of men that are encouraged to embrace hollow consumerism as a substitute for both spirituality and masculinity. Within the film, this empty consumerist world is shown to have sown the seeds of its own destruction by allowing the rebellion of intelligent but uninitiated men that have not been guided by the older generation. Tyler's complaint that his father never gave him any life advice as a young man apart from to get a job and get married reinforces this assertion. Conspicuously, there are very few older men in the film (briefly, there is Lou who owns the bar where the first fights take place and who Tyler allows to beat him bloody, and a police commissioner who is threatened into non-investigative silence), nor any families. Tyler and the Narrator are nihilistic, cynical, lost, physically violent, spiritually hollow, and all the more dangerous for it. The numinous is not obviously present here; one of the thematic concerns that run throughout the film is a mocking of any kind of spiritual seeking. For example, there is an elaborate and deeply symbolic dream/trance sequence early in the film, with the Narrator urged to do a guided meditation to seek his power animal, a totemic figure beloved of new age devotees who tend toward the Native American/First Nation set of beliefs. The Narrator duly does so and ends up in a cavern (the deeper unconscious), where he meets his power animal: a penguin. Deliberately played for laughs (and effectively a symbolic joke), the scene is one of the funniest within the film, but it is a humour that is predicated on a mocking of numinosity. When the Narrator goes into the cavern again, the penguin is absent; instead, Marla Singer (Helena Bonham-Carter) is waiting. Symbolically, this can be read that the Narrator has, in effect, given away, or transmuted, his power to the feminine, this dynamic held to be a common occurrence by psychoanalysis as well strands of male gender theory. As Gunn and Frentz persuasively point out by using a Lacanian reading of the film's Oedipal themes, Marla can be read to be the symbolic Mother presence in the film, and Tyler the Father (2010). Father hunger within the film manifests itself thus: '[It is] . . . less about the Narrator's violent desire for Tyler than it is about his psychotic longing for a father figure' (ibid, p. 279). The lack of the paternal, and the subsequent father hunger, leads to a schizoid Shadow-driven narrative with the film, channelling a dark numinous energy that is contained within the main protagonist/antagonist(s). Tyler is charismatic, intelligent, focused and persuasive, and very dangerous because of it, despite being a split-off part of the Narrator's psyche, revealed to the audience at the beginning of the third act. In place of the missing paternal, Tyler/the Narrator has gone his own way, seen the limitations of a wholly materialistic society and seeks to destroy it without, seemingly, much realistic thought as to what it will be replaced with (there is a brief mention of men hunting elk through the ruins of the Rockefeller Centre).

With the film ending with the destruction of credit card companies in the hope of a fresh start of sorts for society, the film's impact and critique of late-stage capitalism and neoliberal economics have rightly been commented on by critics (Gold, 2004; Ta, 2006; Iocco, 2007; Lizardo, 2007). As Tyler expresses it:

TYLER: Advertising has us chasing cars and clothes, working jobs we hate so we can buy shit we don't need. We're the middle children of history, man, no purpose or place. No Great War, no Great Depression. Our great war is a spiritual war; our great depression is our lives. We've all been raised on television to believe that one day we'd be millionaires and movie gods, and rock stars, but we won't. . . . We're very, very pissed off.

What the film eloquently shows is the Shadow side to this generation (presumably X), and future (Y and millennials) in that the self-destruction, both personal and societal, is an inverted American Dream of social and material success and deliberately downward social mobility. As Ortner crisply summarises, the film taps into a deep vein of dark cultural energy and anger about how the American Dream has been exposed as now mostly unattainable for contemporary generations:

[W]ork in the neoliberal economy has no intrinsic pleasure, nor does it lead to security, happiness, or success. Rather, work today is something that eats your soul and destroys your life . . . the characters are educated people in white-collar jobs who historically could expect to be on the way up but actually are on the way down. The film(s) say to middle class viewers with varying degrees of explicitness, that there is a general and systemic problem here. On the one hand, this means that it is not your fault. On the other hand, you need to wake up and see what's going on.

(2013, pp. 79–80)

The film's Project Mayhem is essentially violent anti-capitalism as a result of a cultural enantiodromiatic psychic reaction, in a large part generated by the lack of intergenerational support and the lack of both father and of proper cultural initiation. As Gunn and Frentz put it:

> As the evil twin of Robert Bly's men's movement in which male "wildness" is reclaimed through spiritual rituals overseen by initiated elders, *Fight Club* traffics more in male "savageness" lead by a neo-Fascist street gang mentality of uninitiated adolescents.
>
> (2010, p. 270)

Whilst this statement is mostly accurate, initiation does, in fact, play a key part in the film. When Tyler draws the Narrator into his plans for Project Mayhem, he uses a homo-erotic ritualistic 'kiss' using a corrosive lye on the Narrator's hand and holds him there whilst the lye burns into a permanent scar. This is effectively a *dis-initiation*, that is to say, a deliberately misused ceremony/ritual which carries, in this case, a dark psychic resonance. Tyler goes on to put each Fight Club member who wants to take part in Project Mayhem through a three-day endurance ritual, another dis-initiation ceremony that is a key representation of the dark numinous energy that permeates the film. This ritual emphasises the difference and 'Otherness' of the subaltern community that Tyler is creating, a direct counterpoint to hetero-normative American society, effectively a Shadow organisation that aims to cause huge societal disruption. When, at last, the Narrator decides that the violence and conspiracy are getting too much, but then discovers that *he* is, in fact, Tyler Durden, he has to take drastic measures to end the madness and shoots himself in the mouth, killing Tyler (read, his Trickster alter-ego) but seriously maiming himself in the process. Here, as throughout the film, pain is represented as both a cleansing force and necessary sensation, whether applied to confused and frustrated masculinities, or societal psychoses (Gunn and Frentz, 2010). When we consider the crisis in masculinity and accompanying (or causal) widespread changes in American social and family structure that the film critiques, then the question of possible solutions are raised. Gunn and Frentz again:

> If *Fight Club* is symptomatic of a larger, cultural decline of the father figure, then what would be the cultural remedy? Many politicians, especially those who identify as "conservative" would argue the solution to contemporary crises of identity and violence among young people is a return to the nuclear family: only a traditional, stable mother and father can properly socialize and shepherd children into mature adulthood. As *Fight Club* makes clear, however, given the way in which late-stage capitalism works to erode the traditional family, such a solution is not simply patriarchal, it's downright impossible.
>
> (ibid, p. 288)

Given the key role that the father plays within American cultural myths, his decline and increasingly socially unstable role are synonymous with the corresponding questioning of the American Dream. The absent father, it would seem, is dangerous to not only families and young men but to cultural and societal dreams too.

## Pa Ain't Here: The lost rural father in *Winter's Bone* and *Frozen River*

In Debra Granik's second feature from 2010, the absent father this time is located within rural working-class America in the Missouri Ozarks, a far from idyllic landscape. Focusing on the efforts of seventeen-year-old Ree Dolly (Jennifer Lawrence in her debut film) to prevent her and her family's home from being taken in lieu of her absent father's bail bond money, the film depicts the desperate poverty and economic plight that poor rural white Americans face on a daily basis. Ree's father, Jessup Dolly, has been missing since being arrested for meth cooking, illegal drugs being the new source of wealth in the area. Like other Shadow fathers who attempt to achieve the American Dream of material success by shortcuts into criminal activity in the absence of more legal avenues of opportunity, Jessup has suffered the consequences, in this case, death at the hands of his former associates when he chose to co-operate with the authorities. Due to his absence and consequently putting the familial domestic space at direct risk, Ree has to act as both parents to her two siblings, her mother suffering from a form of catatonia in reaction to the stress that the family are under. In effect the feminine within this particular filmic family is represented as paralysed in the absence of a caring masculine; Ree has to step into her father's shoes to protect the domestic space, both physical and psychic. In this film, Granik presents the American family, in this case, a white rural American family as being very far from a Norman Rockwell ideal. Drenched in washed-out blue/grey tones reflecting the harshness of the landscape and society, the film's narrative is driven by Ree's search for her father and, by implication, a protective masculinity. The family here is shown as having to pursue a desperate and dangerous hard-scrabble existence on the fringes of American society; the missing paternal has left them vulnerable and unprotected. This is a psychic and physical landscape of rural nightmare, with rampant meth addiction and unemployment, and savage violence meted out to transgressors of Old Testament-style codes of behaviour (Ree is badly beaten by the local crimelord's female relatives). Ree's search for her father, more out of an exasperated and desperate necessity rather than obvious love of the paternal, results in her being taken to his final resting place, a shallow lake where in truly symbolic twist, she is instructed to hold his corpse's hands as his killers cut off his arms with a chainsaw so that she can prove his death to the authorities by virtue of his fingerprints. Ronnberg and Martin summarise the symbolic importance: 'Hands speak with eloquent silence: the clasped hands of lovers, the comforting hand on the shoulder of the grieving ' (2010, p. 382). The grasp of the dead father can be seen to signify his passing of traditional masculine responsibilities on to Ree as a surrogate father, even as he tried his best in life to provide for his family. The paternal within the film is an unseen presence that nevertheless holds the family in its grasp, even beyond death, fatherhood here being an oppressive and endangering masculinity. In a similar vein, *Frozen River* (Hunt, 2008), set in the snowy northern reaches of upstate New York at Christmas, has the absent father forcing the feminine, in this case Ray Eddy (Melissa Leo), having to act as the father when her compulsive gambler husband absconds with the money that the couple were saving for a new mobile home. Forced, along with a Mohawk widow (Misty Upham), into people-smuggling across the titular waterway in order to survive to make the payments, Ray, in effect, acts as a traditional father figure in that she must be the main breadwinner to save her family from penury and potential homelessness. Like *Winter's Bone*, the American Dream is not an option for the main protagonists in this film; rather, their main concerns are to do with survival and impending homelessness, rather than social and material success. The American Dream has been transmuted into trying to survive. It is, perhaps, deliberately ironic that both the narratives are triggered by irresponsible fathers trying to fulfil the American Dream by criminal shortcuts rather than by culturally and socially sanctioned methods.

As Ortner points out, the film also shows how far it is possible to fall in contemporary American society; she makes the point that in the past, the American middle class was perceived as being fundamentally secure in terms of material notions. Both these films show that in contemporary US society it is now possible to fall further than before in social and economic terms. The middle classes' 'fear of falling' (Ehrenreich, 2001) is now a very real prospect within neoliberal economies. Both films show how this is possible:

> The point about people in lower-class positions, on the other hand, is not just that they're poor – have less money, less things – but that their lives are much more insecure. They have less margin of error and are much closer to some edge where their lives may start coming apart.
>
> (Ortner, 2013, p. 194)

In summary, the success myth of equal opportunities for Americans is presented in both these films as being patently false; the rural geographical and social settings are a far cry from the bland, safe suburban locations that Lester Burnham and Frank Wheeler inhabit. The American Dream is shown to be at least partially dependent on geographical location, as well as social location; with *Winter's Bone* and *Frozen River*, the success myth is essentially unreachable for the film's characters. The absent father is depicted as potentially destructive and disruptive to normative American family life; without him, these films seem to be saying, the American Dream is unreachable. Father hunger here is also hunger for survival; the absent father is equivalent to absent dreams, American or otherwise.

## The surrogate father – *Boogie Nights, A Bronx Tale*

The surrogate father is a symbolically interesting figure. Their appearance can signal a number of directions for the narrative of the film and the character trajectory of the child, whether adult or young. Often foregrounded over the biological father (particularly with some directors such as Paul Thomas Anderson), the surrogate father is tasked with providing the child with guidance that the biological father often cannot, or will not, provide. This extended *Logos* energy is a constant feature of the surrogate; if the biological/normative father does not, or cannot, provide life or worldly guidance, then the child unconsciously or, more rarely, consciously seeks this out via another man. This later developmental stage of masculinity (certainly as understood by most mytho-poetic men's movement writers) relies upon the presence and input of a community of (ideally) supportive males to complete the initiation of the young man into the wider community of men and women as the son begins to outgrow the familial father. Amongst others, Keen, (1991); Biddulph, (1995), and to a lesser extent Bly (1990), argue that a male still needs a wider community of older men to support their masculine journey into (ideally) healthy and maturing manhood; in other words, older men play a key role in shaping younger men through their function as masculine mentor and the passing on of external, *Logos*/'Rule of the Father' worldly knowledge that is useful, in some cases held to be essential, for survival. The masculine continuum is therefore held as continuing via the father and paternal surrogates; father hunger can still occur here if there is no strong father figure for the adult son, or if there is not a community of older men to help this supposed societal initiation and masculine constellation.

Whilst the father is still seen as being crucial to this process, the adult son is now regarded as needing the input of older men; in other words the adult son is approaching the position of transcending the father, or at least, held to be carrying out this maturing process. This mytho-poetic men's movement view has strong echoes of Jungian and Classical post-Jungian writers such as Anthony Stevens (1994), but this view is questioned by other post-Jungians such as Samuels (1985b, 1989, 1993) and Tacey (1997). Samuels, for example, reminds us that *Logos* and *Eros* energies can be understood as:

> symbolic terms of psychological factors that are independent of anatomical sex. Logos and Eros exist within a person of either sex. The balance and relation between the two separate principles regulates the individual's sense of himself [herself] as a sexed *and* as a gendered being.
>
> (1985a, p. 210)

Jung himself, at different times, appeared to argue for a much more binary position on this issue, echoing Freud and Lacan, consequently inviting more concrete and commensurately less flexible interpretations of gender, whilst at the same time proposing a vision of both qualities being available to both sexes. If this more flexible post-Jungian approach is applied to the figure of the surrogate father, then a number of challenges emerge against this view of a wider community of father surrogates that the mytho-poetic men's movement hold as being necessary for maturation of manhood:

> [B]ut every archetypal figure brings with it its own set of dangers and difficulties. There is no simple 'integration' of the father, but an ongoing struggle to maintain one's own individual identity in the face of this potentially overwhelming archetypal figure.
>
> (Tacey, 1997, p. 149)

A surrogate father (or fathers) is not without its dangers, it seems. Fathers, including surrogate fathers, can overwhelm the adult son, leading to potentially limited psychological growth and to burden the son with personal complexes. There are also questions around what the mytho-poetic men's movement constitutes as a socio-normative 'healthy' attitude towards masculinity that are more often than not, not always engaged with. Are they promoting a 'reactive' masculinity (Connell, 1995) that seeks a reactionary, conservative return to 'traditional' masculine values as a number of political men's movement writers have proposed (Kimmel, 2000, 2009, 2015; Pfeil, 1995)? Or is it more a case of them attempting to co-opt the archetypal father energy to effect change in masculinities, but falling prey to the Shadow energies that are present within the archetype of the American father, and ignoring any specific cultural discourses and contexts that surround this archetype? As mentioned previously, ideal notions of the mature masculine include actions carried out in a healthy, supportive, life-loving manner towards both men and women. At the same time, there are the Shadow aspects to consider when we examine the role of the surrogate father, for example, and what kind of male mentoring they may (or may not) provide. Tacey again:

> The negative senex [older man] actually fuses with our male ego and our power drive, and men tragically fail to realise that the very thing that presents us with the illusion of power is the source of our crippling pathology.
>
> (1997, p. 166)

Assuming Tacey is correct, there appears to be a clear danger that Shadow surrogate fathers may cause the adult son to enter their own Shadow, a psychological dynamic that arguably shows strong awareness of this danger by the various directors analysed, judging by the commensurate themes and narratives within their output. The role and issue of the surrogate father are also picked up by Goss: 'In Anderson's films, the necessity of surrogate family is demanded by the failure of families of the biological variety and is due largely to patriarchal desertion'

(2002, p. 180). Similarly, Konow reports Anderson as saying, 'I was not really able to notice a pattern in my work until I made three movies. Now I'm starting to decipher that they all have something to do with surrogate families and family connection' (2000, p. 3). Whilst this is certainly true of *Magnolia* and *Hard Eight*, in *Boogie Nights* the son deserts the family, partially due to the weak paternal, and is taken under the wing of the strong negative senex, Jack Horner (Burt Reynolds). Anderson effectively transposes nuclear familial conflicts onto surrogate families, familial conflicts being depicted here as just as common as in normative families. This more nuanced portrayal echoes Halberstam's (2005) work on subcultures – Jack Horner's surrogate family effectively acting within a porn subculture, similar to the gambling subculture in *Hard Eight*: '[S]ubcultures provide a vital critique of the seemingly organic nature of "community" [ . . . through] transient, extrafamilial and oppositional modes of affiliation' (p. 14). Sarah Thornton further defines this point:

> Kinship would seem to be one of the main building blocks of community. By contrast, those groups identified as "subcultures" have tended to be studied apart from their families and in states of relative transience. It is also often assumed that there is something innately oppositional in the word "subculture".
>
> (1997, p. 2)

This assumption of familial oppositional status of a subculture is subverted by Anderson, particularly where he explores this concept of critical subcultural kinship further in relation to the question of surrogate familial incest discourses, discussed at length later in the chapter. This subversion resonates with the point made earlier about archetypal imagery and symbols not necessarily being psychically logical in terms of the experiences generated.

Analysing further, rather than being in opposition to the nuclear family, Anderson portrays the surrogate father and family as functioning as a substitute family structure within an American porn subculture. In both *Magnolia* and *Boogie Nights*, there are nuclear families, but they are depicted as being under pressure and fracturing as the film progresses, with familial discord, disintegration and reconciliation being a large part of the narrative drive. In *Boogie Nights*, the surrogate family and parental figures Jack Horner and Amber Waves (Julianne Moore) are oppositional figures, in that they appear to be welcoming to Eddie Adams/ Dirk Diggler, a depiction which is in deliberately stark contrast with his shrewish, nagging and abusive biological mother and a weak, silent biological father. Archetypally, the surrogate family can be said to embody the familial energy here and acts accordingly in terms of performing as aiding the individuative journey of Eddie/Dirk. This substitute family also performs an archetypal initiatory function for the adult son, in that the son's entry into adult masculinity is facilitated by the surrogate family or a surrogate father figure, discussed and analysed in more detail later. In terms of filmic depictions of this relationship, Bruzzi again picks up the thread:

> The sons, in turn, manifest extreme responses toward these [absent] fathers, wanting to destroy them, become them (sometimes both at once) or wanting to effect a final reconciliation with an alienated father, often as lies in bed ill or dying.
>
> (2005, xv)

Surrogate families and father figures can be dark constructs, seemingly benign, but often with negative cores and features. *Boogie Nights* and *A Bronx Tale* both exemplify this surrogate paternal darkness with Eddie Adams/Dirk Diggler (and particularly his phallus) being exploited under the seemingly friendly paternalism of adult film-maker Jack Horner and his Shadow version of the American Dream. Similarly, Sonny (Chazz Palmintieri) acts both as a surrogate father to Calogero, and, on a bigger scale, to the neighbourhood, despite his position being predicated on deadly violence and crime. The films are explicit in showing how the son can have his masculine journey stunted and stymied by a dark father figure, as well as despite being drawn to the surrogate paternal in the first place to satisfy any feelings of father hunger. This stunting function of the paternal reflects another dark aspect of the father. Tacey accurately describes this situation: 'The negative senex rules best when our psychic energy is not available to challenge him' (1997, 163). Eddie is portrayed as simply not psychically strong enough to resist the dark paternal energy embodied by Jack Horner. The adult son is shown as being unable or unwilling to transcend the father; the paternal Shadow that they are under is essentially ending up acting as their prison. In *A Bronx Tale*, the surrogate and biological fathers are in conflict, the son being subjected to differing aspects of the Father archetype, but the film depicts an interesting psychological truth; namely that both aspects are necessary for the son's continuing psychic development.

## *Boogie Nights:* the surrogate father as pimp

In *Boogie Nights* (1997), Anderson depicts both the adult son and surrogate father in dark thematic tones, layering both masculine performances with sexual complexities and comments on exploitative masculine power relationships within American society. Whereas *Hard Eight* (1996) is more concerned with the guilt of the surrogate father, *Boogie Nights* is more concerned with the depiction of the surrogate father as an exploiter of young and undeveloped masculinity, effectively a paternal pimp. Anderson portrays the American father in the film as both recognising and capitalising the masculine power of the phallus, in effect an exploiter of masculinities as well as femininities (Di Lauro and Rabkin, 1976; Williams, 1999; O'Toole, 1998; Kryzwinska, 2006). Horner is one of the central figures within the film and one of its central constellation points and source of masculine performance. It is this surrogate father figure that feeds the father hunger of

Eddie Adams (Mark Wahlberg), soon to become Dirk Diggler, and the consequent effects it has on both the adult son and the father within the film. In pursuit of portraying these dysfunctional relationships, Anderson mediates a number of symbols, most notably: the phallus, the family and its Shadow (both literal and metaphorical), and also uses time in a symbolic manner, the film neatly dividing into two halves, both of which have clearly demarcated imagery and themes. The film's depictions of exploitative surrogate fatherhood reflect and resonate with wider debates and discourses over the development of the son into an adult as outlined earlier, as well as feeding into ideological debates about the family and patriarchy (Tincknell, 2005).

The story of Eddie Adams (later self-christened as Dirk Diggler), an adult film star, and set in the late 1970s and early 1980s, the film was in part inspired by and loosely based on the real life of adult film star John Holmes.[4] This is the American Dream of (supposedly) guilt-free pleasures of the flesh (sex and drugs), set to a disco soundtrack. Located mainly in the San Fernando valley, the film can be viewed as both a coming-of-age morality tale and a sly critique of the American family structure and Shadow capitalistic mores that prevailed at the time, particularly around the porn industry and the so-called Golden Age of Porn.[5] The film depicts a complete surrogate family structure that contains within it a rendition of the masculine journey as experienced by Eddie/Dirk as he matures from callow restaurant bus-boy through to adult film star with all the attendant temptations and dangers that this role entails. Symbolically, Eddie/Dirk's star power within the film is generated by his famously large phallus, with this most masculine of symbols depicted throughout the film by Anderson by others' reactions to it. Anderson, in effect, teases us with the unseen power of Eddie/Dirk's penis, only revealing it in the very end scene in a self-consciously humorous and yet poignant moment.

## The phallus on film

An ancient symbol, found in various visual forms in all human cultures from the earliest days to the present, the phallus is most often associated with masculine virility and potency. Ronnberg and Martin describe the power of this archetypal masculine symbol in some depth:

> [I]t takes on the ithyphallic form that is worshipped as a numinosum. Seed-bearer, penetrator, begetter, the phallus was also wonderful for its association with not one, but two sacred fluids – golden urine and the semen of life . . . we have venerated the phallus as emblem of rapturous pleasure, inseminating heat and spiritual transcendence.
>
> (2010, p. 406)

It is this aspect of the phallus that Anderson is mainly concerned with in the first half of the film, an approach that resonates with Freudian interpretations. Stevens reports that ' . . . Jung himself quipped that the penis was a phallic symbol' (1998, p. 313). Monick, also quoted by Stevens, declares:

> Phallos . . . has a mind of its own; it will not be dictated to by the ego. It behaves in a way that tangibly manifests the autonomy of unconscious forces. An erection cannot be manufactured by a conscious act of will: either it happens or it doesn't, as the circumstances dictate. As a consequence, an erection can be experienced as an epiphany.
>
> (ibid)

The phallus, it seems, is an organ that will not be dictated to. Chevalier and Gheerbrant remind us that the phallus also 'conveys the sense of the powers of procreation which are worshipped in that particular shape by many religions' (1994, p. 751). In other words, the phallus is not always a literal penis. Cooper agrees and emphasises its polysemous symbolic nature (largely contradicting a psychoanalytical interpretation), as discussed previously: 'It can be merely physical in is symbolism, as in the worship of Priapus, or be spiritual in significance, as in Hinduism' (1978, p. 129). With this in mind, where Anderson mediates this symbology in more complex ways is by linking the phallus with the nature of the filmic gaze and the Shadow. The film is, in effect both a dramatic and occasionally humorous exploration of both the American personal Shadow, the surrogate familial Shadow and the American porn industry's Shadow, in essence an exploration of the American phallic Shadow and its relationship with the father.

The phallus in *Boogie Nights* is first encountered via Eddie Adams (Mark Wahlberg) as he works at Maurice Rodriguez's (Luis Guzman) club Hot Traxx in the San Fernando Valley. Both the location and time are specifically referenced in a subtitle, locating the film and subsequent action in a deliberate context, a point that is returned to later on in the film when he signals a change in attitudes towards his main subject matter. The swooping tracking shot provides the immersion to Eddie/Dirk's world, effectively suturing us into this milieu. As King summarises:

> This is a breathtakingly fast and fluid example of initial multi-strand-narrative exposition, the effect increased through the use of highly mobile camerawork and emphasis-creating zooms, introducing all the major characters in a sustained sequence of about six minutes.
>
> (2005, p. 89)

Jack Horner, Amber Waves, Rollergirl (Heather Graham) and other members (John C Reilly, Don Cheadle, Melora Walters and William H Macy) of Eddie/Dirk's soon-to-be surrogate family are rapidly and efficiently introduced to us with the mise-en-scene accurately capturing the music, clothes and atmosphere of the time. Jack is portrayed as an ostensibly benevolent and authoritative paternal figure, greeting people, giving friendly orders and looking after his colleagues and cast, but his main interest soon becomes clear when he spies Eddie performing his busboy duties and goes to talk to him alone. The camera gradually pulls in closer to Jack and switches between him and Eddie as Jack senses something different and special about the young man. Eddie suspects Jack of being interested in being a voyeur because of his outsized phallus, and is already amateurishly capitalising on it: ('If you wanna watch me jack off it's ten bucks. If you just wanna look at it then it's five'.).

The chance for Jack to be a voyeur that Eddie is offering is arguably self-reflexive, an intertextual awareness being present, given the main subject matter and themes about pornography and the spectator. This nascent self-exploitation of his penis is also indicative of Eddie's growing awareness of his potential phallic power; it is Jack, however, that holds the key to the commercial exploitation, commodification and capitalised gains around Eddie's phallus, in that he can provide access to voyeurism on a mass scale by virtue of his role as producer and director of pornography. Eddie is, in effect, being offered the chance of fulfilling the American Dream in terms of material success and the attendant fame by being a porn star: the ultimate capitalised American phallus. This scene is key in terms of casting Jack as a surrogate parental figure, reinforced as he questions Eddie's ambitions and what he wants to do with his life, typical parental and paternal concerns. From Jack's perspective, Eddie's (as yet unseen) phallus is wonderful (reflected in the dialogue), but mainly only in terms of exploitation and the potential monetary rewards that await him and his backers. From Eddie's naïve perspective (as he remarks to his casual lover): 'Everyone is blessed with one special thing . . . I plan on being a star. A big, bright shining star'.

The phallus is again indirectly referenced when Jack uses Rollergirl to confirm the size of Eddie's phallus. Her reaction shot when she first sees it (a visual motif that occurs throughout the film), as she prepares to perform fellatio on him at his workplace, reinforces the growing off-screen phallic presence. This presence is strongly hinted at again when Rollergirl has intercourse with Eddie at Jack's house, watched by Jack, his head tilting to the side as he sees Eddie's phallus in action for the first time. Before, however, Eddie and his phallus can star in adult films, he has to become an adult; in other words, undergo a rite of passage into the adult world. This initiatory journey is explicitly referenced after a party that Jack holds and where Eddie is introduced to the porn financier Colonel James (Robert Ridgley), who calmly asks to see Eddie' penis. Satisfied with his future investment, and closing the deal with a manly handshake (effectively the cash owning the cock in an informal capitalistic exchange), the Colonel asks Eddie if he has thought of a new name. The archetypal significance of this re-naming is profound when we consider that in primitive cultures, the passage to adulthood for both genders was marked by a ceremonial re-naming.[6] During this sequence, the symbolic nature of water, like *Road to Perdition*, discussed in the previous chapter, is foremost, with the parallels of the Christian christening ceremony strikingly similar to Eddie's initiation into his new surrogate family.

He is depicted as diving into Jack's swimming pool and emerging anew and accepted by his adult co-stars into a new world. Water is depicted here as having spiritual and initiatory symbolic qualities that mark a significant change in Eddie's life. This quasi-initiation (not formalised, but nonetheless archetypally powerful) is completed when Eddie is in Jack's hot tub (more water) and chooses a new name for himself. This particular scene is played for comic effect, with Eddie describing what his new name would look like in blue neon and that his name would be so sharp and conjure up so much (presumably masculine) power that the sign would explode. The film then cuts to the said sign that boldly reads, 'Dirk Diggler' in blue neon which promptly bursts into flame and explodes. Cutting back to the hot tub, both Jack and Eddie's future friend and co-star Reed Rothchild (John C Reilly) give their wholehearted masculine support. From now on, Eddie has transmogrified into an adult who can now star in adult films, as well as engaging with a subcultural version of the American Dream. Greg Singh makes an important point about pornography:

> It is also evident that there is a curious contradiction in terms of gender representation here: The men are often reduced to objects in that emphasis lies on their sexual performance and size of genitalia: the women are often reduced to fragmented body parts through generic framing and camera set-ups.
>
> (2009, p. 138)

Dirk's phallus and performance are both objectified and symbolised within the film. Once the phallus is established as one of the key symbols within the text, the Shadow side of it is depicted, intertwined with depictions of the family, both natural and surrogate. Ronnberg and Martin also describe this dark aspect of the phallus in detail:

> The brutal, violating aspect of the phallus is manifest in the rape of the individual, in the rape of the earth. Phallic power can shatter, uproot and lay waste. There are interior forms of coercive penetration, like self-destructive compulsions and invasive thoughts; or intellectual or religious transfixion, where the phallic presence overwhelms its vessel.
>
> (2010, p. 406)

This Shadow side is explicitly referenced with the move to video coinciding with the advent of a more brutal and explicitly misogynist pornography and Horner's surrogate family's consequent involvement in this new world. Before the key New Year's Eve party scene, Dirk makes a heartfelt plea to Jack Horner, complaining about Johnny Wadd (see previous footnote) and his violence towards women: 'That's not sexy, that's not cool!' Dirk does not want any part of violence towards women in the films he stars in, yet Anderson shows the new decade that Dirk and his surrogate family are about to enter as being much less about pleasure and much more about power, violence and money.

## The father, sex and the Shadow

With Dirk's first adult film under his belt, masculine sexuality in the shape of Dirk and his phallus is ready to be both exploited and celebrated. Yet Anderson has not only shown Eddie's initiation into his new adult world but also (specifically within the first party sequence) set up strong hints of the Shadow aspects of both Dirk and Jack, aspects that grow throughout the film and eventually culminate in violence and near-death experiences before they are resolved. Jung defined the Shadow in 1945 thus: 'The thing a person does not want to be' (Samuels et al., 1986, p. 138). Samuels et al defined it as 'the negative side of the personality, the sum of all the unpleasant qualities one wants to hide, the inferior, worthless and primitive side of man's nature, the 'other person' in one, one's own dark side' (ibid). Hauke and Alister define it thus:

> The part of the personality that one does not identify with or wishes to disown; it usually refers to negative aspects, but may also include positive aspects that – due to family or social beliefs – have remained rejected and unavailable to the individual.
>
> (2001, p. 246)

Bassil-Morozow and Hockley define it thus:

> [T]he Shadow is the 'dark brother' in whom all the negative aspects of human nature are stored. It is home to greed, aggression, envy, jealousy, fear and hatred. Humans' relationship with the Shadow has always been a key *leitmotif* of art and literature.
>
> (2017, p. 39)

These darker qualities, present in the background earlier in the film, begin to overwhelm the characters as the film progresses, lending a darkening tone to the second half of the film. The Shadow aspects of the American porn industry are mediated mainly around the sinisterly avuncular figures of Colonel James, Jack's financial backer (and later on revealed to be a paedophile), and Floyd Gondolli (Philip Baker Hall), another producer who has adopted a more realistic attitude to the new video technology and how it will benefit the pornography business. For these men, surrogate father figures after a fashion, sexuality (both male and female) is itself to be exploited for monetary gain. Jack Horner's delusions of being thought of and feted as a 'proper' filmmaker are depicted to be just that: delusions. The Shadow side of the industry, its exploitation and commodification of both male and female sexuality, is a constant presence within the film and provides a counterpoint to the initial depiction of clichéd 1970s free love and relaxed attitudes to drugs and pleasure. Dirk's initiatory journey into adult manhood develops into a parallel exploration of American attitudes towards sex, pornography and drugs, an exploration, in effect, of an aspect of the American

Shadow and cultural complex. This is articulated by Peter Lehman in a lengthy quote from an article in *Jump Cut*:

> [T]he first part of Boogie Nights characterises the adventures of its hero, Dirk Diggler (Mark Wahlberg), as part of the carefree, anything-goes era of 70s sexuality. Porn chic, casual sex, and nudity a la hot-tubs and drugs are the norm, and everyone seems happy and content. There is no price to pay. The 80s, on the other hand, contain nothing but paying the price. In the 80s those associated with the world of 70s porn commit suicide, lose custody battles for their children, can't get loans to start their legitimate businesses, or get killed in drug shoot-outs. Even porn itself seems degraded from the narrative forms of 35mm theatrical features with stories, production values, and stars to the 80s cheap amateur videos. During the 80s, it seems, we pay the piper for the 70s, and little else.
>
> (1998, p. 37)

Whilst Lehman correctly identifies the film's plot and narrative in this demarcation between the 1970s and 1980s, there is an implied criticism of Anderson's supposed naïve approach to his contextual eras. It is arguable that he is too subtle a filmmaker and auteur to allow the film to be clumsily divided up like this. In the film's first half (the 1970s half, as it were), there are a large number of telling scenes (Amber Waves' phone call to her ex-husband and attempted contact with her young son, Little Bill's wife [real life ex-porn star Nina Hartley] cheating on him, and the constant presence of hard drugs in the background [young girl ODing at the party] that eventually, but inevitably, come into the foreground) that do much more than hint at the tensions and dark side of 1970's porn industry. Whilst Lehman is correct in pointing out that, on the whole, the price of pleasure is shown to be mainly paid in the second section of the film, sharply delineated by the new year's party scene for 1980, the problems are already apparent and implicit within the first half of the film. They become explicit in the second half of the film and are linked in with the Shadow aspects of American culture and society during the Reaganite 'greed is good' 1980s. The surrogate father is shown as being a key part of Dirk's downfall; the adult son in this instance is caught in a trap with a debt owed to the surrogate, yet exploited by him. This is exemplified by one of the last scenes of the film with Dirk as a prodigal son returning home to Jack's house pleading with him to take him back, which he does. Dirk is not psychically strong enough to resist his dark senex father, and he is drawn back into the embraces of his surrogate family.

## A clash of fathers: Calgero Anello

*A Bronx Tale* (De Niro, 1993) provides a subaltern perspective on the American Dream, in that it portrays the working-class Italian-American and African-American neighbourhoods in the 1960s and 1970s, where the American Dream was experienced in very different ways to white, normative middle-class America. To a large degree, the American Dream *is* the multi-generational immigrant dream, as a nation made up of a wide variety of ethnic and racial groups bound together by a supposedly egalitarian constitution and government. The film shows this, however, to be very far from the ordinary lived experience of a large number of American citizens, the different ethnic and racial communities instead exerting their grip, with the figure of the father at their centre. Here, the paternal is shown as conflicted and ambiguous, the male child, Calogero (played at different ages by Francis Capra and Lillo Brancato) effectively having his loyalties split by both his biological, father Lorenzo (De Niro), and his unofficially adopted surrogate father, Sonny (Chazz Palmentieri). In addition, the father's realm, both societal and environmental, plays a key role in determining a father's power and agency. An honest bus driver, Lorenzo does his best to raise his son in an honest fashion, but the neighbourhood Mafia figure, Sonny, and his henchman hold much more of an appeal for Calogero (or 'C' as Sonny comes to call him). Here, the American Dream and its relationship to the father is portrayed as both potentially achievable (Lorenzo is a firm believer in hard work and obeying the law to advance materially and socially, even though he doesn't advance much) and subverted (Sonny is all-powerful in his particular locale of Belmont/Fordham in the Bronx area of New York, in terms of respect, social standing and material wealth, but through wholly criminal means). Ironically, it is Sonny who has, on the surface, achieved the American Dream, in that he has advanced socially and materially and is (relatively) secure in his neighbourhood. That his death comes in his own bar on his birthday is a deliberately dark twist in the story.

For our purposes, *A Bronx Tale* is an acutely accurate example of how the location of the fathers within their social spaces and environment plays a crucial part within the story and themes. The neighbourhood space is deliberately portrayed and contextualised, along with its various denizens, to a high degree of detail, establishing the boundaries for the main characters and playing a key role in the narrative. With Calogero commenting on the action as a young adult via a voice-over throughout the film, he describes his neighbourhood in the opening scene: 'This is the Fordham section of the Bronx; my home. A world unto itself. Any borough is only fifteen minutes away . . . but they seem like three thousand miles away'. Populated by Italian Americans, and with strong social rules that directly affect Calogero and his family, this is a close-knit community, with all the attendant benefits and constraints that such a community can enact. David Coon points out:

> [A] nostalgic vision of community focuses on a sense of togetherness, happiness, and connection. But this vision conveniently overlooks the potentially negative consequences of community formation. Identifying a community usually involves identifying who will be included and who will be excluded.
> (2014, pp. 103–104)

In the film, it is African Americans and figures from the emerging American counterculture (the film is set in the 1960s) who are shown to be forcefully excluded from the community. In the former example, Calogero and his friends regularly see African American schoolchildren bussed through their neighbourhood and angrily verbally abuse them as 'invading' their space, reflective of the historical and contextual civil rights battles occurring at the time. Contrastingly, Calogero's father Lorenzo (a bus driver who, by necessity of his job, has to cross social and geographical divides) is not shown to hold racist opinions, similar to Sonny. Instead, it is Calogero's friends who act in the most hostile way towards community outsiders, to the point where, later on in the film, they physically attack African American schoolmates for cycling through their neighbourhood. Calogero saves one of the teenagers from a beating, who turns out to be the brother of Jane Williams, a female African American schoolmate with whom he falls in love. As their relationship develops, Calogero walks Jane to her part of the Bronx, an African-American neighbourhood, where it is Calogero's turn to be the excluded outsider, his presence resented to the point where local teenagers throw bottles at him, the African-Americans behaving in a mirror-image way to their Italian-American neighbours. The myth of the American Dream and its emphasis on social mobility is explicitly shown here to be wanting. Social mobility is partially contingent on geographical mobility, and in their respective ethnic and racial urban enclaves neither the Italian Americans nor the African Americans are shown to be able to transcend their locations and achieve social advancement. When Calogero's friends go to invade the African-American neighbourhood armed with Molotov cocktails to punish an infringement, Calogero is saved by Sonny, Belmont's mini-Godfather, who stops the car, orders Calogero out against the wishes of his friends, and thus prevents Calogero from meeting the same fate as his friends who are gruesomely burned alive when their attack on their neighbours goes awry. Fire here is symbolically used as a punisher and cleanser: the attack is filmed via claustrophobic close-ups showing the hatred, violence and panic amongst Calogero's friends as they are thwarted in their attempted vengeance but killed by immolation. In attempting to punish outsiders for trespassing, the would-be invaders themselves are punished by death when they transgress another community's space; the American Dream of an egalitarian and level playing field in which to achieve material and social advancement is explicitly absent.

Similarly, Sonny, as the Shadow personification of the caring, protective paternal within his social space, protects the neighbourhood bar from a gang of bikers who ride in from outside. He is shown as attempting to be reasonable towards the bikers (read: the American counterculture) but makes plans as a backup. When the bikers go back on their word and cause havoc within the bar, Sonny's henchmen come in the back door and a vicious brawl starts, ending with the locals victorious against the outsiders. As the bikers are chased outside, Calogero, his friends, and the rest of the neighbourhood kids join in attacking them and their motorcycles. Here, the community has banded together against outsiders, and protected itself; outsiders are to be excluded at all costs if they do not meet the community's rules and standards of behaviour. In a key scene early on in the film, Calogero witnesses Sonny killing a man who started a fight in the street. Coon again describes the Shadow or negative side of a community:

> The perception of community as inherently positive masks a variety of potentially harmful consequences. One such consequence is the exclusion of that goes hand in hand with the creation of any community. In order to designate certain individuals or traits that are part of a community, it is necessary to define those that are not part of it.
>
> (ibid, p. 106)

When the police take him downstairs to perform in an impromptu identity parade, the whole neighbourhood turns to watch. There is a palpable air of tension as Calogero (the camera following closely) works his way down the line of suspects (Sonny and his henchman), each time saying no when the policeman asks him if this man was the shooter. When it comes to Sonny, who did shoot the man, and Calogero still says no, the community's rules against informing outside forces of the state (in this case the police) have held. As Calogero states on the voiceover: 'I did a good thing for a bad man. I didn't understand that, not at nine years old. All I knew was that a rat was the lowest thing anyone could be in my neighbourhood. And I didn't rat'. Calogero, and his father, showed their community that they abided by the community's rules, and social cohesiveness is maintained as a result. Calogero's sense of self, and his father's, are shaped by this moment and their environment, in the protection of the larger father, in this case Sonny. As Coon states: '[T]he difference between self and others must be constructed by a particular community in order to achieve cohesiveness. Anything that threatens group identity must be eliminated or at least neutralised' (ibid, p. 107). The father is shown here as both protected and protector; this could have been a vulnerable moment for Sonny as the head of the neighbourhood, but the figure of the child ensured that his position of power was maintained. Lorenzo understood that if his son was honest, both his position and his family's safety within their community would be under threat.

Linked in with the community and its control over its inhabitants, we can further examine the filmic symbology used; as Tacey stated earlier (1997), the father is seen as a doorway into masculinity through which the son passes. Within the film, Calogero goes through both the doors that are represented by his two fathers and learns lessons from both. This takes place on a metaphorical, symbolic and literal level, with De Niro showing the male child/son passing through doorways denoting safe and unsafe spaces; from his home (a safe space) Calogero accesses Sonny's bar (initially an unsafe space) via a back stairway that goes underneath the street. Symbolically, this works on a number of levels; Calogero descends from his usual apartment above ground that he normally resides in to a darker, underground world, full of unconscious psychic Shadow forces that provide temptation for him, namely respect (albeit resulting from fear), money (resulting from illegal means, e.g. gambling), and violence, both verbal and physical. Sonny inhabits this Shadow world as a dark Father, and he is shown at the threshold of his world giving Calogero, or C as Sonny christens him (itself a symbolic act, similar to Dirk Diggler previously), advice that his biological father is reluctant to. Not surprisingly, within the film, the fathers are portrayed as in conflict; Sonny subverts and undermines Lorenzo's role until, in another key scene, Lorenzo confronts Sonny in his bar after discovering his son with $600 that he earned from waiting on illegal card games, and angrily denounces him as trying to steal his son away from him, a potentially cardinal sin in familio-centric Italian-American society. Here, Lorenzo is secure in the knowledge that the community will back him, in that in their Italian-American community, the bond between children and parents is a strongly numinous one and a relationship that is threatened at one's peril. As father and son leave the bar, united in their love, Sonny looks on from inside and declines the opportunity to have Lorenzo killed or maimed as he recognises and respects the masculine bond that the child and the father have, a bond that he does not possess in the same way. As a surrogate paternal, Sonny is depicted as heterosexual (he tutors C to respect women and to be open to love), but he is not a father the same way Lorenzo is. Despite this, Sonny's role in the film is to tutor Calogero in worldly wisdom, both necessary and valuable for the young man's survival in a larger society that discriminates against ethnic groups. Despite, or even perhaps because of his Shadow qualities, Sonny plays a necessary role to Calogero in that he can deliver life advice that Calogero would not accept from his father; here he is representative of an uncle figure, part of Bly's wider world of men that a younger man can, and must (if Bly is to be believed), learn from in order to be accepted in wider society. By rescuing Calogero from the revenge mission that his friends embarked upon, Sonny acts as Calogero's protector and can be viewed as an embodiment (albeit a Shadow version) of Jung's *Logos* energy, similar to Lacan's Rule-of-the-Father, an active masculine force that saves Calogero's life.

The film's ending is a conventional one in that the dark Shadow paternal, Sonny, is murdered by the son of a man he killed (itself deeply symbolic of filial vengeance mythology) but that a new Mafia boss Carmine (Joe Pesci) introduces himself to Calogero prior to taking over Sonny's role within the neighbourhood. The narrative circularity here appears to be deliberate; the community status quo is maintained, and life continues on. Coon once again:

> Forming a community, whether suburban, national, or otherwise, generally necessitates the creation of a false sense of unity and homogeneity. Norms do not simply exist – they are constructed over time and their maintenance requires a great deal of effort.
>
> (ibid, p. 118)

With the cultural myth of the American Dream reliant on the notion, contested or otherwise, of a unified national community in which to flower, *A Bronx Tale* is an example of how communities, and the subsequent father figures within those communities, exact their price for the stability of a society to be maintained.

## Conclusion

What is, perhaps, most noticeable about Hollywood films concerning the father is that the masculine journey of the father-son relationships within the films is often depicted as taking place within psychic darkness. Whilst the father can (potentially) achieve redemption in terms of the father and child relationship (*Magnolia, American Beauty* and *Road to Perdition*), in both *Revolutionary Road* and *There Will be Blood*, father figures end their journeys in a psychic void, bereft of support, isolated and disconnected from their families, the masculine continuum being portrayed as largely broken. The American Dream is shown here to be a dangerous illusion that entrances and traps the father in restrictive models of relating, as well as damaging the child. In addition to this, the absent father in *Fight Club, Winter's Bone*, and *Frozen River* demonstrates that the American Dream appears to be largely contingent on the active presence of the paternal. *A Bronx Tale* shows how dependent the American Dream is upon location, both geographical and societal. In addition to these arguments, Jung's definition of psychological and visionary art applies in that the visionary is strongly referenced; for example, *Road to Perdition* shows Michaels Snr and Jnr having to make spiritual choices, reflected in the deliberately ghostly and otherworldly shades of grey, white and black used throughout the film. Similarly, *There Will Be Blood* also references spirituality, but it is in terms of false prophets and psychic and spiritual darkness As Izod reminds us, '[F]ilms are vehicles for symbolic energy' (Hauke and Alister, 2001, p. 16). Bruzzi has this to say about the desire and hunger for reconciliation in the masculine continuum:

> Reconciliation with the father remains the ultimate goal of the children within these films . . . reconciliation is by no means the same as closure; the former is a state of individual understanding, the latter is a definite narrative end.
>
> (2005, p. 180)

It is significant that there is no closure in any of the films, only a partial reconciliation (if any at all). Bruzzi again:

> This need to apportion blame and importance to the father and the concomitant desire to reach a rapprochement are all features found in these millennial films, although in none of these films is there a happy/child/father reunion. The fathers in these films hurt and hold back their children because their offspring cannot work out how to disentangle themselves from the oppressive patriarchal relationship.
>
> (ibid)

It is this struggle both to connect and to separate, to transcend the American paternal and, in many ways, to transcend the strictures of the American Dream, that mark the masculine journeys within the films discussed. Linked in with these visions, the Child archetype, in this case, the child son, is also developmentally symbolic. Bassil-Morozow notes: 'Jung theorised that the child motif corresponded to a specific psychological process: the birth of the personality and its development and survival in the world' (2014, p. 145). The presence of the child in these films can be seen as allowing mediation and depiction of father hunger as a necessary process of masculine development (both psychological and spiritual). Where this hunger to be a father in both these cases is thwarted, it turns in on itself and is destructive in the extreme, both personally and societally. Given how important the Child archetype is within these films, and that it is the Child that essentially qualifies a father to be a father, we can now turn to analysing this figure in the next chapter.

## Notes

1 The Trickster is an archetype that Jung wrote extensively on throughout his work and is often cast as a truth-teller, a disruptor of the norm and a user of humour and satire to upset the status quo. The Trickster lives within the Shadow and is often encountered as a shapeshifter (Bassil-Morozow, 2010, 2011, 2014).
2 The rule of the father (*logos*) is discussed at length by Jung and is compared and contrasted to *eros*, the rule of the mother. In a sense, it is the delineation of a binary set of worlds, the interior and the exterior.
3 The puer aeternas, or flying boy/eternal youth, is an archetype that epitomizes arrested masculine development. Peter Pan is a prime example of this figure, someone who cannot deal with the adult world and who significantly has no Shadow and subsequently does not recognise (or ignores) unconscious and earthy drives. Jungian writer and analyst Marie Louise von Franz (2000) wrote extensively about the puer.
4 John Holmes starred in approximately 2,250 adult films including the *Johnny Wadd* series of films which is specifically referenced with *Boogie Nights*. Like Eddie Adams/Dirk Diggler, he was (in)famous for the large size of his penis, his star power within his chosen profession being entirely dependent on it. The attempted heist and theft scene towards the end of the film is loosely based on the Wonderland murders which took place in 1981 in Los Angeles in which he was directly involved.
5 The so-called Golden Age of Porn is widely held to have started with the 1972 theatrical release of *Deep Throat* (Damiano) and continued into the early 1980s. It was characterised by relatively high production values, use of professional equipment by professional operators, starred performers who (in the main) consented to be constructed as adult film stars and scripts that constructed (or at least made a pretence of) a viable narrative structure. Anderson's film purports to show the end of this phase of porn production being a direct result of the advent of home video and a lowering of production values, budgets and narratives with the express aim to maximise the enormous profits that were to be made.
6 Naming ceremonies that are a part of formal rites of passage ceremonies are a consistent feature within pre-industrial and primitive societies and have been documented, by, amongst others, Charles (1951) and D'Alisera (1998). Jung discussed these as part of initiation and posited that they were evidence of processes contained within the collective unconscious.

# Chapter 4

# The Child – living under the Shadow of the American Dream

The Child is, first and foremost, the key symbolic signifier of the father; the paternal cannot be paternal without issue. What is also inherent in the Child archetype is the journey that the Child must embark go on in order to become adult; in other words, to individuate as a developmentally healthy man or woman. It is this psychic journey that can be differentiated using a post-Jungian methodology, as we saw in the earlier chapters, but this is also complicated by the father, his wounds and his role within the family and American society. Similar to the previous chapter, we can examine and analyse the figure of the Child via different archetypal features and reveal how the Child is also depicted as carrying much of the Shadow of the American Dream. For example, in the earlier analysis of *The Pursuit of Happyness* (Muccino, 2006), the son of the main protagonist Chris Gardner (also called Chris, similar to *Road to Perdition*'s Michael Sullivan Snr and Jnr) is, ostensibly, the father's hope, reason and motivation for his relentless social and career advancement. He is also a burden, given to Chris to look after by a conveniently feckless mother (Thandie Newton), the maternal being completely sidelined and cast, arguably misogynistically, as a gender villain within the film. Chris Jnr is deliberately adorable and provides a convenient foil to his father's social Darwinist homilies (one of the cheesier lines in the film is: 'I'm an Ameri-can, not an Ameri-can't!') but simultaneously acts as an inconvenient reminder of the more shadowy aspects of American society in that his presence can act as a brake to the fulfilment of the success myth, whilst paradoxically at the same time being a key part of it. The child is, in effect, often acting (in a memorable phrase from a 1990 *Guardian* review of *Iron John*) as 'psychic copper', transmitting the darker familial and societal emotions and energies. When we also consider more transgressive films such as Todd Solondz's divisive and controversial *Happiness* (1998), analysed later, with its focus on deeply damaged characters such as Dr Bill Maplewood, the paedophile psychiatrist that abuses his sons' friends, the child is shown within American cinema as having to deal with any number of darker adult energies during the course of a film. This aspect of the child resonates

DOI: 10.4324/9780429199684-5

with Jung's analysis of the child archetype as fulfilling both future and past psychic patterns of behaviour:

> He (Jung) writes of the child motif (and we can begin to now to consider 'child' through narratives and developments of emergent and inceptive digital and electronic media born from previous cinematic technologies and histories) as linking to forgotten experiences within a collective rather than individual context'.
>
> (Fuery, quoted in Hockley, 2018, p. 441)

Also, as correctly pointed out by Knight, quoting Jung: 'Viewed through the lens of Jungian thought, one of the essential features of the child archetype representation is its futurity (Jung, 1940, p. 278), that is to say that the child is the potential future' (Hockley, 2018, p. 106). This futurity is echoed by other definitions of the Child as a symbol of renewal and innocence (Chevalier and Gheerbrant, 1994; Cooper, 1978). The temporal nature of the child archetype within American cinema, arthouse and mainstream, is a symbolic signifier in itself and points the way to the importance to the father; the child is, in many ways, a second chance for a father to transform themselves by a kind of proxy individuation. In many ways, the Child symbolically acts as a way to highlight the father, partly by throwing the figure of the paternal into sharp relief.

We now need to turn to how the filmic symbolic images and imagery of the American father relating to daughters, namely the child, adolescent and adult female, are mediated. Whilst the son's journey has been covered earlier, and given the profoundly different nature of the father-daughter relationship and the female gender journey (described in more detail later), there are a number of reasons why father hunger may have arisen. When we consider post-Jungian theory and its flexibility around interpretation of gender imagery (similar to symbolic imagery) and the corresponding archetypes (anima, puella, etc.), a number of perspectives and insights into this perceived parental need emerge. However, before we can discuss this figure any further, the developmental relationship between the father and daughter needs to be examined, in a more general sense, and differentiated from the relationship between the father and son, as there are markedly different features that are unique to this dynamic. Linked with this is analysis and discussion of the anima and the animus, two of the best-known Jungian terms, and how the American anima in particular is symbolically mediated and depicted within the father's psyche by Mendes in *American Beauty*. Portrayal of the damaged adult daughter's relationship has been already been indirectly analysed in Anderson's *Magnolia* in the previous chapter, with the American paternal Shadow once more being seen to affect the child in a detrimental way, albeit with the tentative hope of healing also being shown.

## Daughters and paternal 'otherness'

According to Jungian and post-Jungian perspectives, as well as psychoanalytical perspectives (Herzog, 1983; Williamson, 2004), the father and daughter relationship is fundamentally different to that of the son for a number of social, psychological and cultural reasons (Herzog, 1980; Samuels, 1985, 1993; Stevens, 1994). Whereas previous chapters dealt with the relationships of fathers and sons being constructed as indicative of a masculine continuum, the imagery that depicts fathers and daughters are different, in that they show the cinematic paternal depicted as an opposite to femininity, represented in this case by the daughter. Bassil-Morozow and Hockley make this point: 'Judging by myths and fairy tales in which the protagonist is a woman, female individuation is structurally different from the traditional hero myth' (2017, p. 136). The father, therefore, exists for the daughter as a primally important representation of masculinity, both in real life and within the psyche since he is the very first man in her life (both in terms of him playing a fundamental role in her creation, as well as, in most cases, being the first man she is aware of being present on a daily basis). Even if he is not present, his absence (Herzog, 1983, p. 2), or, perhaps more accurately, his lack of *presence*, is held to have far-reaching consequences for the psyche of his daughter. The classical influenced post-Jungian writer Anthony Stevens makes this point in his analysis of parental hunger when he highlights the importance of the father-figure to a female child:

> For the girl, the father's presence is no less important [than the boy], for it heightens her sense of being female in contrast to the essential 'otherness' of the male, and so profoundly influences how she experiences her femininity in relation to men.
>
> (1994, p. 69)

This 'otherness' of the father to the daughter (rather than the psychoanalytical *lack*) is a crucial difference when we consider the question of father hunger. Whereas the son feels this hunger due to a gap, or hole, within the psyche that he has to fill or bridge (essentially *re-join*) in order to be part of the masculine continuum alongside his father, and perhaps one day his own son, the daughter feels father hunger as partly a need to know herself in an *oppositional* sense; in other words, an experience of the masculine as a (ideally) well-balanced 'Otherness' in complement to her femininity, feminine energy, feminine presence and feminine power. Rather than a part of the masculine continuum, her relationship with her male parent is defined by both its opposition and complementarity. Similar to the son, there is a gender journey to be made here, but it is a profoundly different one, compared to the masculine journey. Whereas the son's gender journey is held to separate from the mother and join the father to complete his experience of his own gender and accompanying sense of self-identity (certainly in terms of gender), the daughter's gender journey is to travel from the mother[1] to the father, *already* knowing her own gender, and to experience and understand the masculine, initially as an Other (Singh, 2009; Izod, 2001, pp. 71–74). This Otherness can be located partially by virtue of the fact that the daughter is fundamentally dissimilar biologically to the father, a profound difference that also throws the similarity of the daughter to the mother into sharp relief. Bassil-Morozow and Hockley identify the goal of the father-daughter relationship thus: 'The meaning of the female journey is "relating" (as opposed to "discovering", which is the focus of the male journey)' (2017, p. 137). Whilst the mother–daughter relationship is of primary importance, the daughter also finds herself having to relate to, negotiate and accept the father and his presence, and to absorb it into her psyche and personal consciousness.

There is, of course, a challenge with this gender journey. If this complementary aspect of the masculine is not present in the shape of the paternal presence through absence, unavailability, or worse, inflected or shaded by abuse, then the 'Otherness' of the male and by larger implication, masculinity as a whole will be perceived as missing, unreliable, abusive, violent, dangerous and by implication, the daughter will feel unloved and unprotected. The 'Otherness' of the father (and by extension other men or masculine presences) can become a fundamental source of guilt, anger, frustration and fear, powerful enough to colour her experiences of the masculine throughout her life. Mitscherlich's conclusions around this supposed parental 'hole' in the psyche,[2] highlighted by Bly (1990); Reiter, (2008); and Biddulph, (2013), and referred to before when discussing the son, could be argued to apply equally as strongly here. To summarise, if the daughter does not have a clear idea of who her father is, what he is like, and what he does, then a space can open up by virtue of his absence which can be filled by negative feelings. Bly states that these feelings for the son are in the main feelings of suspicion; for the daughter they can be feelings of anger, longing, guilt and fear that can grow to fill this psychic space. Anger, because of her not feeling her father is there for her in terms of protection and love; longing for a safe and life-giving masculine presence; guilt because of feelings that she may not be good enough for him as a daughter and therefore be undeserving of his presence as Maine puts it: 'Guilt pervades the female psyche, the way that isolation haunts the male psyche' (2004, p. 101); and fear for the potential or actual danger that he may represent.

The Otherness of the father, therefore, can become a threat or, in some cases, a source of contempt and anger towards the masculine, with a weak or absent father also generating the hunger for a stronger masculine presence who will perform the role of a safe/strong father figure for the female psyche. Just as the emerging male psyche has to negotiate the mother and all of the powerful feminine energies that she represents in its journey towards individuation, so too does the female psyche have to deal with this often problematic father-energy. A psychoanalytical perspective corresponds closely with the post-Jungian view; as Herzog reminds us with reference to both sons and daughters:

> The father is the organizer and modulator of intense affect paradigms. He beckons to the child like a knight in shining armour, not only pulling him or her out of, or assisting in the dissolution of the intense mother-child relationship . . . but actively intruding upon it.
>
> (1983, p. 51)

This perceived need for a robust paternal presence, which helps to enforce both psychic and physical boundaries for the female psyche, echoes powerfully with Jung's concept of the father being a representative of, or indicative of, *Logos*, or the organising force in the world, the erstwhile rule of the father being a consistent presence within the outside environment, the world outside of the domestic sphere where *Eros*, the force held as being mostly associated with the mother energy, is to be found. Jung referred to these broadly male and female energies with characteristic vagueness: 'The animus corresponds to the paternal Logos just as the anima corresponds to the maternal Eros. But I do not wish or intend to give these two intuitive concepts too specific a definition' (Storr, 1983, p. 111).

As the female psyche develops, the encounters with the father and his archetypal *Logos* energy (whether or not it is the woman's biological father, as Samuels judiciously reminds us[3]) becomes increasingly important. This purported psychic need for a safe man who is there for her as support, as a role model and as a powerful presence with which to activate and nourish her psyche is arguably the essence of father hunger for the feminine. In addition to the father functioning as an oppositional figure, as stated at the beginning of the section, the father also fulfils an apposite role to the daughter in that he is often presented, or depicted, within film as complementary to the mother, and by extension to the daughter, when normative depictions of the standard Hollywood American nuclear family are considered. (Bruzzi, 2005; Hamad, 2014). One of the features of American cinematic output is the subversion of this construction of the American father as complementary, which will be explored in more detail later on in the chapter. To explore this relationship further, the problematic area of the American father and his sexuality is now examined and how he and it relate to the daughter.

### Daughters and the father's body

In his book *The Political Psyche*, which deals in some depth with cultural perceptions of the image and positions of the UK father at a particular juncture in the early 1990s, the post-Jungian author Andrew Samuels makes the uncomfortable observation that whenever fathers and daughters are mentioned within a number of cultural discourses, there is an assumption made, bordering on a cultural complex, that this relationship is very likely not always a healthy one '[I]t has become very hard to write about the positive, loving flexible father and his political impact as well as about the sexually abusing, violent, abandoning or absent, authoritarian father and his political impact' (1993, p. 126). Later on, he expands his theme:

> It is difficult to stay close to positive images of the father without tipping over into denial and idealization. There is very little description of the ordinary, devoted, good-enough fathering; our preoccupation is with the sexually abusing or violent father.
>
> (ibid, p. 135)

This realisation was prompted by a related request for a newspaper illustration to show the positive aspects of the physical relationship between a father and daughter in an article that he had written. Subsequently, the picture provided was an overwhelmingly negative one, despite the original brief. Samuels later came to an interesting conclusion:

> It follows that, in order to stay with positive images of the father, one has to stay with the negative images as well . . . *sex and aggression constitute the good father as well as the bad father*. The central implication of this is that we are now required to pay maximum attention to the *father's body*. When the media concentrate on incest, they are expressing a fascination with the father's body. In its positive form, frolicking in the swimming pool; in its negative form, touching the child in an abusive way in the pool.
>
> (ibid, p. 136; italics in the original)

This point is mentioned in depth as an example of how deep the associations of the father being a danger to the daughter can run. Putting aside the often idealised, but at the same time conflicted, notions of American fatherhood that are contained with much mainstream Hollywood fare (Bruzzi, 2005; Hamad, 2014), the father, and particularly the father's physical presence in the imagery surrounding his body and his physical and symbolic relationship with his daughter, are often negative.

Bruzzi highlights this point when discussing the father's body and the father's desires in *American Beauty*:

> Although Lester harbours illegal desires (Angela is still under-age) *American Beauty* is not 'about' them, for these sexual longings are merely symptoms of – and in some ways a metaphor for – his middle-aged malaise. It is symptomatic of this distancing of Lester's perversity that his sexual fantasies are visually stylised and [deliberately] non-naturalistic.
>
> (2005, p. 185)

This assertion by Bruzzi around Lester's desires is not necessarily true (and subsequently undermines her argument somewhat) as neither Jane Burnham nor

Angela Hayes's ages are made explicitly clear in the film. However, Ball's script does mention that Jane is sixteen, both of them are shown as attending senior high school (normal ages between fifteen and eighteen), and Jane embarks on a sexual relationship with Ricky Fitts, who is mentioned as being eighteen within the script. They are depicted as being both sexually maturing and sexually aware and most likely above the age of consent. This point is made to highlight that Lester's desires (whether or not they are legal or illegal) are still depicted to be perceived as, at best, deeply inappropriate, given the age difference (he tells us he is forty-two and his daughter's best friend is at most sixteen or seventeen). In a sense, illegality does not factor as much as Bruzzi would assert, rather the fact that he is (to echo a cliché) old enough to be her father, inviting questions of problematic incestuous desire. Bruzzi's point above around Lester's fantasies being a symptom of his mid-life crisis is well made and certainly resonate with the post-Jungian position highlighted by Chachere (2003); this is explored later in the chapter, along with the concomitant film imagery. Suffice to say that in the 1990s, the father-daughter relationship (in both the US and the UK) was culturally widely perceived to be vulnerable, fragile and threatened by potential paternal incestuous desires.

Where does this fear and fascination with the father's body come from, particularly in relation to his daughter? The answer, at least partially, appears when the daughter begins puberty and the growing realisation her sexual potential and power in relation to the males around her, including her father. Margo Maine, in *Father Hunger*, makes a telling point that a male mid-life crisis (that may or may not be catalysed by sexual self-doubt and age-related anxiety) can often coincide with his adolescent daughter's puberty:

> When a man is experiencing such conflicts, which often arise just as his daughter is going through puberty, the relationship between father and daughter may suffer. His discomfort with himself and insecurity or impulsivity regarding sexuality may frighten her. If he seems preoccupied by sex or becomes more overt in his own sexual behaviors, she becomes confused, not knowing how to react because her needs for parental support and stability during her adolescence are strong. In addition, a father's tendency toward separation and denial may make him oblivious to his daughter's needs and reactions. The widening chasm in their relationship results in the deepening sense of father hunger.
>
> (2004, pp. 92–93)

Maine maintains that the dangers of a father's timidity in facing up to his daughter's burgeoning sexuality as a maturing young woman can be considerable:

> So as the typical father watches his global girl mature and become increasingly sexual, he may be worried about [physical] boundaries and withdraw from her even more. Dad's anxiety compounds the daughter's own fear of

her body's changes and becomes a powerful deterrent to a close supportive relationship and to her sense of herself as a young budding woman.

(ibid, p. 131)

When it comes to the daughter's father hunger experienced as an adolescent/pubescent, Maine warns that the dangers are serious:

> Father hunger becomes increasingly detrimental when girls enter puberty, because this is the developmental phase during which their curiosity about men and the male perspective, their interest in hetero-sexual relationships [if so inclined] and their physical attractiveness emerge and intensify. When a father responds by withdrawing and being aloof, his daughter suffers from low self-esteem, and her confidence in her sexuality is undermined. She is denied valuable opportunities to gain experience and practical knowledge about how to act around men and how to talk to them.
>
> (ibid, pp. 131–132)

This purported fragility of an adolescent daughter's understanding of the masculine that Maine proposes appears to resonate when the depiction of this relationship within American cinema is considered. Another aspect of father hunger is the hunger for the man to be a father to a daughter. If this desire to parent his daughter is frustrated due to internal and external challenges, then the father's paternal potentiality is frustrated and his love and nurturing will be stymied. *American Beauty* depicts this fatherly frustration via the figure of Lester Burnham (Kevin Spacey) and goes further in explicitly linking this paternal frustration as a fundamental masculine spiritual challenge, which Lester is depicted as nearly meeting. Mendes and the screenwriter Alan Ball articulate this situation with arguably a large degree of accuracy, with Lester Burnham's mid-life crisis[4] coinciding with Jane Burnham's adolescence and individual journey of sexual and spiritual discovery in conjunction with Ricky Fitts. Post-Jungian writer Tacey articulates this soul search:

> In much cinema and popular culture, the pursuit of the soul turns a man away from his wife, toward either another woman or to an emotional or spiritual undertaking that for the time being appears to be a working vessel for soul-making.
>
> (1997, p. 182)

*American Beauty* accurately portrays this definition of a search, but with a crucial difference, in that Lester still tries to connect emotionally and sexually with his wife, Carolyn (Annette Bening) and is finally 'woken up' to the benefits of his family by his rejection of Angela (Mena Suvari), before he is killed. Before we engage with further textual analysis, the sexual presence of the father, as theorised by Samuels (1993) and Bruzzi (2005), needs to be examined in more depth if the imagery and narrative drive of the film is to be understood on a deeper level.

## The erotic paternal

Samuels proposes in *The Political Psyche* (1993) that the father plays a number of roles to his daughter, in that he enables (along with the mother) the daughter to become psychologically pluralistic:

> My view is that the father's affirming physical response to his daughter at all stages of her life helps her to achieve a kind of psychological pluralism (to be one person and many persons). It is the father who communicates this to his daughter that 'You can be this . . . and this . . . and this . . . and still be your (female) self'.
>
> (p. 152)

One feature of this pluralistic theory is that the father provides erotic communication of a sort to the daughter that affirms that she is not just a maternal, or potentially maternal creature. Echoing the above statement, Samuels posits:

> The daughter is *not* liberated by the father in the sense of being led into pastures new. Rather, his positive physical and erotic communication fosters and brings out potentials in her which are already there. 'You are this . . . and this . . . and this . . . and you're still you'.
>
> (ibid, p. 153)

This erotic playback between father and daughter is a delicate matter, and Samuels recognises the dangers inherent at this stage of a developing relationship in a section that is quoted at length:

> A father whose own sexual development has been damaged may not be able to keep the physical element within bounds. But there's a paradox here: the father-daughter relationship has to be physical enough to allow for the experiential – and political – outcome I have been depicting . . . the good-enough father plays a full part in providing it. . . . Quite understandable concentration on erotic excess, for example, child sexual abuse, has made it very hard to stay with erotic deficit . . . there is the risk of being misunderstood as advocating incest. . . . we begin to think of *an optimal erotic relation between father and daughter and, hence, of the pathology of a failure to achieve that.*
>
> (ibid, p. 154; italics in the original)

Assuming they have veracity, these arguments are challenging in terms of the father-daughter relationship. According to this view, the paternal figure needs to provide enough physical, sensual and erotic presence for the daughter to feel that she can be whatever she wants to be, and also feel that she has erotic viability as her own woman to be in the psychologically strong position of being able to sexually renounce the father, which, paradoxically, allows her to be able to be close to him. In terms of her developing awareness of eroticism (both her own erotic potential and the erotic masculine, assuming heterosexuality), the father (as the primary man in her life) needs to have a safe sexual presence around the daughter so that her erotic boundaries develop in a healthy way and that she gains an understanding of the erotic potential of the masculine (the so-called erotic playback), constellating and assimilating this aspect of life within her psyche. When we consider, as we did at the beginning of this chapter, the oppositional and appositional aspects of the father, erotic playback can be viewed as a vital part of the father-daughter relationship in the sense of the daughter establishing a clearer idea of herself due to the various *presences* of the father. Father hunger can arise when this erotic playback is either not provided, as in the fathers described by Maine who shy away from the reality of the evidence of their daughters maturation or when damaged fathers fall into their Shadow and take the erotic playback too literally, such as in *Magnolia* (discussed earlier) and sexually abuse their daughters. Samuels' point appears to be backed up by Herzog's case studies: 'All the fathers of girls in my study roundly insisted that they favoured total freedom of choice for their daughters professionally, but they tended to interact with them predominantly in the model I would call *protoerotic endorsement*'(1983, p. 52; italics added). *American Beauty* also shows Lester Burnham as an American father who is in danger of remaining in his Shadow, but who (with the help of his anima) manages to contain his erotic playback and mature as a man as a result, achieving redemption by the end.

## Archetypes and the daughter

When discussing the female-male dyad, particularly from a Jungian or post-Jungian viewpoint, the terms 'animus' and 'anima' need to be defined. For the purposes of this project, it can be held that the term '*Animus*' is for the male contrasexual archetype that Jung held to be present in all women. Correspondingly, the term '*Anima*' is the contrasexual female archetype that Jung held to be within all men. Jungian scholar Anthony Storr describes these archetypes as follows

> This psychological bisexuality is a reflection of the biological fact that is the larger number of male (or female) genes which is the decisive factor in the determination of sex . . . anima and animus manifest themselves most typically in personified form as figures in dreams and fantasies ("dream-girl", "dream-lover"), or in the irrationalities of a man's *feeling* and a woman's *thinking*.
> 
> (1983, p. 414; italics in the original)

Jung himself is initially quite specific about these primally important archetypes and where they belong, hence the need to quote him at length:

> Every man carries with the eternal image of woman, not the image of this or that particular woman, but a definitive feminine image. This image is

> fundamentally unconscious, an heredity factor of primordial origin engraved in the living organic system of the man, an imprint or 'archetype' (*q.v.)* of all the ancestral experiences of the female, a deposit, as it were, of all the impressions ever made by woman.... In it's primary 'unconscious' form the animus is a compound of spontaneous, unpremeditated opinions which exercise a powerful influence on the woman's emotional life.... Consequently, the animus likes to project itself on 'intellectuals' and all kinds of 'heroes', including tenors, artists, sporting celebrities etc.
>
> (ibid)

The exact purpose and reason why these two archetypes exist is then discussed in more detail:

> The natural function of the animus (as well as of the anima) is to remain in (their) place between individual consciousness and the collective unconscious (q.v); exactly as the persona (q.v.) as a sort of stratum between the ego-consciousness and the objects of the external world. The anima and the animus should function as a bridge, or as a door, leading to the images of the collective unconscious, as the persona should be a sort of bridge into the world.
>
> (ibid, p. 415)

As a mediating psychic structure between the collective unconscious and the material world, the animus for a female certainly makes sense when we consider that this particular archetype is influenced greatly by the individual's experience of the father. Whilst we have to ensure that we do not confuse the two (the animus for a woman also includes the collected and constellated experiences of other encounters with males and the masculine such as brothers, sons, other family members as well as non-familial male figures), it is the father most of all that influences the development of the animus the most. In addition (and as mentioned previously), the rule of the father, the *Logos* energy, is hinted at when we consider the purported organising nature of the animus, a resonance that carries into the material realm and its perceived structures, whether this is actually the case or not.

When discussing the animus, we must also be mindful of the nature of archetypes, in that they are essentially unknowable in and of themselves but are held as only really being known through the archetypal images that are produced by them. Post-Jungians, among them Singh, urge caution in that Jung's writings on the animus in particular betray his own personal foibles and 'rather blasé perspective on sexual difference' (2009, p. 131). It seems to be a feature of writing on Jungian theories that archetypes can quickly become stereotypes, not least by Jung himself when we consider his, at times, essentialist language on the sexes. Indeed, it can be argued that Jung edges closely towards essentialist thinking around the animus and anima when we consider his assertion about the complementarity nature of the anima in men, an assertion that could be argued to be a personal projection:

> [The anima] contains all those fallible human qualities his persona lacks. If the persona is intellectual, the anima will quite certainly be sentimental. The complementary character of the anima also affects the sexual character as I have proved to myself beyond a Shadow of a doubt.
>
> (ibid)

Whilst the latter assertion from Jung in the quote just cited borders on arrogance, the central theory of a contrasexual complementary archetype of the psyche that is held to help maintain balance within the individual is an attractive one, in that it explains the individual's approach to the opposite sex and gender, as well as the individual's attitude to its own sex and gender. It is also in sharp contrast to psychoanalytical gender biases which have arguably disadvantaged Freudian psychological perspectives. Bassil-Morozow and Hockley also highlight a number of (qualified) advantages to the post-Jungian approaches to psychologically analyse the feminine and its presence:

> The good thing about Jungian psychology, however, is that it accounts for the active, aggressive and masculinised forms of female behaviour when it discusses the 'whore' aspect of the anima. Although it still objectifies the feminine and brands it 'mysterious' or 'dangerous', it nevertheless does not try to diminish its importance or restructure it to suit the patriarchal order. . . . Jung's approach to the feminine, although largely tainted by the general patriarchal attitude to women prevalent at the time, nevertheless accounted for its power – not passive power, but the active and unpredictable type of power.
>
> (2017, p. 152)

Bearing these points in mind, we can identify where dangers lie within this theory. When discussing symbols and archetypes, there is a danger of falling into stereotypes when discussing the male-female dyad. This point is picked up by a number of post-Jungians, among them Izod and Singh. They hold that it is more than likely that *both* contrasexual archetypes are present within the individual psyche, a more flexible proposition than the somewhat restrictive binary position that Jung originally proposed, and which has led, perhaps understandably, to charges laid against Jungian theory as essentialism. This proposed archetypal duality is termed 'syzygy', similar to the montage definition in that it is a structure that allows for oppositional forces to be held together. Singh quotes Izod when he describes it in more post-Jungian terms:

> 'the conjunction in opposition of the sexes', characterising 'many images of the unified self'. (2001: p. 142). Although Izod acknowledges that syzygy is only one image of this kind of deep unification, there is a case to be made

for the power of this specific conjunction that is both overwhelmingly other and yet utterly reasonable. As many commentators have noted, post-Jung, there is a general consensus that both men and women should be considered to have both anima and animus *aspects* (my emphasis) of the psyche present. This makes sense in terms of the overall consensus in cultural theory that gender is performative, is not static within identificatory practices, and is a social construction. However, this conjunction flies in the face of normative assumptions, surrounding the sex/gender alignment that have changed little since Jung, in popular representation.

(ibid, p. 147)

Bassil-Morozow and Hockley add to this definition: 'Psychological wholeness is a matter of equality and enlightenment, not a retrospective exercise in eliminating difference or an immature search for similarity and perfect mirroring' (2017, p. 146). Post-Jungian writer Susan Rowland identifies another advantage that post-Jungian theory has when it comes to assigning gender meanings and culture:

Jung's originating principle is that the unconscious is independently creative of the ego and in part unknowable. Such a belief means that the human body cannot fix meaning. Gender becomes a dialogical process between the creative unconscious . . . and the cultural meanings bestowed upon the sexed body.

(Hauke and Hockley, 2011, p. 149)

I would support these positions with regard to this theory of syzygy and its dynamic interplay of the anima and animus, particularly in representations within cinema. Whilst it would be reasonable to assume that in women, the animus would hold more sway that the anima when dealing with any Shadow energies and when dealing with the opposite sex, the anima would no doubt also be presented when questions or complexes regarding the individual's own gender surfaced. When we factor in cultural and societal reinforcement of gender roles, there are clear reasons why imagery of feminine gender roles are so prevalent. In particular, and with specific reference to daughters, we can see this syzygy at work within American cinema. For example, Jane Burnham's troubled relationship with her mother in *American Beauty*, and with Claudia Gator with her outwardly normal parents in *Magnolia*, particularly Jimmy Gator (Phillip Baker Hall), the erstwhile respectable host of the ambiguously titled gameshow *What Do Children Know?* Having outlined the main points and features of the father-daughter relationship and the potential for father hunger therein, we can now engage with more detailed analysis of the symbols and themes used in Mendes' *American Beauty*, a text that is explicitly about father hunger, its source and the consequences of it.

## American beauty: the anima and the inadequate paternal

The redeemed father is the subject of Sam Mendes' first feature film[5] (1999) and specifically references father hunger at the very beginning of the film and from the perspective of a teenaged American girl at the turn of the twenty-first century. The film opens with grainy home-video footage of Jane Burnham (Thora Birch), who is lounging sulkily on her bed with her lover Ricky Fitts (Wes Bentley), an initially unseen presence whom we hear talking to Jane as he films her. In this opening scene, we have Jane's current situation and relationship with her father Lester Burnham summarised pithily as only a teenaged daughter can:

JANE: I need a father who's a role model, not some horny geek-boy who's gonna spray his shorts whenever I bring a girlfriend home from school. (Snorts). What a lame-o.

This bitter and seemingly world-weary commentary echoes Margo Maine's (2004) regarding the emergence of the daughter's sexuality clashing with the American father's uncertainty and sexual self-doubt, brought on by age-related anxiety. Lester Burnham's (Kevin Spacey) journey of self-discovery, both spiritual and sexual, coincides with his daughter's own similar journey, with Jane's anger at her father for not being an adequate, or even as D.W Winnicott has termed it a 'good enough parent' (1973, p. 10) or, in this case, a male adult. In both an oppositional and appositional sense, Lester is explicitly depicted as not up to fulfilling his role as father to his daughter, which is portrayed as having detrimental effects on Jane (her respect for the masculine and, in post-Jungian terms, her animus, is lacking). This subsequently provides much of the dramatic and narrative drive of the film as Lester's journey towards a state of self-conscious awareness is depicted. Lester is depicted as failing to provide sufficient presence to Jane (erotic or physical), which consequently contributes to Jane's feelings of father hunger. This sexual awareness of both Jane and her friend Angela (with whom Lester experiences an anima-inspired fixation) must be understood in context with Samuels' point about the father's erotic presence for the daughter (1993). For a daughter's healthy psychological growth, Samuels argues that he needs to be erotically present to provide an erotic male presence for a daughter, but paradoxically also be available for eventual erotic rejection by the daughter in order that she can grow and develop her own eroticism in relation to men (or women) nearer her own age. Symbolically the daughter's body also acts as one of the main sites where father hunger is mediated; in *American Beauty*, the daughter is sexualised by her maturing relationship to both her body and her first lover, Ricky, who calmly informs her that she is beautiful. The daughter's body image, and more specifically Jane's body image, is depicted as fluid and fragile, to be changed, altered and shaped in accordance with a faceless and unaccountable set of influencers that are located online in cyberspace (Maine, 2004) as well as in the schoolyard of her high school, as strongly hinted at in a scene where her friend

Angela Hayes (Mena Suvari) is boasting about allowing herself to be seduced by a fashion photographer.

Returning to the main relationship between father and daughter, Lester (through his voice-over at the beginning) is surprisingly aware of his daughter's troubles: 'Janie's a pretty typical teenager. Angry, insecure, confused. I wish I could tell her that's all going to pass. . . . But I don't want to lie to her'. This cynical, yet poignant, awareness of his daughter's needs and his own inability to connect with her is portrayed throughout the film, especially at the dinner table. This domestic space is transformed as a key location for family conflict in two scenes, the first of which Lester announces that his job is under threat, an announcement that does not have the impact on his family that he'd hoped for. He is sarcastic: 'You couldn't possibly care any less, could you?' Jane bites back: 'Well, what do you expect? You can't all of a sudden be my best friend, just because you had a bad day. I mean, hello. You've barely even talked to me for months'. It is this hinted-at back story detail that builds a bigger picture of their strained situation; they had a better relationship, but for some reason it has changed, and not for the better. It is not made clear who is responsible for this decline, but given the timing of the daughter's adolescence and Lester's slowly growing mid-life crisis, Maine's theory of the daughter's developing sexuality and adulthood clashing with the father's re-assessment of his life is particularly pertinent and resonant at this juncture. Richard Chachere reiterates that:

> *American Beauty* is a very American film and it is very American about the disaster of married life. It is also the all-American Jungian mid-life crisis film. In the story, Lester is having his mid-life crisis, and sure enough, the *anima* comes and pops him on the head. He looks stupid. He looks especially stupid to his daughter, Jane.
>
> (2003, p. 5)

It can also be posited that Jane's anger towards her father is shown to be born out of frustration that her emotional needs as a developing young woman are not being met by her father who is shown as being unconscious on a number of levels. Lester's self-described emotional and mental somnambulant state therefore is depicted as being damaging to both his marriage and his daughter. He is shown as unavailable to the people that need him to be available; his depicted journey to a state of awakened awareness is all the more poignant when we are confronted with his death at the end of the film. If we analyse the symbolic imagery that is used in this particular scene, more is revealed. The mise-en-scene is carefully composed on a number of levels beginning with the deliberate seating of Caroline Burnham (Annette Bening) and Lester opposite one another, with Jane being placed forlornly in the middle. Given what we have already experienced of the Burnham's familial unhappiness, the chances of a parental confrontation are high, and Jane is likely to be caught in the verbal and emotional crossfire. The scene also contains a number of photos of the family in (presumably) happier times to give contrast and heft to the drama that is being played out. These pictures are also directly referenced at the end of his film when Lester's end-of-life coda is being played as a montage and he experiences powerful archetypal images and imagery of happier moments (his wife laughing and joyous, his daughter excited at her birthday party) from his family's life played out as he dies.

The dining room is cast by Mendes and the film's cinematography (tightly framed composition of the Burnhams to enhance the sense of pressure, with red flowers present, a constant palette choice and significantly symbolic motif, discussed in more detail later) as the space and emotional cauldron, the temenos[6] as it were, where the family dynamics of the Burnhams are played out. This scene is tragi-comic and revealing in that it shows the state of the father's status as fallen. To paraphrase Bly (1990) and Moore and Gillette (1992), at this point early in the film, Lester's King archetype as weak and lacking purpose. He is shown to have abrogated his responsibilities, and it is this weaker energy and the resulting lack of conscious presence within his family that his daughter identifies and complains about. Lester is shown to be dimly aware of the situation, but instead of recognising it, lashes out at his wife instead: 'You treat her like an employee!' When challenged by Caroline Burnham, he backs away from what could be a useful confrontation in terms of seeking conscious emotional truth with his wife, instead seeking solace in a bowl of ice cream. The scene ends with the Burnhams still unhappy, despite Lester's belatedly feeble attempts to connect with his daughter, and the attention cleverly shifting to Ricky Fitts' perspective as he films them from his bedroom window. The next time, however, we encounter the Burnhams again in the family space of the dining room, a major shift has occurred in consciousness on the part of Lester as he begins to wake up from his spiritual and emotional torpor and starts to challenge the status quo of his family life.

What awakes Lester from his emotional coma presented to us at the beginning of the film? Mendes and Ball consciously locate the catalyst for Lester's awakening in his initial encounter with his *anima* via the figure of Angela, Jane's friend and fellow high-school cheerleader at a high school basketball game. As Chachere correctly identifies earlier, Lester's *anima* is shown as striking him awake, both locating itself both within Angela, or to be more accurate, simultaneously projected *onto* her by Lester. This is a pivotal moment in the film on a number of levels and raises a number of serious questions to consider, not least of which that issues of incestuous desire are raised when we consider that the object of Lester's desire is his daughter's friend. Lester, in Heyraud's words 'fumbles around the fringes of life, morbidly bound by his death-like depression' (2000a, p. 144). The next scene cuts to the darkened interior of the basketball court, the camera focusing in on Carolyn and Lester as they (in Lester's case, clumsily) take their place on the bleachers with Lester plaintively asking if they can leave after Jane's cheerleader performance, another culturally specific moment. We then switch to Lester's POV as the cheerleaders, Jane and Angela included, begin their cheerleading dance to staccato music that mimics the ticking of a clock, reflected in their automaton-like dance moves and lit up to emphasise them and them alone.

We then switch back to Lester's POV as the deliberately dream-like image of Angela Hayes is revealed, prompting an accompanying deliberate and distinct change in tempo of music, colour, sound and camera angle as the mise-en-scene changes dramatically and explosively. This theatre stage-like change (a throwback to the director's previous role as a theatre director)[7] employing harsh lighting on both Lester and Angela to reinforce the psychic connection between the two is deeply symbolic as the initial archetypal image of Lester's *anima* is revealed in all its power. This is Lester's first encounter with the sexually powerful aspect of his *anima*, and it is this power that manages to finally grab his attention and begin the process of his psychic awakening, or individuation. As Chachere has already succinctly pointed out, 'it pops him the head' in order to wake him up. Adding to the definitions discussed earlier, Jung defined it:

> Every man carries with him the eternal image of woman, not the image of this or that woman, but a definitive feminine image. This image is fundamentally unconscious, an hereditary factor of primordial origin engraved in the living organic system of man.
>
> (1954, CW 17, par 338)

As Tacey describes it: 'A flight that does not soar upwards, but hovers near the things of the earth, is not governed by puer, Zeus, or Icarus, but by anima' (1997, p. 179). There is also another side to the emergence of the *anima*. Tacey manages to provide a summary of the film in one sentence:

> Notoriously, the arrival of the anima in a man's life is associated with the mysterious or desirable 'Unknown Woman' who breaks up marriages, disrupts conventions, and throws a man's life into a mixture of erotic excitement and moral and personal chaos.
>
> (ibid, p. 180)

He expands more, less it be misunderstood that it is somehow the fault of the woman who has anima projected onto them that causes the disruption:

> [W]omen act as the convenient carriers for the emotions, passions, energies and feelings that are part of the psychic reality of the anima-complex. If this complex is carried by others, then one is relatively free from the challenges that anima poses to male consciousness.
>
> (ibid, p. 181)

Bassil-Morozow and Hockley expand these points:

> The woman is thus both the anima and the container of the animus. Either way, she is the victim: patriarchal culture sees her animus as 'the loud evil thing', and, as the anima she is not even a real woman – she is a cluster of

someone else's fantasies. The anima needs to be restrained lest its uncritical opinions destroy the aura of mystery surrounding the feminine; and the anima needs to be maintained in order to keep the woman a suitable vessel for projection.

(2017, p. 154)

Tacey's definition of the psychic space that the anima provides is what is initially valuable for Lester's spiritual and psychic journey. Mendes depicts Angela as acting as carrier of the anima-complex, allowing Lester to 'wake up' and rebel, abrogating his adult responsibilities, which in turn catalyses the narrative drive of the film. That this anima is also, in a sense, blended with his daughter's presence is one of the more sophisticated and disturbing aspects of the film; Lester does not, or chooses not, to see how falling for a girl his daughter's age is problematic (Arthur, 2004; Karlyn, 2004; King, 2009). Returning to the scene, and after an increasing series of camera close-ups on Lester's comically astonished face, the sequence progresses with the main motif and image being depicted. Angela is shown as both objectified as Lester's focus of desire, her unambiguously sexual look towards him culminating in her opening her jacket to reveal not her body and breasts as an audience might think, but instead a shower of red rose petals which fly out at a shocked Lester, at which point his dream/revelation ends abruptly and he (and the audience) is shown as returning to the reality of the basketball court. Bruzzi claims that the petals are 'vehicles of disavowal. That they both stand for Lester's lust and deny access to Angela's pubescent body means that the audience never has to confront the raw obscenity of the sexual situation' (2005, p. 185). Perhaps, but from another perspective, the scene and aesthetics also function symbolically as a way marker of Lester's imminent psychic journey.

Why is the red rose used as the symbol of transformation in particular? Aside from the obvious and well-known popular romantic connotations that are near universal, the rose can be symbolically analysed on a number of levels. With the petals not only resembling female sexual organs, the flower also carries a pleasing scent or perfume, both physical attributes that resonate strongly with desire, sexuality and life; on a visual level, the rose is generally held to be a deeply libidinous blossom. Cooper defines the rose as standing for 'perfection; the pleroma; completion; the mystery of life; the heart centre of life; the unknown; beauty; grace; happiness, but also voluptuousness; the passions and associated with wine, sensuality and seduction' (1978, p. 141). Exploring further on an archetypal and symbolic level, the rose has been reported as being found (Ronnberg and Martin, 2010, pp. 162–163) in a large number of cultures and mainly linked with goddess worship, particularly goddesses of love and fertility, reflecting the earlier assertion about its culturally recognised symbolism. The rose is also held to allude strongly to more than just feelings of romance:

> For alchemists, the entire process of psychic transformation takes place sub rosa (under the rose). . . . In alchemy the crossed branches of the white and

red rose not only allude to the "love affair" of opposite natures, and to the albedo and rubedo as understanding and realisation of psychic processes.

(ibid)

In other words, the rose is a strongly symbolic signifier of psychic transformation; in this case Lester's symbolic psychic re-birth and partial awakening from immature and asleep father and husband to a more self-aware and mature man and parent. This symbology is developed in a number of ways, from our first glimpse of Carolyn Burnham tending to her ruthlessly controlled and pruned 'American Beauty' rose bushes (her handling with gloves of her flowers can be read as indicative of both a distrust of the symbolic power of the rose, as well as an appreciation of their thorny nature) to the continuation of Lester's individuative journey. The rose, then, is both a symbol of both beauty (referenced throughout the film and on the film's paratextual publicity materials – adverts, posters etc. – upon its release) and, as Stevens has noted it is also:

The Western equivalent of the lotus (allegorical symbol of creation and individuation), its mandala form representing the wholeness of creation, the perfection of the deity, and the individuation of the Self. For the Christians, it refers to the chalice, the blood of Christ, the promise of redemption and resurrection, and the certainty of divine love. . . . Aphrodite caused the red rose to grow from the blood of her slain lover, Adonis.

(1998, p. 389)

This Shadow side of the rose (that it sprang from spilled blood, and that its thorns can draw blood as in various fairy tales) and its accompanying psychic power is also explored in the final scenes of the film in which the dramatic narrative come to a climax.

Returning to the follow-up scene to what can be described as the anima scene, we are then shown (for Jane) an excruciatingly embarrassing first encounter with Angela where Lester stutters and inadvertently humiliates himself. For her own part, Angela displays preternatural awareness of the true state of the Burnham's marriage. Jane is humiliated: 'Could he be any more pathetic?' Angela smiles. 'I think it's sweet. And I think he and your mother have not had sex in a long time'. At this point, Mendes and screenwriter Alan Ball deliberately depict Angela as fulfilling, at first glance, Lester's sexual anima fantasies about her. She is initially depicted as sexually experienced, worldly, aware of her sexual capital and power over men via the agency of her looks and her body, referenced particularly in a previous scene with Jane where she recounts confidently her growing awareness of her sexuality and beauty and the effect it has on men. This depiction of Angela as a Lolita-esque figure continues throughout the film, with her true state of virginity and sexual inexperience only revealed at the end of the film in another pivotal scene with Lester. To emphasise the journey that Lester is embarking upon, the scene after the encounter discussed earlier, we are then shown Lester in bed in a highly stylised dream sequence, grinning in amazement and wonder as red rose petals (presumably of the American Beauty variety) fall gently all around him from above. His POV then shows a magical version of Angela floating above him on an inverted and literal bed of roses, her body coyly covered up by strategic petals, Mendes deliberately stylising Lester's fantasies in all of the dream sequences within the film. With this particular sequence Mendes references directly (and literally) the phrase 'sub rosa' as quoted above as they show Lester starting the process of awakening due to his anima resorting to desperate measures to awaken him. Lester has found himself under the power of the rose, under the power of his anima, and it is working its psychic magic upon, bringing him out of his mental and emotional torpor.

Alongside the obvious symbol of the rose, there are a number of other symbols within the film that are used here to generate affective power, namely rain (water), blood, and doorways. The background to significant scenes is dominated by water in the form of rain, with darkness falling in the evening to add to the imagery. As discussed previously in the chapter around fathers and child sons using *The Road to Perdition* as an example, rain is a primal indicator of spiritual cleansing and soul revitalisation:

> Rain is a miraculous visitation of heavenly power, natural and immense, necessary and feared, cleansing, releasing, dissolving, flooding, relieving and sweet. . . . Beneficial healing by the celestial influence of such "rain" cleanses that which is dark and trapped in emotional blindness, or in the parched earth within, inert, barren of life, stuck in unconsciousness or in uncertainty, and in need of the dissolving and propagating rains. The alchemists saw the falling rain as the "washing" of the *nigredo* state, illuminating and reanimating what felt dead and dark. This divine intervention of grace occurring at the darkest point preceded a new *coniunctio*, a psychic union of emotion, body, imagination and mind in a new level of consciousness.
>
> (Ronnberg and Martin, 2010, p. 62)

This lengthy quote reinforces the importance of water as a transforming symbolic force within the film. Up to this point, the narrative has been built around Lester's awakening, and the effects of his awakening upon those around him, both constructive and destructive. Rain symbolises a coming renewal of Lester's psyche and his maturation towards individuation. Interestingly enough, the imagery used is highly reminiscent of horror films when analysed, his encounter with Angela (after her fight with Jane and Ricky in which her repressed ordinariness is revealed to her by Ricky) is lit by light with rain clearly visible on window glass and stark Shadows, with occasional rumblings of thunder being heard as well. This direct hint at Shadow aspects (the *nigredo* state) is indicative of and evinced by the mise-en-scene, which references claustrophobic framing, close-ups, a darker palette of colours and harsher expressions of Shadow from the actors; forces, both repressive and expressive, are on the march here. Within the house, Lester is in the position of having his sexual fantasies fulfilled with Angela as she needs reassurance from someone that she is not ordinary after her fight with Jane and Ricky:

> Lester starts unbuttoning Angela's blouse. She seems disconnected from what's happening. Lester pulls her blouse open, exposing her breasts. Lester looks down at her, grinning, unable to believe he's actually about to do what he's dreamed of so many times, and then . . .
>
> ANGELA  This is my first time.
> LESTER  (laughs) You're kidding.
> ANGELA  (a whisper) I'm sorry.
>
> Lester looks down at her, his grin fading. Angela lies beneath him, embarrassed and vulnerable. This is not the mythically carnal creature of Lester's fantasies; this is a nervous child.

Confronted with the raw and uncomfortable reality of the situation, Lester subsequently does not follow through with his desires. This is a key moment within the film and for Lester's development as a man and, more importantly, as a father. His anima-inspired fantasies about Angela (which are all they have been up to this point) have collided with the reality of his position that he finds himself in that he realises that his desires have led him not to pleasure but to a truth about himself. The erotic playback (as defined by Samuels earlier) with a girl his daughter's age that he nearly gets so wrong fulfils its role in jolting him awake to become a mature man. The implications of this are played out later, but before we can turn to a more in-depth analysis, we need to focus on the linking scene. This next scene focuses on a different but no less important symbol: the doorway, or portal. Ronnberg and Martin have this to say about the symbolism of this feature:

> Gates [and doors] stand between here and there, between the known and the unknown. At a psychological level, gates are found between the inner and the outer world, between waking and sleeping . . . the gate-doorway is a dangerous and numinous place, rich in protective rituals and superstitions.
>
> (2010, p. 558)

Stevens largely concurs: 'They are both a barrier and an invitation to proceed. When open, they lead to the centre. . . . They are thus linked to the symbolism of initiation (entrance) and transition from one state to another' (1998, p. 244). This feature is used symbolically in a brief scene but it is a telling one. When Caroline returns home from her stint on the firing range (another specifically American cultural reference), she has been motivating herself with affirmations about not being a victim. As she pulls up outside the house, the camera centrally frames the bright red doorway set against stark white, lit harshly. The palette choices here are interesting and deliberate; the door can be read as both a vaginal symbol, particularly due to its red colour and connotations of desire, sex and life, as well as a metaphor for spiritual awakening, of another psychic state to be entered into, a threshold to be crossed over (as described earlier). This is particularly relevant as within the house, Lester is about to experience a brief moment of spiritual enlightenment, albeit abruptly terminated. It occurs after he is in the role of caring parent towards Angela after their earlier encounter:

> Lester crosses to the kitchen table, where he sits and studies the photo. He suddenly seems older, more mature . . . and then he smiles: the deep, satisfied smile of a man who just now understands the punch line of a joke he heard long ago . . .
> LESTER     Man oh man. . . (softly) Man oh man oh man . . .
> After a beat, the barrel of a GUN rises up behind his head, aimed at the base of his skull. There is an arrangement of fresh-cut ROSES in a vase on the opposite counter, deep crimson against the WHITE TILE WALL. Then a GUNSHOT suddenly rings out, ECHOING unnaturally. Instantly, the tile is sprayed with BLOOD, the same deep crimson as the roses.

This mature realisation and the deep joy it is hinted at bringing is both underscored and catalysed by Lester's last action, that of picking up a photo of his family and studying it (despite the chaos his hitherto largely anima-inspired selfish actions have wrought within his family up until now). It seems that, despite his wife and daughter on the verge of abandoning him, he perceives that there may be a way out of the situation that he has helped to create. This contemplation is cut short, however, with his violent death, the red and white colour scheme that has been used consistently throughout the film echoed in his last moments as his brains are spread across the wall by Colonel Fitts's bullet, accompanied, naturally by the ubiquitous roses in an arrangement by the white wall.

As detailed earlier, one of the Shadow aspects of the symbolic Rose is that it was held as springing up from the blood of a slain lover; both petals and thorns are therefore present, a reminder of the dangerous aspects of desire and of Eros energy. Blood, the symbol for both death and life, of sex, desire, etc., is used here by Mendes in conscious conjunction with the rose; as Ronnberg and Martin express it: 'Blood symbolises our feeling for the sacredness of life before we distance ourselves in bloodless, abstract thought – it is the soul of embodied life, forming our essential character' (2010, p. 396). Alerted by the gunshot, Ricky and Jane discover Lester's body in a pool of dark red blood, with Ricky, far from being repelled, bending down to try and see what Lester is smiling at. The conjunction of matter and spirit is invoked in this image, with Lester's red blood acting as the connecting factor, the coniunctio as it were, invoked not only by the rain outside, as quoted earlier, but the mortal fluid that Lester is losing. This 'psychic union of emotion, body, imagination and mind in a new level of consciousness' (ibid, p. 62) is expressed as the film concludes with Lester's voiceover reassuring us of the benevolent spiritual force behind everyday life (similar to Ricky Fitts's earlier realisation) we are led through a poignant montage of images, deliberately invoking the hackneyed phrase, 'life flashing before your eyes'. As an example of the mature paternal, Lester is a brief, but interesting example as he finally realises that his role as husband and father is in itself a sacralised and spiritual role that he is now fully ready to embrace and inhabit. The film, and the spiritual themes within, are the closest to Jung's definition of a visionary piece of art from all the films analysed so far, containing, as it does explicitly spiritual and numinous references and sequences.

This redemption has been critiqued by, amongst others Arthur (2004), Karlyn (2004) and King (2009), who argue persuasively that Lester's death is a dodge when it comes to his, at best, deeply inappropriate desires towards a girl his daughter's own age. King has this to say:

> If *American Beauty* was seeking to create genuine discomfort in its viewers, this might be considered a cop-out. It lets the viewer off the hook, which seems retrospectively to license the earlier indulgence in the sexual fantasy, safely removed from any eventual consummation.
>
> (2009, p. 214)

This issue, perhaps, is best addressed in terms of the depiction of Lester's anima fantasies. The first point to make is that they are clearly deliberately depicted *as* fantasies, and therefore unequivocally indicated as not real. No actual physical or sexual harm is shown to have been perpetrated by Lester, although the film deliberately flirts with incestuous themes throughout. Indeed, when he gets the chance to have his fantasies fulfilled (as described earlier), he is shown to refuse, fantasy and reality colliding, but with fantasy explicitly depicted as coming off worst. It is telling that Lester is also shown as *not* getting to have any sex in the film,[8] unlike both his daughter and his wife, who enthusiastically commits adultery, although there is enough ambiguity in the narrative and script for the responsibility for this marital unhappiness to be at the door of both husband and wife. The second point to highlight, to paraphrase Juliet Mitchell's argument (1974), and echoed by Tacey (1997), is that the psyche is not politically correct:

> Masculine and feminine are not only a cause for intellectual confusion and embarrassment, but also, strangely, a source of spiritual power. The psyche continues to use male and female, man and woman, as symbols of the polar opposites that move through the personality. We continue to dream in the archaic and concrete language of ancient symbols, and we cannot rail against the psyche for using sexist or stereotypical language.
>
> (p. 35)

Unconscious forces within the psyche operate simultaneously both on a deeper and more transcendent level than culturally and contextually approved notions of gender imagery. Whilst the chosen imagery is deliberately provocative, the psychic processes that it hints at resonate at more profound levels. Karlyn, Arthur and King's points, whilst wholly valid in their contextual setting, also miss the point, in that Lester does *not* take advantage of Angela, and it is this depicted conscious choice that pulls him back from the brink of falling into an anima-inspired trap, which would send him back into his paternal Shadow. This non-action is depicted as indicating that Lester, as a father, finally manages to achieve a form of redemption. Jane's situation at the end of the film is deliberately left ambiguous; in earlier versions of the script, she was imprisoned due to a mistaken belief that she and Ricky had killed Lester (the opening scene being a key part of this plot). Jane's journey within the film is an interesting one, and intimately interwoven with Lester's journey as a father. The film self-consciously plays with suburban normative notions of the American Dream in terms of white picket fences, red, white and blue colour schemes and restrictive socio-economic normality (Caroline Burnham subscribes too enthusiastically to the success myths present in American society). Jane is initially portrayed her as entangled within these myths as well (her second scene depicts her viewing cosmetic surgery websites), but the film also depicts her journey towards psychic authenticity, catalysed in part by her relationship with Ricky Fitts, a state of being that transcends her socio-normative surroundings. This comes to head in her clash with Angela, a deeply uncomfortable moment of truth for both young women that leads to an awakening of sorts for both of them.

## The exploited child – Eddie Adams, Stanley Spector and Anthony Swofford

We now turn to the figure of the exploited child that features heavily in American 'indiewood' (King, 2009) director Paul Thomas Anderson's oeuvre. In *Boogie Nights* (1997) and *Magnolia* (1998) there are, like Mendes' *Road to Perdition* (2002), a number of complex and blurred relationships around fathers, men and children, in *Magnolia* particularly. Ostensibly drama-comedies, both films feature children (juvenile and adult) who are exploited by fathers within the entertainment industry, albeit in very different ways. Symbolically within these films, the Child archetype is both initiated into new worlds by a father figure, both biological and surrogate, yet simultaneously exploited as well; neither film ends with any kind of happy ending or life lessons learnt. In both films, there is only a partial resolution of the problems that the various protagonists face; fathers are shown to be an intrinsic part of the child's pain and a barrier to individuation.

*Boogie Nights* is essentially the coming-of-age story of porn star Eddie Adams, re-christened Dirk Diggler, inspired by the true-life figure of John Holmes. Dirk's journey into adulthood is overseen by surrogate father Jack Horner (Burt Reynolds), a saturnine, largely unflappable, benevolent and indulgent patriarch, both shepherding and exploiting his surrogate son and his particularly large penis, for financial gain. Masculinity and male sexuality ceases to be problematised (see later) and starts to be celebrated, indulged and ultimately commodified (hinted at earlier in the film), when Eddie turns up at a party at Jack's house and in effect begins his masculine transition into adulthood via his sexual prowess and physical attributes, taking place within his rapidly adopted surrogate family. This focus on male sexuality within the film is labelled by Guttman as 'a desperate assertion of masculinity in its most fundamental terms. All of this stems from a sense of maleness under pressure, under hostile review' (1997, p. 72). Whilst it is arguable that the portrayal of maleness and male sexuality within *Boogie Nights* contains an element of masculinity under pressure, it is contestable that it is a *desperate* assertion of maleness, the film acting as a far more nuanced depiction of male sexuality that Guttman's statement allows for. This said, Eddie/Dirk faces many challenges around his phallic status, not least of which is the exploitation by his surrogate father and, by extension, his surrogate family. There is also a sly inversion of the American Dream that Anderson depicts, with Dirk becoming a classic American success story (a crisply edited montage sequence shows Dirk's rapid rise to the top of his chosen career, the money, the house, clothes, women, and most important of all, his dream car, a bright orange Corvette Stingray).

Symbolically from here on in the only way forward for Dirk is down. This is emphasised by a pivotal New Year's party scene, where Dirk is initiated into cocaine use for the first time by his co-star Amber Waves (Julianne Moore), who also tells him that she really loves him, not just for their performances on screen. The use of hard drugs (previously portrayed, but until now never used by Dirk) marks the beginning of the end of the carefree period that has been shown so far, with Todd Ingram (Thomas Jane) making his first appearance, acting as a Shadow catalyst for Dirk. *Boogie Nights* skilfully depicts Eddie/Dirk being partially initiated into adulthood via Jack in the first half, but he has to deal with both his Shadow and Jack's Shadow in the second half of the film. Dirk's Shadow emerges as the 1980s get into full swing, with his drug use, specifically cocaine and later freebase cocaine, rapidly escalating out of control. The cinematic power of drugs to indicate emotional repression and damaged personalities in film characters has a long and well-researched history (e.g. Shapiro, 2003) and *Boogie Nights* is no exception. As surrogate son, Eddie/Dirk is skilfully depicted as initially innocent and willing to please both his surrogate director-father and his surrogate mother and sister actresses (Amber and Rollergirl) to descending, via his cocaine abuse, to an abrasive, troubled and impotent young man. It is Dirk's impotence (indicative of non-functioning and Shadow masculinity) that threatens both his deluded self-image and earning power and is the catalyst for a symbolic break with his surrogate father figure, depicted in a scene at Jack's house and garden. Dirk is threatened not only by his self-inflicted impotence due to cocaine use but also by Johnny Doe (Jonathan Quint), a young actor, very much like himself when he was first recruited by Jack. His explosion of anger at his director-father is encapsulated in the following exchange:

DIRK YOU DON'T TELL ME ANYTHING!
JACK Get the fuck outta here.
DIRK YOU'RE NOT THE BOSS OF ME!
JACK Yes I am.

Jack's own Shadow emerges from this encounter as he is faced with a son that needs disciplining but that won't stand to be disciplined. His Frankenstein's Monster-like penile creation, has in effect, run amok. In Jungian terms, this is the start of a descent into the underworld for Dirk as he has to face up to his Shadow and Shadow-induced emotional and mental trials. His putative music attempts with co-star Reed (John C Reilly) end in failure due to the pair of them squandering money on drugs that could have rescued their tapes from the recording studio; he gets badly beaten by homophobic thugs in a parking lot when he tries to raise money by gay hustling, and finally he is nearly killed in a drug deal initiated by Todd that goes terribly wrong. This particular sequence ends with him having to push his prized but shot up Corvette home as he has run out of fuel, a close-up shot on the flashing red low fuel light an apt but a somewhat heavy-handed symbol from Anderson about Dirk's internal state of mind and soul.

His homecoming to Jack as the prodigal son returning is captured in a short but pivotal scene where he appears in a doorway, Jack in extreme foreground which effectively frames Dirk as he stammers out his apology to his surrogate father, ending in a desperate plea for help and a corresponding embrace from Jack. Tacey (1997, 158) maintains that the senex will dominate the puer unless the puer develops the psychic strength to resist, something that Dirk is shown not to do, lacking the willpower to grow past his surrogate father. The final sequence of the film is dominated by a long tracking shot (reminiscent of the opening tracking shot), with all of the surrogate family coming together at Jack's house, ready to shoot another picture, this time on the once-despised videotape format. A form of balance has been restored, with porno-normative family life reigning once more. The very last scene has Dirk, dressed in a *Miami Vice*-like ensemble of pastel T-shirt and white linen jacket with rolled-up sleeves, firmly established the mid-1980s context, rehearsing his lines, clearly having learned some acting skills by this point. He then undoes his fly and finally shows the spectator his overlarge penis, which has been the hitherto unseen presence throughout the whole film, ending with his words from the beginning: 'I'm a star, I'm a star, I'm a star, I'm a star. I'm a star. I'm a star, I'm a big bright shining star'. The 'melodramatic phallus' (Lehman, 1998, p. 36) finally makes its appearance after teasing us for most of the film, and we can finish watching the film satisfied, having finally seen our own symbolic phallic money shot.

Following on from the familial reconciliation discussed earlier, the surrogate familial dynamics contained within the film are also mediated as being symbolic, albeit in an arguably deliberately subverted form. As mentioned by Goss (2002), Anderson portrays surrogate families taking over when biological families breakdown or are shown to be too restrictive. In *Boogie Nights*, Eddie's natural family consists of him, his mother and his father (no siblings are present). The mother is portrayed as a nag who, in our first encounter with them, rejects her mild-mannered husband's affections and instead verbally attacks her son for not having a job closer to home and for not finishing school. Later on, once Eddie returns from his job late one night, crucially having been introduced to the rest of Jack's 'family', his mother first verbally attacks him over his life choices and his choice of girlfriend, attacking the reputation of his lover Sheryl Lynn, calling her a 'little slut' and 'whore' several times. This is a significant choice that Anderson makes in psychological terms, casting the American mother here as a Shadow mother, in essence a maternal catalyst for Eddie to leave home and begin the process of adult maturation. Her shrill denunciation of her son as stupid and useless and her verbal attack on his lover point towards a fundamental inability to deal with her son's burgeoning sexuality, reminiscent in a maternal sense of Bruzzi's earlier point (2005, p. 191) around the problems Hollywood and American culture has of portraying the father as being sexual or sexualised.

In a telling cutaway edit, Eddie's father is sitting on the edge of his marital bed, listening to the fight unfold but unwilling or afraid to intervene or interject. In short, he fails to stand up for his son and to stand up to his wife. As Tacey reminds us: 'The son may be required to reject the style and consciousness of the father, but the psychic life or 'spirit' of the father must be continued. This is a deeply paradoxical realisation' (1997, p. 45). There is no masculine support for Eddie within his biological family (Gross's earlier quote being proved here); Anderson depicts the natural/biological nuclear family as unhappy and stressed, with masculine sexuality problematised for mothers. Eddie, at this point, is still materially owned by his mother, a situation that he deals with by violently rejecting her and her maternal rule, and leaving home to take up Jack Horner's offer. Masculinity, and in particular male sexuality, is initially problematised, deliberately ironic, given that Eddie's talents and the narrative impetus rely on male sexuality.[9]

Subjecting the surrogate family to refraction through both psychoanalytical and post-Jungian frameworks, Anderson posits an interesting symbolic revisionism (another advantage of a post-Jungian approach) with the traditional Freudian theoretical interpretation of the child-parent developmental dynamic, namely the Oedipal and Electra complexes,[10] being slyly and deliberately subverted. Eddie Adams' masculine journey to becoming Dirk Diggler is portrayed as being centred on his relationship with Jack Horner, a clear substitute, and eventual surrogate, father figure, prompted by his unconscious father hunger due to the depicted inadequacies of his timid biological father, first seen early on and never referred to again. The family structure that Eddie, now Dirk, is subsumed into is depicted as consisting of Jack as the father, Amber Waves as the mother (they are a couple away from the film sets), Dirk as the son, Rollergirl as daughter, and the other cast and crew as extended family. This familial dynamic is explicitly reinforced at several points during the film, Jack himself, stating to Eddie at the beginning that Amber 'is a wonderful mother to all those round her', Amber's cry of 'Yes, my baby boy!' referred to earlier, her explicit positioning of herself as Dirk's older combined mother/lover when she introduces him to cocaine during the pivotal 1980 New Year's Eve party scene, and Amber and Rollergirl's cocaine-fuelled conversation where Rollergirl asks Amber 'Will you be my Mommy?' and Amber acquiescing, albeit with both women crying as they do so. The obvious symbolism around the Oedipus complex and its dynamic make for an interesting deconstruction. Far from repressing the wish to sexually possess the mother and kill the father as is normatively held in classic psychoanalytical theory, Dirk is shown to be not only encouraged to sexually join with his substitute mother and sister time and again, but at the behest of his father figure, rather than against his wishes. The family that Anderson portrays here is a fundamentally permissive sexually incestuous one and one that does not repress these urges but instead revels in them to the point where they are commodified and capitalised by Jack, the patriarch. The Oedipus complex is, in effect, being depicted here by Anderson as being overturned and subverted in a case of deliberate symbolic and semiotic revisionism. The demarcation between the sign and the symbol, explored by Fredericksen (Hauke and Alister, 2001, pp. 27–29), is effectively blurred here with both signs (sophisticated images of the production of pornography) mixed in with the symbols (images of existential despair, masked by drugs) mediated by Anderson.

Exploring this further, if we examine this family dynamic through a post-Jungian lens, other dynamics and complexes emerge. Ronnberg and Martin describe incest as 'the muddying of emotional waters, the defiling or dishonouring of another, the closing off of naïve spontaneity and trust through the breaching of sacrosanct psychological or physical boundaries' (2010, p. 416). This breaking of boundaries points towards other issues and complexes. The image of and the action of joining with the mother on a sexual level could be interpreted as pointing towards a desire to be reborn on a mental and spiritual level for Dirk. He has already taken a step towards adult maturity with his symbolic renaming, overseen by his father figure in the hot-tub scene, a universal rite of passage that is held to be contained in the collective unconscious or objective psyche. Where his individuative progress is halted is by his continuing exploitation by his paternal and, to a lesser degree maternal, figures of Jack and Amber. By effectively owning and commodifying Dirk's phallus, Jack is delaying his surrogate son's maturation, resulting in psychic pain that is shown as being numbed by increasingly heavy drug use. This in turn leads on to Dirk's reluctant experience of the Shadow journey detailed earlier. By the end of the film, Dirk has returned to the family fold as the prodigal son, but he has still not matured fully and has not been able to satiate his father hunger and break free from the paternal influence and control. Anderson shows us the cost and price of Dirk not engaging fully with his complexes as he prepares at the very end of the film to go out and shoot yet another exploitative film for his exploitative director-father, who arguably represents the Shadow American Dream. As Tacey identifies by quoting Neumann, the father can engage with the 'patriarchal castration' (1997, p. 157) of the son, either deliberately or unconsciously. Dirk is portrayed as not consciously recognising nor engaging with his father-hunger complex, and he is effectively trapped under Jack's influence until he does so. His partial breakaway from Jack and Amber earlier in the film, which marks his downward psychic trajectory, where he undergoes a semiconscious awakening of sorts resulting in a statement of fact about his familial situation; ('You're not my father! You're not my mother!')[11] is doomed to fail as he is portrayed as not having the inner psychic resources or emotional strength to fully separate. Eddie/Dirk's father hunger is too strong for him to fully let go of his paternal exploiter. Tacey comments again:

> As Robert Bly has said, the father is a kind of doorway through which the son must pass, and if the doorway cannot be found, or is closed for some historical and/or personal reason, then the son suffers the condition of ongoing and chronic immaturity, living life as an Oedipal man, effeminate, incapacitated by guilt, and alienated from his own spirituality.
>
> (ibid, p. 52)

For his part, Jack Horner is also not up to the task to fully play the surrogate father role that he has (unconsciously) chosen. His persona and role of seemingly benevolent chronicler of the contextual pleasures of the time (consequence-free sex and the associated pornographic voyeuristic pleasures that accompany it) is partially a false one. The polyvalent and polysemous nature of this symbolism is contradictory, in that he acts in a paternal way, but this paternalism is predicated on capitalistic exploitation of his surrogate family. Anderson shows him as exploiting the substitute family that has gathered round him mostly without consequence; he is largely untouched by the pain that the other characters undergo. When his financier, Colonel James, is arrested for drug possession and child pornography, Jack is quick to abandon him to a brutalising legal system. The only difficulties that Jack faces are his reluctance and slowness in embracing the change in technology and the fact that he will never be taken seriously as a storyteller. By the end of the film, everything is back to normal for Jack; the only difference being that they are preparing to shoot on video[12] instead of 35mm film. *Boogie Nights* displays the consequences of not recognising father hunger by charting both Eddie/Dirk's dark journey into his Shadow, alongside Jack playing the dark Father, a controlling exploiter of his surrogate son and his surrogate family. Dirk is shown at the end still not being able to break away from his exploitative adopted family; he has not grown out of his Shadow and individuated past his father. Anderson has demonstrated that his surrogate father has blocked Dirk's growth into mature masculinity, issues that resonate with Anderson's next film, which we will now analyse.

## What kids *do* know – the exploited child in *Magnolia*

Anderson's third film, *Magnolia* (1999), also explores a symbolic approach to the father-child son relationship, operating in 'Indiewood', the blurred realm where the American indie fringe blends with mainstream Hollywood, and is deliberately self-reflexive and self-referential. Anderson brings an interesting sensibility to his depiction of masculinities, particularly the complexities of the many father-son relationships that abound in the film, all eventually to be revealed to be connected with the symbolic process of a dying elderly father, namely, TV patriarchs Earl Partridge (Jason Robards) and Jimmy Gator (Philip Baker Hall). This is revealed by Anderson's depiction of the quiz show (deliberately entitled: 'What Do Kids Know?') boy genius Stanley Spector's (Jeremy Blackman) relationship with his father Rick Spector (Michael Bowen). Echoing our earlier points in Chapter 1 about shortcuts to achieving the American Dream of material success, Spector Snr is portrayed as a venal and pushy man who reveals his greed about what his son can do for him. In an uncomfortable scene as he watches his son effectively perform as a cash cow for him, he exclaims: 'My little fucker! I have no idea where he gets this stuff!', Anderson's portrayal of Rick calls to mind one of the four broad types of negative father that John Lee outlines in his book *At My Father's Wedding* (1991) and that Biddulph summarises thus:

> The Critical Father – Full of put-downs and nit-picking, driven by his own frustrations and anger. This father was certainly active in the family, but in totally negative, frightening ways. 'Is that the best you can do?' 'Can't you get anything right?' 'You stupid idiot, look what you've done!' Whatever was frustrating him – his job, his own father, his lack of success in life, even just his hopes for his children – even the sweet wine of his love was turned into an acid which ate away at his family's well-being.
>
> (1995, p. 108)

Rick Spector certainly fits this description; he is first shown in a hurry for an audition (perhaps he's an actor; it is not made clear); he then berates his son as they travel to the TV studio where Stanley will perform for money that Rick will take. Ostensibly Rick is acting as a parent, and fulfilling a paternal role, but in actuality Anderson symbolically portrays him as a kind of paternal pimp who uses and intellectually prostitutes his own son for material gain. Rick is driven by the rewards of the American Dream, but his paternal love has fallen into the American Shadow and its love of material success. Anderson depicts a deeply troubled father-son relationship here; arguably drawing inspiration from his time working on a very similar children's TV quiz show in the 1980s (Sperb, 2013). The father's boasting to other parents in the studio viewing gallery displays not only his misplaced pride but also his arrogance and ultimately his impotence, with his income being earned by his son, rather than by him. This parental insecurity grows the more when the film starts to build to the multiple narrative denouements and Stanley's climactic on-air rebellion articulated by him when he is denied a much-needed toilet break:

STANLEY: I AM NOT A DOLL . . . I'M NOT SILLY AND CUTE. I'M SMART SO THAT SHOULDN'T MAKE ME SOMETHING, SOMETHING SO PEOPLE CAN WATCH HOW SILLY IT IS THAT HE'S SMART? I KNOW. I KNOW THINGS. I KNOW I HAVE TO GO TO THE BATHROOM I HAVE TO GO TO THE BATHROOM AND I HAVE TO GO!

Anderson uses the symbology of the boy's body and its physical frailty and basic needs as an effective brake and reality check to his father. In particular, the use of urine has several symbolic and semiotic aspects. Stanley's outburst is him finally breaking through his emotional barriers and expressing his anger; he is literally 'pissed off'. Ronnberg and Martin also note that urine can:

> denote(s) the urgency of emotional and creative self-expression, the feeling-toned "yielding or allowing the flow of what needs to come through one" . . . we find urine also representing affect that is hot, intense, personal and sometimes not ideally contained.
>
> (2010, p. 426)

After this outburst, Stanley gets into trouble with both his father (who displays a sudden and shocking violent streak when he throws a chair at the viewing window after watching his son's pleas) and the floor manager of the TV studio. He also arouses the ire of the other two child contestants who are depicted as spoilt and venal as most of the adults around them, the greed and dysfunction of the entertainment industry being effectively generationally passed down. In effect, the sacred space of the studio (signed as sacrosanct within the film for diegetic performative and commercial reasons) is symbolically defiled by the physical realities of the child's body. The voyeuristic nature of television is reinforced here as all gazes are on Stanley and, symbolically, the vulnerable aspect of the Child archetype. Later, after the climactic rain of frogs has brought the film to a conclusion; Stanley displays almost preternatural levels of maturity in a short but intense scene with just him and his father, shot by Anderson with the father lying on a bed in the foreground, his anger largely spent, contemplating his life after Stanley's meltdown has cost him any future appearances on the show, and therefore an income.

STANLEY: Dad . . . Dad.
    Rick opens his eyes, but doesn't move.
STANLEY: You have to be nicer to me, Dad.
RICK: Go to bed.
STANLEY: I think that you have to be nicer to me.

As Carmago summarises:

> The focus on the present means that, although the characters in *Magnolia* clearly have pasts, they do not have histories. We do not know . . . what has happened to Stanley's mother, or whether his father is successful in his career.
>
> (2002, p. 1)

All that Anderson shows in the film is that there is just Stanley and Rick, a masculine unit of two, with no mother present or referred to anywhere in the film.

Their history is a blank one; the feminine not being present, with a dysfunctional masculinity centred around Stanley's now unstable TV career as a quiz kid on display. Symbolically speaking, there is no feminine energy in their relationship; and the future trajectory of the child son is in doubt without this (presumably) more caring presence to negate the darker aspects of the father. Stanley's possible future fate is symbolically indicated by Anderson by the presence of former quiz kid Donnie Smith (William H Macey). He is a now washed-up salesman, his past glories of TV celebrity a long time behind him. Stanley's final request to his father, delivered with an unsettling urgency, hints at a possible different future than Donnie, who the audience learns had parents who also exploited him and cast him adrift after spending all the money he earned for them.

Anderson depicts the relationship between Stanley and Rick with a high degree of ambiguity; this vaguely hopeful scene shows that Stanley is maturing in knowing what he needs from his father and asking for it. Rather than a fixed symbol and dynamic that a psychoanalytical approach would apply, we can analyse this particular relationship as containing the capacity for the previously mis-used Child to transcend the American father and the focus on material gain. Stanley is starting to outgrow the paternal and move towards transcendence of his father and his father's materialistic American Dream values. Like the Colonel and Ricky Fitts in *American Beauty*, the presence of both Donnie and Stanley in the film (although they never meet) strongly hints at an eternal present when it comes to the son – both are portrayed here as vulnerable, exploited and in a space of potential change, a position that has a strong symbolic and archetypal echo about it, again a post-Jungian perspective containing polysemous symbolic aspects. Anderson invests *Magnolia* with this potential for change and for healing; the American fathers in the film may be dark and dysfunctional, but the damage that they have wreaked on their children may just yet be healed in time.

## *Jarhead*: welcome to the suck

The adult child's exploitation can also be societally approved, particularly when we consider the role that state institutions play in the misinitiation and disinitiation of young men. The 2005 film *Jarhead* (Mendes) is an example of this state-sanctioned warping of masculinities via a mostly masculine surrogate family, namely the US Marine Corps. This familial structure, not surprisingly, contains powerful surrogate father figures, in the shape of Staff Sergeant Sykes (Jamie Foxx), Lt Colonel Kasinski (Chris Cooper) and Major Lincoln (Denis Haysbert), who all perform familial paternal functions and act as father figures. Sykes, in particular, is shown as caring for his men, as well as acting as a punitive father, arguable acting as a 'male mother', by setting appropriate punishments for various infractions. Despite *Jarhead* being an atypical war film, in that it is a war film without much of a war (Cromb, 2007), or for that matter, very little combat action, it is still concerned with soldiers and the effects of war on men and masculinities. Based on the eponymous bestselling memoir of Anthony Swofford, a US Marine

Corps scout sniper during the first Gulf War,[13] it is ostensibly a war film about a war that, according to Jean Baudrillard's infamous assertion,[14] did not happen. Contextualising Swofford's experiences via a constant voiceover, the film takes as its focus an ordinary Marine's perspective on the direct experience of war as essentially tedium, rather than action and heroism. Indeed, the failure to engage in combat is a major thematic issue within the film and one that is analysed in more detail later. What in main distinguishes the film from similar offerings such as *Three Kings* (Russell, 1999), *Courage Under Fire* (Zwick, 1996) and *Live from Baghdad* (Jackson, 2002) is the deliberate direction of attention away from actual combat and towards the more mundane and everyday details of a soldiers life. Rather than employing a conventional narrative and plot, it is the inner psychological journey of a soldier that is under scrutiny here. It is this focus on the psychological and the study of unformed masculinity under pressure within patriarchal American social subcultural spaces that marks this film of interest.

The film also references a strong sense of self-reflexivity in terms of both war films that are consciously used within the film's narrative and accompanying music from the same era.

The film treats the Vietnam War as deeply symbolic (both deliberately referenced directly and indirectly by cultural products such as films like *Apocalypse Now* (Coppola, 1979) and *Full Metal Jacket* (Kubrick, 1987) in particular).

This conflict hangs over the film like a combative ghost, giving the film a sense of never quite managing to escape America's past military trauma and shame. As Joosten notes, '[T]he haunting presence of Vietnam lingers in these modern works in the confusing nature of nature of the conflicts depicted, in both direct and indirect references, and in the ambiguity concerning enemy identity' (2011, p. 1). Indeed, *Jarhead* can be viewed as casting a subtly critical eye over the attempts by films from the 1980s (Reaganite or otherwise) such as *First Blood* (Kotcheff, 1982), *Missing in Action* (Zito, 1984), *Platoon* (Stone, 1986), etc. to reclaim the Vietnam War as a victory in the sense of individual heroism and so regain some sense of collective honour for America. The major difference between the previous war films and *Jarhead* is that Mendes' effort is devoid of any actual combat action, symbolically recasting this crucial aspect of a war film in new light, combat being present by its absence, so to speak. This recasting of the Persian Gulf War by Mendes and screenwriter William Broyles Jnr as not so much as a chance for heroism but as a missed chance to fulfil an ostensibly patriarchal masculine agenda was, not surprisingly, unpopular with audiences.[15] As a psychological perspective in terms of its treatment of masculinities within a subculture, however, it is concomitant with contemporaneous masculine themes, particularly when we consider the treatment of the archetypal process of initiation.

Initiation occurs in the opening moments of the film in a crisply edited rush of imagery and sound as we are introduced the hyper-aggressive masculine social space that Swofford will inhabit for the duration of the film: the US Marine Corps. Almost immediately upon entry, Swofford is being insulted, challenged and bellowed at by a verbally dextrous and abusive drill instructor, highly reminiscent of the performance from Drill Instructor Hartman (R Lee Ermey) from *Full Metal Jacket*, a film that *Jarhead* is inevitably compared to in that it contains similar depictions of boot camp, an officially endorsed and led version of the initiation process, but from a psychological perspective, a mis-initiation and arguably a dis-initiation ceremony.

Interestingly Swofford's father is brought up by the drill sergeant almost immediately as this powerful dialogue reveals:

DRILL INSTRUCTOR: Swofford!
SWOFFORD: Sir, yes, sir!
DRILL INSTRUCTOR: You the maggot whose father served in Vietnam?
SWOFFORD: Sir, yes, sir!
DRILL INSTRUCTOR: Outstanding! Did he have the balls to die there?
SWOFFORD: Sir, no, sir!
DRILL INSTRUCTOR: Too fucking bad! He ever talk about it?
SWOFFORD: Sir, only once, sir!
DRILL INSTRUCTOR: Good! Then he wasn't lying!

Death and mortality are facts of life for a soldier; this has arguably become fetishised in that true courage for the drill instructor involves dying. Anything less is somehow lacking bravery. Swofford's presence as a new Marine is an echo of his father's presence in the same tribe, and he is reminded sharply of it, along with the honourable fate of dying as a Marine. In the film the Marine has his individuality broken down (he is no colour except either light green or dark green, the colour of a Marine); his head is shaved so that he is de-individualised, and he is put through a physically demanding and painful process of training so that he is integrated into his new sub-culture. As the army as a subculture deals in state-sanctioned killing and wounding, it follows that pain and wounding is a feature of its initiation process. This wound also has a psychological purpose and function to perform, in that the wound marks a break with youthful notions of invulnerability, notions that need to be outgrown if one is to become a mature adult, and a successful soldier. Bly quotes the anthropologist Mircea Eliade when summarising the characteristics of initiation and how a wound is given during initiation:

> The second [feature] is a wound that the older men give to the younger boy, which could be a scarring of the skin, a cut with a knife, a brushing with nettles, a tooth knocked out. But we mustn't leap to the assumption that the injuries are given sadistically. Initiators in most cultures make sure that the injuries they do give do not lead to meaningless pain, but reverberate out of a rich centre of meaning. Where a man's wound is, that is where his genius will be.
>
> (Biddulph, 1995, p. 200)

In other words, a wound can be seen as an entry point to the soul, although this has to be contextualised in terms of the subculture or tribe in which the initiate is socialised into. Swofford's soul and vulnerabilities are what the USMC are after, although they are seeking them so that they can toughen him up and get him to discard them. Wounds can also be psychic as well as physical; Bly differentiates the various wounds that mothers and fathers can give out to children during the course of an upbringing:

> The father gives a son a vivid and unforgettable blow with an axe, which has a hint of murder in it; many a mother makes sure the son receives a baptism of shame. She keeps pouring the water of shame over his head to make sure.
> (1990, p. 32)

These psychic wounds can add up to many small and not-so-small hurts within the psyches of men and women. Where the mytho-poetic men's movement has a different perspective on initiation is that the wound is contextualised. The untreated or ignored wound runs the risk of turning the recipient (to paraphrase Bly) into a 'grandiose over-achiever' or a paralysed and depressed victim (ibid, p. 33). As Bly points out, 'initiation prevents such a fate, by reframing the wounding into a bigger picture – giving it meaning and channelling its intensity into a positive force' (Biddulph, 1995, p. 209). Once initiated, an adult can give his or her wounds meaning and place them in a psychic context in terms of wholeness. Bly again:

> The ancient practice of initiation then – still very much alive in our genetic structure – offers a third way through, between the "natural" roads of manic excitement and victim excitement. A mentor or "male mother" enters the landscape.
> (1990, p. 36)

Swofford's various wounds and pain are received via training at the same time as his fellow boot camp inhabitees; Mendes show these wounds as a collective pain, received and officially endorsed, by that most patriarchal of structures, the army. Lehman identifies the USMC as one of several American 'formidable national fathers' (2001, p. 264) that carry out this wounding. It is this collective wounding that provides a focal point for their individual masculinities to coalesce around; each of them knows first-hand what the other has gone through. It is, in effect, a brotherhood based upon and mired in pain. There are also psychic wounds being inflicted here; in effect, to join the USMC, each Marine must submit their individual nature to the group consciousness. If they don't, there is a price to pay, namely some kind of punishment that is decided by their surrogate father figures (the NCOs performing the role of 'male mother') ranging from physical training exercises (twenty press-ups) to degrading tasks (cleaning out latrines). This deliberate sacrifice of individuality is a necessary price that the army must extract from its soldiers in order to efficiently carry out its main function; that of executing war upon perceived enemies. Individual consciousness is neither desirable nor useful in a soldier. Mendes shows Swofford quietly resisting this de-individualisation process; in a semi-comic scene, we witness him in the latrines reading Camus' *L'Etranger*. The main male mother figure in the film, Staff Sergeant Sykes (Jamie Foxx) then enters, solemnly notes (with half-hidden approval) Swofford's choice of reading material: 'That there's some heavy duty shit Marine!' and informs him that his shooting scores have qualified him to attempt to pass the Scout Sniper training program. This sequence marks the beginning of Swofford's further initiation into his new world in that he is specialising in a weapon (sniper rifle) that can bring death to enemies without them being aware of his presence. This paternal presence is a constant one throughout the film and a presence that arguably shows the Shadow side of patriarchal social structures, in that developing masculinities of the young soldiers are being moulded for aggression and potential bodily sacrifice for patriarchal purposes.

So far we have analysed the official initiatory process that Swofford goes through, but there is another, *unofficial*, initiatory process at work within the film, and it is arguably equally as strong in terms of the initiatory drive. Early on in the film, Swofford turns up in his new bunkhouse, where a group of Marines (his new companions) are wrestling an unwilling new recruit to the ground for the purposes of branding him with a hot iron to mark his entry and membership of their world. Swofford looks on from a distance, his trepidation masked as best as he can, as they appear to brand the new Marine. They then turn on him as another new member and wrestle him to the ground (not without fierce resistance from Swofford), heat up the iron and go to brand him, at which point he faints. When he comes round (alone apart from one Marine), he remains unbranded. The situation becomes clear when the remaining Marine, Troy (Peter Sarsgaard) informs Swofford that a Marine has to *earn* a branding by his fellow Marines and that what Swofford initially witnessed was staged for the purposes of scaring him; a hazing ritual that is dished out to all new recruits. Troy then laconically delivers the line 'welcome to the suck' to Swofford, meaning that Swofford's new home, his new male space has its dangers (it sucks in the sense of it being disagreeable as well as perhaps in a homoerotic sense), but it also has its true price of entry, namely fellow Marines have to accept you. In other words, the unofficial fake initiation, or more accurately dis-initiation, is deliberately acted out as a tool of fear, as well as a reminder that a 'true' Marine is not made on the parade ground or even in the boot camp process, but in combat when they kill. With death, indeed with any soldier's first credited 'kill', their initiation into the masculine social space of the army is completed. As Tacey reminds us, '[I]t is beyond doubt that war has long acted as cultural site for the making of men' (1997, p. 121).

Crucially, the film shows the frustrations experienced by the soldiers when they are denied performing their primary function as soldiers, that of killing the enemy in combat. When Swofford and Troy are assigned a sniping mission, they are ecstatic to be able to perform as soldiers and fulfil their full initiation into the USMC. When they are ordered by another surrogate father figure, Major Lincoln (Denis Haysbert), to step down in favour of an air strike, despite having Iraqi Republican Guard officers in the scope of the sniper rifle, Troy loses control and pleads with his superior officer the chance to perform as a soldier, all to no avail. When they return to their platoon camp, the war is already over, but Sergeant Sykes recognises the pent-up frustration of his men and allows them to discharge their weapons in a deeply symbolic and ritualistic phallic manner. The primary colours that Mendes uses for this scene (night black with yellow gun flashes) combine with the soldiers in a near-naked state of dress to create a disturbing effect, but are also deliberately ceremonial and ritualised.

This recognition of the need to finish his men's initiation into the USMC demonstrates Sykes as the 'male mother' performing his initiatory duties. In addition, Mendes depicts the dubious honour of the unofficial initiation being extended to Troy when (due to him not reporting that he had committed a crime prior to joining the Marines and so cannot continue to be one) about to leave his new brotherhood, he is held down and branded by his fellow Marines. This accords him their (unofficial) signal honour and inflicting a deeply symbolic wound upon him to remind him that he once belonged to them. For them, it does not matter that he is no longer officially qualified to remain a Marine; it is more that he did once belong and was recognised by them as belonging. As Janssen reminds us:

> Ritual here is seen as a dramatized part of generally dramatic constructions of gender that implicate a double necessity: that of staging of the cultural plot, and that of resolving the psychostructural problem of early life feminization. Necessary action is essential (ontologically critical) reaction.
>
> (2007, p. 216)

This unofficial ritual (along with the official initiation dispensed by the army) is therefore another indicator of the initiatory drive and its push towards a form of adult masculinity. The pain received by the initiate is a strong sign and symbol of his removal, or exit from the civilian world (we can read this as a feminised or feminine world) and his consequent entry into a recognised masculine space, or at least a masculine space recognised by his fellow men. This initiation is carried out in lieu of Troy getting a credited kill, a clear case of a substitute ceremony. More tragically, Troy is denied a continuing role in the army, despite being an exemplary soldier, his pain at this official and patriarchal denial of purpose leading to his eventual suicide at the end of the film. The patriarchal structure of the US army therefore exacts a heavy price from its members; Troy is, in essence, depicted as a victim of other men and a masculine structure that has used him but ultimately rejected him. He is effectively betrayed by his surrogate family and the surrogate father figures therein.

## The wounded child – Frank Mackey, Billy Maplewood and Mikey Carver

Similar to the children so far described, *Magnolia* presents the wounded Child in a different guise, this time in the shape of an adult son finally reconciling with an absent dying father in the form of Frank 'TJ' Mackey (Tom Cruise). With this highly self-conscious rendition of a classic filmic narrative, namely that of the dying father attempting a reconciliation with an estranged adult son, Anderson manages to depict a strong sense of archetypal masculine pain as father hunger in the American adult son symbolically resulting from the masculine continuum being fractured, and by the end of the film only partially redeemed. Early on in the film, Earl Partridge's nurse Phil (Phillip Seymour Hoffman) has a conversation with one of Frank's assistants (instigated by Earl), outlining the situation and how similar it is to previous melodramatic film scenarios:

PHIL: I know this all seems silly. I know that maybe I sound ridiculous, like maybe this is the scene of the movie where the guy is trying to get a hold of the long-lost son, but this is that scene. Y'know? I think they have those scenes in movies because they're true, because they really happen. And you gotta believe me: This is really happening, you can check this with, but don't leave me hanging on this – please – please. See; see; see this is the scene of the movie where you help me out.

This deliberate self-awareness is indicative of a conscious subversion of the dying father narrative trope, and at the same time, he also employs it to generate affective and emotional impact when Frank Mackey does finally visit his father. Up to this point, Mackey has been depicted as an example of toxic hypermasculinity, to the point where, after his male 'self-help' seminar[16] entitled 'Seduce and Destroy' has finished, and he is being interviewed by the female journalist, Gwenovier (April Grace) he is shown to be revelling in and sporting a very obvious erection. However, as the interview progresses and her subtle and gradually relentless questioning begin to unravel the holes in his purported history, we are allowed to see his hypermasculinity as being exposed as an act. Carmago comments about this history and how unique it is to this particular character within the film:

> This lack of history makes it difficult to make moral judgements about them [the other characters]. The single character in *Magnolia* who explicitly attempts to create a history for himself is Frank Mackey, the male empowerment guru played by Tom Cruise. Mackey says that a focus on the past is an excuse for not progressing in the present, further thematising the importance of the present.
> 
> (2002, p. 1)

Mackey's deceit, and avoidance about his past, and his exposure by Gwenovier, causes him to explode in anger at her when she calmly states that his mother is not alive but died when he was a teenager. This is a pivotal moment within the film as Mackey's hyper-masculinised persona slips, emphasised by an unflinching and unforgiving close-up shot on Cruise's face as he retreats into a blank mask, only to erupt in self-righteous ire at his questioner, accompanied by the line: 'I'm quietly judging you!' with an accompanying violent snap of the fingers very close to Gwenovier's face.

It is this moment that marks a turning point for the character, and another part of his masculine journey begins (initiated by feminine intervention); he finally visits his estranged father, Earl Partridge (Jason Robards), on his deathbed. Peberdy (2011) identifies Mackey's performance up until this point as being reminiscent of Bly's Wild Man (1990), although this is arguably more of a Savage masculine performance, with Bly clearly differentiating the Wild Man and the Savage[17] in *Iron John*. Tacey argues that Bly's idealisation of the Wild Man can lead to potentially reactionary thinking, a consistent critique of Bly's position, and a position that is more than hinted at in this scene. This next stage of Mackey's masculine journey is the unexpected descent into what Bly and Biddulph describe as the time of Ashes. Before this particular scene is analysed in depth, it is worth defining what the time of Ashes actually is and its symbolic value and resonance. Biddulph describes this period:

> Eventually though, all men learn that not everything works out in this life. The mid-thirties seem to be the time that this often happens. The trigger can be anything. Perhaps a baby is stillborn. Or your wife stops loving you. A once-sturdy father shrivels and dies before your eyes. A lump becomes cancerous. A car accident smashes up your body. Or your carefully built career tumbles like a pack of cards. Suddenly there is shame, error and grief all around you. Welcome to the Ashes.
>
> (1995, p. 222)

Symbolically, the time of Ashes is when the masculine is humbled by greater forces than it, including direct knowledge of mortality, through either personal or indirect experience. Chevalier and Gheerbrant have a stark definition of what ashes may represent: 'In spiritual terms what remains is valueless, thus from the eschatological point of view, ashes symbolise the nullity of human life, deriving from its transience' (1994, p. 49). Ronnberg and Martin broadly agree, and call attention to the initial qualities ashes are associated with: 'On ash we project finality, irrevocability, what has gone cold after the heat and light of desire, hope, creativity or generation has been extinguished' (2010, p. 728). Later they also highlight the more ritualistic and positive qualities:

> Yet ash is also associated with the sacred and the essential. Ash is the extract from a completed life or an achieved process, the substance that can go no

further decomposition. . . . Alchemy perceived ash, like salt, as an emblem of the albedo, the "white foliated earth", resulting from the burning off of impurities – desire freed from compulsion, bitterness become wisdom.

(ibid)

Echoing these definitions, Cooper also highlights their explicit signing of humiliation and penitence (1978, p. 16). Symbolically, ashes can be found throughout the film, as the emotional energies and narratives are eventually resolved after crises have burned themselves out, with the processes and griefs experienced by the characters resulting (in some, but not all, cases) in healing and wisdom.

These statements notwithstanding, a significant proportion of what the time of Ashes is defined as is grief. Anderson portrays this hitherto unexpressed masculine grief within Mackey as a counterpoint to the hypermasculinity and narcissism that has so far been expressed by the character. As Izod notes, '[N]arcissism shows itself in a psychological predisposition to gather the outer world to the self in order to sustain a pretentious persona that cover up feelings of emptiness' (2000, p. 271). Returning to the symbolic journey of the estranged adult son confronting his dying father, this is depicted via a number of cinematic techniques within the consequent deathbed scene. The scene (cutting to and from the other scenes that track the other characters and story arcs) is filmed fixed and in medium shot, encouraging deep focus editing on behalf of the spectator. Phil and the dogs are initially all we see, only hearing Mackey off camera as he converses with Phil, establishing who he is before he deigns to enter his father's house.

The mise-en-scene here is dark and the lighting harsh, and mainly lit from above, a visual motif that is consistent throughout the scene and in all the rooms, emphasising the starkness and mood. Cutting in to a closer angle on Mackey's entrance, his body language is defensive and aggressive, consistent with his previous portrayal, as is his language to Phil when he sets out his expectations around the meeting: 'I need you to be around, because I'm not gonna help him. And I will drop-kick those fucking dogs if they get in the way'. These ground rules established, he goes forward to meet his father. At this point, Mackey is still overly identified with his overwhelmingly macho, narcissistic, and hypersexual persona, a psychic construct that is slowly revealing to have been built to protect him from the pain of his history. Stevens defines the persona as a construct that has a social element to it; therefore: 'There is always some element of pretence about the persona, for it is a kind of shop window in which we like to display our best wares' (1994, p. 63).

The meeting of father and son is shot from underneath, close-up and from Earl's side of the encounter, with the camera focused, again static and still, on Mackey, Phil quietly standing in the background. The encounter between father and son is deliberately and palpably awkward, with Mackey first denying his father's illness ('you don't look that bad') to specifically masculine and phallic terms of verbal abuse ('You prick. You cocksucker'.) as he castigates his father for not responding when his mother, Earl's former wife, lay dying, waiting for a visit that never happened. The focus of the camera, however, starts to prove relentless as his hyper-masculine persona at this point starts to break down as his hitherto suppressed grief and pain gradually erupt from within his Shadow, repository of all suppressed feelings and complexes, as stated earlier. He starts to cry, even whilst denying that he is going to, as his feelings begin to overwhelm him and exposes his vulnerability, the emotion of the situation affecting both himself and Phil. Mackey's childish rage is on now fully on show ('I hate you, you fucking asshole'), but this is shown as being born out of fear, grief and abandonment, an assertion that is borne out by his next utterance ('don't go away, you fucking asshole!') as Mackey regresses to a frightened child again that we (presumably) suppose he must have been when his father abandoned him and his mother the first time around. As Fredericksen notes: 'We could say that a false self has no resonance with a nascent true self, and therefore does not activate the true self's manifestation' (2014, p. 135). Peberdy also picks up on this point: 'Hard and soft masculinity should instead be seen as a sliding scale; a hierarchy of masculine tropes demonstrated both across roles and within them' (2011, p. 103). Mackey is forced into soft and vulnerable masculinity by realisation of his father's mortality at this point in the film.

This scene breaks down Mackey's false-self masculine façade, his specifically masculine and narcissistic arrogance, to reveal his latent father hunger, psychological hunger that he can only painfully admit at the end of his father's life. Subverting the dying father trope to the end by refusing to use speech or sentimental clichés such as 'I forgive you' or 'I love you Dad; I love you son' as analysed by Bruzzi (2005) in other films such as *The Great Santini* (Carlino, 1979), Anderson shows Earl Partridge regaining consciousness one last time and gazing at his son, but unable to speak, has him gasping out unintelligible sounds. Mackey's face, symbolically framed by this point by Anderson in extreme unforgiving close-up and half-lit so there is both light and dark on it, struggles to understand, but the scene eventually ends with the paternal and the filial energies on display here connecting via the gaze, a continuation of the fragile masculine continuum being conveyed by visual means. As the drawn out montage of scenes at the end of the film show us Earl's body being taken away, the film's narrator reminds us that: 'We may be through with the past, but the past ain't through with us', a direct contradiction of Mackey's earlier confident dismissal of the power of the past, a past that he is forced to confront due to his forced engagement with the symbolic power of ashes. Anderson demonstrating here the power the senex (Earl Partridge) still has over the puer (son), as Tacey correctly identified.

With this key scene, the masculine trope of the father on his deathbed reconciling with a son is simultaneously and symbolically subverted and re-invented. The performance of masculinity depicted here by the damaged adult son being forced to deal with his father hunger is deeply revealing. Mackey's almost comically hyper-masculine behaviour from earlier in the film during the self-help seminar scenes ('Worship the cock! Tame the cunt!') are exposed by this scene to be a sham, a hollow pretence of male dominative power that lacks any credibility, by Mackey's regression to frightened, insecure boy when he has to deal with his own father's mortality. His unacknowledged masculine wound is due to paternal abandonment as having left him in a dark masculine space, where masculine domination is a substitute for masculine depth of feeling. Echoing Carmago, the film focuses on the present; what happens to him afterwards is not made clear, although in the closing scenes of the film, Mackey is shown as beginning to connect with his late father's widow (Julianne Moore) at the hospital after her unsuccessful suicide attempt. It is arguable that in *Magnolia* the father's death is depicted perhaps the ultimate catalyst for the adult son to deal with any father hunger; the reality of a dead or dying father is, essentially, a numinous symbol for the son to engage with in confronting his own father issues and wounds.

Ang Lee's *The Ice Storm* (1997) is an unmerciful portrayal of wounded adults in turn wounding their offspring in suburbia, itself an aspirational location for American families, but depicted here as a coolly bland social prison where numinosity and life are gradually crushed. The film features both sons and daughters as symbolically wounded by their self-centred baby boomer parents, who themselves are wounded by the ending of the 1960s idealism (the Watergate hearings – the film is set in 1973 – are a constant background feature). Mostly self-absorbed, the parents in the film are depicted as nominally successful (they all live in comfortable wealthy suburban Connecticut) but are also spiritually lost, lacking any kind of numinosity and cynically choosing adulterous hedonism over a more functional family life. Not surprisingly, their teenage children are adversely affected, unconsciously imitating their parents, with tentative (and arguably premature) sexual exploration mixed in with idealistic outbursts of rage at the shortcomings of American society. As Paul Hood (Tobey Maguire) wryly asks his sexually precocious sister, Wendy (Christina Ricci): 'How are the parental units functioning these days?' The answer is sad, but knowing: 'Dad's like doing his Up with People routine, mom hasn't been saying much'. The other main family in the film, the Carvers, are equally bereft, Janey Carver (Sigourney Weaver) seeking emotional stimulation via an affair with Ben Hood (Kevin Kline), Jim Carver (Jamey Sheridan) being a classic case of the absent father. His cross-country business trips that take him away from his family are detrimental to his sons is borne out by the awkward scene when his three-day absence is completely missed by Mikey Carver (Elijah Wood). His mother comments afterwards that Mikey 'has been out of it since he was born'. This self-preserving numbness that Mikey experiences is only slightly alleviated by his crush on Wendy that is knowingly manipulated by her for her own amusement, although this is depicted as essentially unmalicious. These are children cast adrift by the Shadow side of the American Dream; materially wealthy, privately educated, but they are also experiencing an acute case of parental emotional poverty, with both their parents too self-absorbed in their own pain to provide engaged attention. This largely hidden parental pain culminates in the key party, where local suburban couples get to pair off for the purposes of wife-swapping (although it is the wives who are given the choice of keys which pick out the men) is a pivotal scene in that Ben's affair is exposed. This in turn catalyses Ellen Hood's (Joan Allan) own clumsy attempt at a fling with Jim Carver, leaving Ben Hood to make his own way back home, during which journey he discovers Mikey Carver's body, electrocuted by electricity pylons brought down by the ice storm. His death is heavy-handedly symbolic, the deep freeze that precipitates it being depicted as equivalent to the emotional coldness and frustration of most of the characters.

Given this, it is not surprising that both drug and alcohol use and abuse are quietly rampant throughout the film. For example, Libbets (Katie Holmes) – Paul Hood's prospective lover – self-medicates via her mother's well-stocked medicine cabinet (essentially abandoned by her wealthy family as they go travelling in Europe. For his part, Ben Hood always has a drink close at hand, and the key party is well lubricated with alcohol, Ben getting very drunk and as a result inadvertently revealing his affair with Janey Carver. The numbness engendered by the intoxicants is necessary for the protagonists to get through their quietly desperate lives, their society and cultural myths not serving them any kind of spiritual or numinous comfort. In a key scene, a painfully trendy priest, Reverend Edwards (Michael Cumpsty) attempts to flirt and simultaneously give spiritual guidance to Ellen Hood, but to no avail. His role as religious representative in his community is fundamentally undermined by his presence at the key party. The film is full of frustrated numinosity; the suburban landscape and the bland lives are shown to exact a terrible toll on the inhabitants. The American Dream exists within the film, but it is shown to be under tremendous pressure from within and without; the children, Wendy in particular, act as the moral centre of the film, especially when it comes to identifying societal corruption. Overhearing his daughter insulting Richard Nixon during the televised Watergate hearings, Ben Hood lashes out with a reminder that: "Hey, that's the president of the goddam United States you're talking about, Wendy!' He betrays a blind, almost naïve, trust in the standards and institutions of his country, seemingly immune to the cultural and societal changes and fractures that are taking place in front of him (the Vietnam War is also mentioned in passing, but casually commented on, rather than condemned or confronted). Denial, it seems, is much easier to slip into in suburbia, than deal with the truth. The film is a deceptively gentle, but ultimately raw, expose of fractured suburban families, with both mothers and fathers shown as wounded, and inadvertently wounding their children due to their unhappiness.

With Todd Solondz's scabrous *Happiness* (1998), both suburbia and the American nuclear family are depicted as dangerous spaces for children and adults. Released to critical acclaim, but predictable tabloid outrage due to its unflinching portrayal of an outwardly respectable psychiatrist Dr Bill Maplewood (Dylan Baker), who is a paedophile, *Happiness* mercilessly skewers the toll that suburbia and attempts to fulfil the American Dream takes on people. Focusing on three sisters and their respective relationships, the film is disturbing due to its quiet insistence that, in Stella Bruzzi's pithy analysis, '[i]n *Happiness*, as in *Magnolia*, the father is the font of all neurosis, although in [this] film this is worked through as shared perversity as opposed to shared hysteria' (2005, p. 185). Fathers in this particular film are only ever a source of pain for their sons, the father of the boy that Bill Maplewood first abuses ponders around getting him a sex worker to show him how to be a man, even though his son is only eleven years old. During the film, Bill and Billy Maplewood are shown to have several exquisitely uncomfortable and increasingly extreme conversations about sex that affect Billy in a wholly negative way. By the end of the film he is shown to be a voyeur who masturbates whilst wearing makeup. His announcement to his family that he ejaculated marks not only his entry into adulthood in a sense but also his entry in a potentially perverse masculine identity. Bruzzi makes the point: 'Like *Affliction*, Happiness has no stabilising or normative image of contented, conventional patriarchy. . . . The omnipresence of perversity is the exorcised father's ultimate bequest' (ibid, p. 184). Paradoxically, this is part of the film's strength, as well as its weakness, the film being easily categorised as a 'feel-bad' movie, exposing only the perversities of American culture and the American father at the expense of showing its strengths or positive aspects. The American father needs to be viewed as a multi-faceted symbolic presence; this encompasses positive aspects of his presence and paternal wisdom; any cultural product that shows exclusively positive (*The Pursuit of Happyness*) or only negative (*Happiness*) fatherly attributes runs the risk of an unbalanced perspective.

## The rebellious child – Ricky Fitts, Frank Abagnale, Freddie Quell

Moving on from the detailed analyses made earlier, we can also look at more general examples of the Child in other films. The archetype contains the figure of the naughty rebel, the wayward child who yearns for paternal control and family stability, but whose behaviour would, on the surface, appear to indicate otherwise. *American Beauty*'s Ricky Fitts can be viewed as a quieter version of this archetype; his discreet dealing marijuana operation is ostensibly a rebellion against his deeply repressed martinet of a father, Colonel Fitts (Chris Cooper), but more importantly is for Ricky's own psychic benefit in that by rebelling he keeps the connection with the underlying beauty of the world that he is dimly aware of. His rebellion is against conformity and, by implication, against his society, an environment that consists of suburban dullness and stultifying boredom. Ricky has achieved his own version of the American Dream that bypasses the usual conspicuous material success (although he has quietly amassed $40,000 through dealing) and social progression (he is unperturbed by having few friends and being thought of as strange). The key driver of the American Dream is to be happy, or at least experience happiness; Ricky appears to have achieved this state within the film. He recognises that the actual pursuit of happiness is a pointless exercise. Out of all the characters, he, at least *appears* to be the most balanced and calm with a preternaturally clear-eyed view of the world and his place within it. Expanding on this perspective, his habitual use of marijuana would appear to bely this state of grace; in fact he needs to be medicated to deal with American society and its socio-normative restrictions and driving cultural complexes such as the American Dream. In addition to Ricky's quiet rebellion, there is also a Trickster quality to him (Bassil-Morozow, 2011), in that he is a deliberate disruptor of the norm within the film; Lester falls under his spell to a certain degree, and his subsequent dope smoking is a presented as being a key part of his own rebellion against normative societal expectations. In a sense, Ricky is subverting and disrupting the paternal, or at least normative paternalistic expectations, by encouraging Lester to rebel. Whether or not this is an unconscious decision on Ricky's part to attack the paternal and thereby get vicarious revenge on a physically and emotionally abusive father or whether to help to heal the paternal by making the father aware of how trapped he is within American society and its expectations is left to the spectator to decide.

Steven Spielberg presents us with another rebel child with the real-life story of Frank Abagnale (Leonardo Di Caprio), main protagonist of his 2002 film *Catch Me if You Can*. A serial con-man and forger who stole $2.8 million during the course of his criminal career, Frank is a teenager when he carries out the majority of his crimes and successfully poses as a Secret Service agent, a doctor, an airline pilot, and a lawyer during the film. Frank's opponent in the film is Carl Hanratty (Tom Hanks), an FBI bank fraud specialist who becomes obsessed with catching him, partly due to wounded pride after Frank successfully dupes him during their first encounter, and partly, it is strongly implied, because Carl has become a father figure to his quarry, Frank's own father (Christopher Walken) being distant and unavailable. Frank is a classic example of a needy but rebellious child, crime being the main way that he is able to get attention from a father figure, in this case, Carl. The object of his father hunger is the correct age for a father, and additionally shows an understanding and compassion for Frank that Frank is portrayed as needing. Crucially, Carl's own family is split by divorce; he rarely sees his own child and is portrayed by Spielberg as deeply lonely, a man married, in effect, to his job and the Bureau, itself a kind of surrogate family. This adoption of a man's workplace colleagues as acting as a form of substitute family is a common trope across American cinema (e.g. *Wall Street*, 1988 Stone; *Revolutionary Road*, 2008, Mendes). What is explicit within the film is that Spielberg shows father hunger exerting its grip on Carl as much as Frank. The film is overt in its portrayal of the relationship between the two men as strikingly paternal and filial; Carl is aware that he is playing the father figure to Frank, but Frank is less mindful of the true nature of their relationship. When Carl has to tell Frank that his biological father has died, it is done so with a certain avuncular, bordering on paternal, tenderness. After Frank manages to abscond from Carl's custody having received this devastating news, Carl instinctively knows where to look for Frank: his estranged mother's new home. This is where, in a heavy-handed show of symbolism, Frank is shown outside of the family home, hopelessly gazing in to where his half-sister, mother and stepfather are preparing for Christmas, his own presence explicitly excluded. Other fathers appear throughout the film, Frank's own dad meeting him in a bar to have a painfully terse and forced conversation about the past. Rejecting his biological father, Frank's father hunger motivates him to unconsciously seek out more paternal figures. He ends up connecting powerfully with his putative father-in-law Roger Strong (Martin Sheen), the Louisiana District Attorney, when Frank falls in love with his daughter, Brenda (Amy Adams). In a scene that is deliberately directed by Spielberg in a suspenseful way, Frank is nearly uncovered as an imposter by Roger's shrewd questioning but is saved at the last minute when Roger declares that: 'Frank, you're a romantic, just like me!' Having inadvertently fooled his new father-in-law, Frank undertakes legal training and passes the Louisiana State Bar exam to work on becoming a lawyer, a neat and symbolically inversion of his criminal career so far but is nearly caught by Carl at his engagement party. Frank rebels against normative American society in two ways: one, he commits sophisticated crime (cheque fraud) to fund his lifestyle, and two, he pretends to be other people in order to carry out his crimes. This identity theft, arguably itself a reaction to lack of psychic identity on Frank's part, goes both for and against the American Dream, in that there is an expectation of self-reliant authenticity when achieving the American Dream, yet there is also a strong sense of, and indeed expectation, of self-invention within the American Dream, an aspect that Frank takes to heart in order to avoid his own psychic pain, itself located in his lack of paternal guidance and family connection. Frank has been taken in by the American Dream's message of material and social success, but he cannot hope to fulfil it in a societally approved way. His crimes can be argued to stem from his father hunger and being excluded from normative family life; he is trying to manufacture the appearance of normality and success by bypassing the usual routes in favour of cheating and disguising his true identity.

Rebellion can, of course, go too far, a blindly rebelling son embarking on a dark psychic journey in their struggle to avoid responsibility and psychic pain. Such a journey is depicted in *The Master* (Anderson, 2012); Freddie Quell (Joaquin Phoenix), being such a rogue son, is also portrayed as being a victim of paternal betrayal. A troubled and violent drifter, in effect both a potent metaphor and symbol for post-war marginalised American masculinity, Freddie is depicted by Anderson as being betrayed twice by American patriarchal masculinity. First, the US army who, having failed with half-hearted attempts at re-socialisation and rehabilitation, cast him aside to drift aimlessly through mundane jobs, anaesthetising himself and his pain with home-brewed alcohol. When he stows away on a random ship, he encounters his second betrayal courtesy of the paternal in the shape of the surrogate father figure of Lancaster Dodd (Philip Seymour Hoffman), who tries to help him by initiating him into his quasi-spiritual cult, The Cause,[18] to prove that man is not an animal. When Freddie proves both resistant to Dodd's brainwashing methods and challenges the cult's theories, he is also cast aside as being beyond help and unworthy of Dodd's attention. The self-invention aspect of the American Dream here is represented by the Cause, the hubristic Dodd declaring that similar to Jay Gatsby (Leonardo Di Caprio) in *The Great Gatsby* (Luhrmann, 2013) that anyone can be anything. It is a key plank of Dodd's theories that the re-invention of the self is possible; this echoes the transformational aspect of the American cultural myth being a key part of the American Dream. What *The Master* does is depict the boundaries of this delusion, the rogue son showing up the limits of the father's control, despite Dodd's best efforts to the contrary. The film's subtext is also effectively stating that American masculinity, and specifically father hunger, is best served by an authentic masculine presence that has integrity and is grounded within the culture and material presence, rather than Dodd's clever sham show of esoteric knowledge and supposed wisdom.

Similar to, but different from *Jarhead*, initiation plays an integral role in the film, with Anderson depicting Quell as being subject first to a face-to-face initiation process (named Processing by Anderson in a possibly satirical nod to Scientology's 'Auditing'), akin to a formal interview. This particular scene is deliberately starkly lit to emphasise the symbolic movement of Freddie from the darkness of his animal instincts to the light of 'reason' represented by Dodd and his acolytes. Here, Freddie symbolically represents the Freudian Id or Jungian physical Shadow in terms of animal instincts and drives; his alcoholism masking a compulsive, primitive and almost barely controlled libido, expressed in both comic scenes (mock-copulating with a giant female sand statue at the beginning and end of the film) and more dramatic moments (Dodd's daughter groping him surreptitiously during one of her father's speeches). Later in the film, Quell undergoes a lengthier formal initiation process in front of the whole group, which succeeds in allowing him full entry into The Cause. As such, he dualistically represents both a direct threat and opportunity to Dodd. Cavalli makes the point that Quell also symbolically represents: 'Dodd's false self, and at the same time, he represents the outer reflection of Dodd's Shadow, all that he must keep under wraps in order to maintain his role as leader of his cult' (2013, p. 57). As a surrogate father who is depicted as exerting patriarchal control over his disciples, Dodd views Freddie primarily as a project to work on as proof of his ideas around Man not succumbing to animalistic urges, a clear case of a subcultural version of *Logos* energy establishing 'the Rule of the Father'. Before long, however, their relationship develops into a classic Shadow father-and-son relationship that begins to challenge Dodd's own psychic malaise and provokes his wife Peggy into urging him to drop Freddie due to suspicions that he is either an agent or a danger to The Cause. In a brief but revealing scene, Peggy asserts her control over her husband by masturbating Dodd in front of their bathroom mirror, and orders him to, first stop flirting with other women, secondly, stop drinking with Freddie and lastly, get him to join their group or quit.

This scene is used to depict Peggy as an increasingly powerful matriarchal figure who is revealed here to control Dodd, and therefore the group. The paternal phallus, and by implication the paternal itself, is symbolically used here as a tool by the matriarch of the group to manipulate the patriarch; Dodd's own physical and sexual vulnerabilities being exploited and utilised by Peggy to protect their subculture from perceived threats. As with the USMC in *Jarhead*, The Cause is portrayed as a substitute American familial social structure that exacts a price upon its members; any questioning of the patriarch Dodd earns the questioner potential humiliation and exile. In the end, Freddie proves to be temperamentally unsuited to his surrogate father and mother figures; he is given the choice of one last chance of joining The Cause, or permanent exile. He chooses exile, having been betrayed by both patriarchal subcultures and surrogate father figures. The rogue son stays rogue, being cast adrift upon American society with unknown results. Echoing Connell (1995), Freddie's encounters with alternative subaltern masculinities have not resulted in any masculine dividends for him; The Cause's familial support was conditional on unquestioning loyalty and belief in its theories, similar to the army and its reliance on its members unconditionally following orders. So far, the American fathers in filmic subcultures, it seems, are strangely similar to fathers in depicted mainstream American society, with the films under analysis showing and reiterating the controlling and damaging effect patriarchal social groups can have upon masculine children (both immature and adult) via archetypal mis-initiation and dis-initiation processes.

## Conclusion

As a potent symbol in and of itself, the Child archetype is key to understanding both fatherhood and father hunger. As explored earlier in the book, symbolically, the Child fulfils both a polyvalent and polysemous function, as it not only contains different symbolic aspects, all of which make appearances within various films, but, more importantly for our purposes, these aspects can be analysed within both film and psychoanalysis. For example, the child can act as a catalyst for father hunger. This is a key theme explored in the comedy-drama *About A Boy* (Weitz and Weitz, 2002). The story of how a self-confessed man-child Will Freeman (Hugh Grant) is catalysed into growing into adult masculine maturity by the attentions of an eleven-year-old boy, Marcus Brewer (Nicolas Hoult), the film shows how the child is depicted as a force for changes within masculinity. The child is presented within this film mainly as a catalysing presence that ignites previously dormant father hunger within the adult male, and, more importantly, represents father hunger as a necessary drive for a man to act successfully as a man. The film, although ostensibly British (a UK cast and crew, but made with American funding), contains a sly critique of the American Dream, in that material success is presented as being hollow and largely worthless in terms of emotional and cultural capital. Will is explicitly shown as slowly realising that his comfortably materialistic life (symbolically significant in that it is only possible via the royalties from his deceased father writing a popular Christmas song) is ultimately unsatisfying and that heteronormative family life is more emotionally sustaining. The child archetype in the film is portrayed as a partially numinous figure that activates a gender energy change within masculinity, the masculine continuum being revitalised by the child to the point where a balance is restored to both the child and the surrogate father figure of Will. The biological parents here are portrayed as barriers to the child, the surrogate paternal as much more engaging. For example, Marcus's own father is not deceased, but passively absent, and with another family. Marcus's mother, Fiona Brewer (Toni Collette), is portrayed dualistically as a barrier to Marcus's maturation (she is both overbearing and emotionally needy as well as suicidally depressed) and as a gateway (her membership of a single parents group is the narrative device to introduce Will to Marcus). Being at the age where, in classic archetypal terms, he starts to individuate, Marcus is shown to need to detach from the mother towards a father figure, thereby being in the energetic grip of father hunger, as well as gradually catalysing it within Will. The subtext of the film also contains more sly humour, in that Will, who is childless, joins a single parents group under false pretences (he pretends to have a two-year-old son called Ned) specifically to meet single mothers and enjoy casual sex without responsibility. The irony of pretending to be a father and then slowly becoming a surrogate one against his better judgment is perhaps obvious, but nonetheless a key part of the film's humour. Coupled with pithy comedic swipes at British middle-class pretensions and notions of parenthood, the film is an intriguing example of how the Child archetype can be shown to subvert and engender father hunger, whilst simultaneously critiquing it.

To finally conclude this chapter, we need to highlight and differentiate the approaches that are taken with male and female children within American cinema. The American father-daughter relationship and the accompanying father hunger is consciously depicted as both substantially and subtly different from the father's relationship with the son. As highlighted in the earlier chapter, the daughter has to go on her own gender journey from the mother towards the father knowing the masculine as an opposite, his absence, or, as mentioned earlier, his lack of *presence* (e.g. *American Beauty*) can damage the daughter and her perception of the masculine just as much as too much presence in a daughter's life can also cause damage (*Magnolia*). The American father has to do more than just provide material comforts and success; he has to provide psychological support and presence to a daughter. As *American Beauty* explicitly shows in its opening scene, Jane's crisply expressed longing for a role model father is what Lester finally becomes in his last moments, although, tragically, his daughter doesn't get to experience this more balanced mature father energy, robbed of her paternal by the other, more damaged and repressed father in the film, Colonel Fitts. Her father hunger is paralleled by Lester's own innate individuative journey as he confronts and learns from his anima via the symbolism of the rose. The erotic playback function that the father performs, as Samuels has theorised, has become deeply confused for Lester as he unconsciously projects his anima onto his daughter's best friend and results as a chaotic dance with his Shadow, only redeeming himself at the end of the film. As an example of the redeemed dark father, Lester Burnham is a prime example. By sharp contrast, Jimmy Gator is a deliberate example of the unredeemed Shadow paternal. The depicted results of him breaking one of the most primal human taboos is sobering. His refusal to face up to his actions and the truth about his own inner darkness damns him; the psychic forces that Anderson shows at work do not brook denials. Jimmy is punished here by what could be described as a classical Greek tragic device, the rain of falling frogs, sent by the gods. Unconscious forces are depicted here by Anderson as being directly visible; they will act against transgressors and bring punishment, Jimmy's presumed final fate being a salutary lesson.

By contrast, the father's role with regard to the son is to act as a gender bridge of sorts to adult masculinity; examples of this bridge that take the son to darker destinations include *Boogie Nights*, *Happiness* and *Magnolia*; fathers within these films are far from the idealised American paternal presented by cultural myths such as the American Dream. Sons are depicted as potentially at risk from oversexualised fathers (*Happiness*), exploitative surrogates (*Boogie Nights*) or emotionally unavailable and absent fathers (*Magnolia*). The paternal road to masculinity is either blocked, or is more often than not a journey to Shadow masculinity and often Shadow sexuality. In a wider context, Lester Burnham, Jimmy Gator and Bill Maplewood are examples of the sexualised father, as mentioned by Bruzzi (2005), where Hollywood has a tendency to problematise the father's sexuality, ironic given that it is sex that creates fathers and fatherhood. She goes further:

> Although Hollywood's disillusionment with the father is painfully widespread, within these scenarios of loss lie its ultimate masculine melodrama: just out of reach for these flawed fathers lies the perfected image they aspire to but know they cannot match. It is this disparity between the real and the symbolic father that Hollywood finds impossible to resolve, perpetually hoping to instead to effect their coalescence.
>
> (p. 191)

Picking up on this point about the perfected image of the father, as a symbolic relationship, both the father-daughter dyad and the father-son dyad are revealing, in that they help to show the sexual father, sex being a function and feature of the American paternal that are mediated symbolically in differing ways. These aspects tie in with our conclusions around the American cultural complex and the presence of the American father within wider society, explored in the concluding chapter.

## Notes

1 Samuels 'a girl does not have to surmount her relationship to her mother in the same way [as a boy does] to achieve femininity' (1985a, 209).
2 Reiter in his book *Fathers and Sons in Cinema* (2008) describes this father as 'a dragon-obstructor, the same archetypal ogre found in many myths and fairy tales' (p. 14).
3 Samuels makes a powerful argument that the biological father does not have sole rights to being the father figure within the psyche or indeed within the nuclear family, this role often falling to another male figure or in some cases, a female figure as in gay female couples (1985b, p. 23).
4 Maine makes an interesting argument when analysing the definition of crisis. In *Father Hunger* (2004), she points out that the word 'crisis' in Mandarin Chinese is represented by the two ideograms for 'trouble' and 'opportunity', seemingly antagonistic and contradictory elements that can, on reflection, perfectly define what a crisis can be.

5 Both King (2002, 2009) and Waxman (2005) note how critically and commercially successful the film was (£15 million budget against a £130 million gross) and attribute this to what they term as conspicuous 'quality' directing and casting.
6 *Temenos* in a Jungian sense can be defined as a sacred or emotional space where unconscious issues, pain and energy are brought into consciousness.
7 King (2009) argues that part of the raison d'etre in hiring award-winning theatre director Mendes was make the film a self-consciously prestige project: 'From its inception as a project, then, *American Beauty* was treated and positioned as something special, as an individual creative work that needed to be handled as such rather than as just another commercial/industrial 'product'' (p. 197).
8 An earlier version of the script had Lester consummate his desire with Angela, a far more transgressive proposal, and one which may have negatively impacted the commercial chances of the film (King, 2009, p. 215).
9 In *Iron John* Bly makes the generalised (and therefore contestable) point that whilst fathers prefer to wound sons physically, mothers wound sons with words and shame.
10 Freud developed the theory of the Oedipus complex early on his work on psychoanalysis (1897–1909), and it remains a cornerstone of his theories ever since. The female version of this, the Electra complex was proposed by Jung later in 1913.
11 In an earlier version of the script of *Boogie Nights*, Eddie/Dirk visits his former family home to attempt a reconciliation with his mother and father, only to be told by Cheryl Lynn, (who has since moved into his old residence) that both his parents are dead, the result of a car accident that also involved Johnny Doe, his replacement after he stormed off set following his argument with Jack.
12 In another script revision, a scene involving Jack and cameraman Kurt Longjohn discussing how to use a new video camera, was dropped from the final edit. This scene contained the immortal lines from Kurt: 'We can still tell good stories, Jack'. Jack responds: 'No. It's about jacking off now Kurt. No more stories . . . that's over'.
13 Also known as Operation Desert Shield, which then segued into Operation Desert Storm when the coalition forces under a UN mandate invaded Iraq in January 1991, following the Iraqi invasion of Kuwait in August 1990.
14 Baudrillard's pronouncements not surprisingly caused controversy at the time. Whilst provocatively interesting to a point regarding issues over the emergence of digital and hyperreal warfare, it can be argued that his argument is merely another reinforcement of Western-centric perspectives about warfare when we consider the amount of Iraqi dead (hundreds of thousands) compared to US and Coalition soldiers (dozens). In other words, despite the war being absurdly one-sided in terms of casualties, it can still be classed as a war.
15 The film grossed $96.9 million against a $72 million dollar budget. (Ref. www.boxoficemojo.com).
16 The seminar depicted appears to be based on contemporary 'seduction community' seminars that are promoted and led by a number of self-appointed seduction experts, including Ross Jeffries whom Anderson is said to have credited with inspiring the character of Frank Mackey. A popular account of life within the seduction community is *The Game* (2005) by Neil Strauss.
17 Bly attempts to locate the Wild Man within and connected to the natural world; the Savage Man, can, in effect, be read as the Wild Man's Shadow, leading to, as Tacey points out, darker psychic territory.
18 There was a widely held rumour, denied by Anderson, that his film was based on the early days of Scientology with Dodd standing in for Scientology's founder, L. Ron Hubbard.

# Conclusion – the future of the father

The previous chapters have demonstrated how widespread and pervasive the father is as a presence in American cinema; Bruzzi's original point about his filmic ubiquity being comprehensively proved here. What is, perhaps, more noteworthy is how pluralistic and multi-faceted the American paternal has proven to be. We have variously analysed him as castrated suburbanite (Frank Wheeler), re-potentialised suburbanite (Lester Burnham), tyrannical and murderous dictator (Daniel Plainview), and redeemed assassin (Michael Sullivan Snr). He is a dying abandoner (Earl Partridge), a sexual exploiter of masculinity and femininity (Jack Horner), a would-be sexual transgressor (Lester Burnham again), and an actual sexual transgressor (Jimmy Gator). He plays the role of guilt-ridden patricide (Sydney Brown), a harsh nurturer (Staff Sergeant Sykes), repressed and repressing homosexual, (Colonel Frank Fitts) and nervous father-to-be (*Away We Go's* Burt Farlander, analysed later in this chapter). His numinous absence (*Fight Club*) and his economic absence (*Frozen River; Winter's Bone*) are sorely missed, and his potency as both a light and dark provider and protector (*A Bronx Tale*) are telling. This plurality of American paternal performative gender roles and identities proves that there are multiple masculinities within American cinema and within screen texts such as television, discussed in more detail later.

## Post-Jungian sensitivities

In terms of the advantages in using a post-Jungian methodology and sensibility, we are now less restricted (compared to more reductive semiotic approaches) to interpret and analyse how paternal performances are actually portrayed, rather than shaping texts to fit in with theory. One advantage of thinking about the American father in terms of archetypal symbolism is the flexibility it affords us when analysing it within both cinematic and American cultural contexts. As Bassil-Morozow and Hockley state:

> [T]he psychological meaning of the symbol can never be fully understood . . . we are moving along the scale of the fixed-ness of meaning here and its degree is always socially and culturally determined. The less fixed the meaning, the

DOI: 10.4324/9780429199684-6

less indexical the sign/symbol is as indexicality is lost in proportion to the loss of the link between the signifier and the signified.

(2017, p. 69)

This explicit recognition of the symbol's inherent unknowability highlights that within the symbol, there will be what can be termed 'meaning-space' that allows for fresh interpretation. This meaning-space allows future signs to be produced from the symbol within future cultural and social contexts and analysis and resonates with what Fredericksen (1979) and other post-Jungian writers, Izod (2001, 2006) et al, have discussed. For example, the sequence in *Road to Perdition* where key paternal symbols (wallet, keys and gun) are viewed by the son can be pluralistically interpreted as symbols of archetypal masculine security or symbols of insecurity. Is the masculine here safe or under threat? Why the need for the gun, if not under threat? The father's pistol here is not necessarily a sexual phallic symbol but also a dark spiritual symbol in terms of death. Another view is that it is an archetypal economic symbol, in that it could be seen to represent a ruthless version of gangster-capitalism, enforced by potential violence, and so on. In *A Bronx Tale*, doors and portals act on a number of levels symbolically, allowing social, cultural and personal ascents and descents for the characters, and so on. This inherent symbolic flexibility calls attention to the parallels between pluralistic post-Jungian symbolic approaches to the pluralisation of masculinity, effectively one mirroring the other in that we have a flexible method of analysing multiple portrayals of gender. What the semiotic and symbolic imagery around the American father appears to tell us is that there appears to be an ongoing struggle with negative masculinities taking place within American culture from the mid-1990s onwards, a result of the crisis in masculinity leading to fundamental questioning of masculine roles. We can conclude that in many of the films, the American father is shown as not only located within the cultural Shadow, both personal and societal but also engaging with transcending it, a clear sign of cultural individuation. In broader symbolic terms then, the father can be said to occupy a number of dark spaces, both within the personal psyche and as a cultural complex within American society. Being such as fundamental part of the American Dream, in terms of being a main source of familial and economic power within the American family, the American father is logically a key site of signalling a change within the American cultural complex. This understanding of the American father enables us to start to position the paternal as both a polysemous sign and a symbol of masculinity itself, a key link in the chain of masculine continuum and a gender figure that has been portrayed by filmmakers as being in need of redemption, a clear case of individuative and teleological psychic and cultural motion. This motion is also reflected within the medium of television, particularly given the rapidly evolving modes of media consumption, for example, the rise of streaming services that enable cultural textual consumption almost anywhere. Whilst the media landscape is rapidly changing, it is arguable that the figure of the father is still making himself known via the multiple narratives being currently broadcast. For example, both *Sons of Anarchy* (2008–2014, Sutter, 20th Television) and *Mayans M.C.* (2018–2020, Sutter, 20th Television) have numerous multiplicities of the father-son relationship at their core, driving the characters and the narratives in profound ways. In *Breaking Bad* (2008–2013, Gilligan, AMC), Walter White's (Bryan Cranston) relationship with Jesse Pinkman (Aaron Paul) is essentially a surrogate father and wayward son dynamic that lasts throughout the five seasons and involves surrogate familial tensions, pleasures and betrayals, very similar to the films analysed previously. All three shows involve self-consciously symbolic filmic style visual language to transmit their narrative and involve the paternal throughout. All three shows also reflect the Shadow version of the American Dream, or lack thereof, with Walter White, for example, initially deluding himself that his meth lab money is for his family after he dies from his lung cancer. As the show progresses, the thrill of his new criminal life is intoxicating, and he enthusiastically pursues his own Shadow driven version of the national myth.

American cinema and media show us then, via depictions of father hunger, that the father himself is simultaneously portrayed as being within a masculine crisis and also shown as contributing to it by not challenging culturally and socially damaging patriarchal expectations. For their part, we have shown that the father is struggling with negative masculine performances, which in turn reflects deeper patriarchally inflected American cultural attitudes. When a major archetype such as the father is put under such pressures to change, the process does not happen immediately; more, it is a masculine work in progress, and part of the masculine continuum. Tacey argues that this work is fraught with dangers, Bly having fallen victim to some of them:

> [T]here is a real tendency to equate the senex or father with the archetype of the Self (Bly's mistake). The prevailing view is that the inner father will heal psychological pain and create wisdom and wholeness. The inner father is a God-father, an old, smiling, bearded presence who works ceaselessly for the health and development of his fragile, battered, alienated sons.
>
> (1997, p. 59)

Father hunger then manages to be both a symptom of this over-identification with the figure of the father (American cultural complex) and an unfulfilled psychological need (personal complex), filmmakers successfully portraying this dualistic phenomenon. Tacey continues to warn of potential consequences of not seeing past conflated notion of masculine and feminine archetypes: 'Acknowledging the power and might of these figures, without falling victim to them in unconscious domination, is the real challenge facing men today' (ibid, p. 189). Expanding on these points, and also addressing questions around mother hunger and the maternal (which would, no doubt, be another suitable topic for research), the post-Jungian approach to the analysis of gender symbols (viewing them as archetypal) has much to recommend it. Going further, the post-Jungian emphasis on how critical and central the image is to the psyche also makes sense when we consider how images can trigger an affective response[1] within audiences, an area of study that has already been analysed by post-Jungian theorists and writers (Singh, 2009, 2014; Izod, 2001; Bassil-Morozow and Hockley, 2017; Hockley, 2018) to add to the existing discourses on the subject (Merleau-Ponty, 1945, 1964; Sobchack, 2004; Grodal, 1999, 2009; Shaviro, 1993, 2010, etc.). With Jung's definitions of psychological and visionary art inviting discussions around symbols and alchemy, and analytical psychological approaches even arguably being applicable to commercial and industrial cinematic discourses and reception studies,[2] a post-Jungian approach is potentially able to reveal new and vibrant perspectives on existing debates within film studies.

## *Away We Go*: the balanced father?

When we consider future representations of the American filmic paternal, we can link in cultural changes to changes in representation. From the mid-to-late 1990s, American cinematic representations of the father were located mainly in the Shadow aspect of the American cultural, social, and personal unconscious. As it progressed and developed, there was a gradual transition in terms of paternal portrayals, in that the American father partially moved out of psychic darkness and struggle and began to be located in more light-hearted and comedic positions. One example of this is Sam Mendes' *Away We Go* (2009), his last film before he signed on to direct the James Bond franchise. A drama-comedy that took the form of a road trip for two prospective parents, it followed the then-current trend of what has been termed 'mumblecore' films,[3] with Mendes attempting to depict contemporaneous parenthood via the figure of a thirty-something father-to-be, Burt Farlander (John Krasinski) and his heavily pregnant partner, Verona De Tessant (Maya Rudolph). Travelling the country to visit friends and family to try and decide where to raise their soon-to-be-born daughter, the film depicted both fatherhood and motherhood as a maturation process (the couple constantly ask themselves the pithily posed question: 'Are we fuck-ups?'). Encountering a number of other parents, including his own (hers are both dead), they are in turn amused, mildly horrified, confused and saddened by the differing models of American parenthood on offer. Finally choosing Verona's parents' house as a final place to settle down, the couple commit to raise their daughter as best they can, demonstrating themselves as, paraphrasing D.W. Winnicott's earlier term: 'good enough parents'(1973, p. 10). Here, fatherhood is shown as a performance that is inflected by an active rejection of both the selfishness of his parents, baby-boomer generation, and an equal determination to avoid the more extreme modes of modern 'continuum' parenting as evidenced by his adopted cousin, LN (Maggie Gyllenhaal), who angrily (and hilariously) rejects their gift of a pushchair as developmentally damaging.

In attempting to steer a middle course between the older generational parenting mode and the overly involved mode of LN, Mendes paints his version of modern American fatherhood as a balancing act between external (work and social) demands and internal (familial and domestic) demands, and between the excesses of previous and contemporary parenting models that represent generational perspectives. The American Dream (and American cultural complex) is depicted within the film to have transformed to more modest parental ambitions and a desire to raise their daughter with a more balanced approach. Material success, and competitive parenting as evidenced by Roderick and LN, are depicted as being rejected, indicating a potential change in cultural attitudes. Echoing Modleski's point about modern masculinities borrowing, or even appropriating, feminine qualities (1991), Burt is depicted as a caring and sensitive father who eschews traditional and outdated modes of masculinities, and, in a telling pre-credit sequence, divines that Verona is pregnant due to her tasting different whilst performing cunnilingus.

This is a clearly signified shift in terms of the American father performing as a sensitive and considerate lover, a far cry from the abusive (Jimmy Gator) or frustrated (Lester Burnham) sexual fathers that have been portrayed previously. This depiction also runs counter to Bruzzi's point about the action film essentially displacing masculine sexual frustration: 'That masculinity in cinema is so often predicated upon sexual frustration is one notable paradox of men's cinema' (2013, p. 119). Symbolically, Mendes depicts the American father in *Away We Go* as embarking upon an individuative masculine quest for responsible fatherhood, but it is a quest that is intimately involved with his partner, not a lonely or difficult masculine journey through his Shadow as portrayed in other examples, analysed earlier. The feminine has a strong and visible presence within the film, indeed; the film centralises the pregnancy as a key narrative driver and agent of the maturation process for both the feminine and masculine within the film, a gender syzygy that is portrayed as ultimately resulting in a satisfied, balanced and idealised state by the end of the film. Whilst this signifies a distinct shift in representation, there is an unwillingness, or at the very least a reluctance, to engage with the Shadow that Jung held to be within every psyche. How far this depiction of the new paternal accurately reflects current American cultural and societal discourses around fatherhood is highly debatable, but given the increasing and sustained attention that the 'new' fatherhood attracts (referred to in the literature review) in the media and in recently in print (Perry, 2016; Hemmings, 2017; Urwin, 2017; Webb, 2017), it can be argued that just as there are multiple masculinities being performed, so there are multiple paternal performances also on offer for adoption. With *Away We Go*, Mendes would have us believe that, in response to the calls of father hunger, the performance of a more balanced American fatherhood by modern men shows that they have duly responded.

To finally conclude, we can return to Jung and post-Jungian methodology for a fresh perspective on current discourses. Quoted in *The Frankenstein Myth*, Rushing and Frentz state that: 'Every period has its bias, its particular prejudice, and its psychic malaise. An epoch is like an individual; it has its own limitations of conscious outlook, and therefore requires a compensatory adjustment' (1989, p. 98).

## 158 Conclusion – The future of the father

The inadequacies of the American post-war fathering models depicted in film, as outlined by Bruzzi and others (Chopra-Gant, 2005; Kord and Krimmer, 2011; Hamad, 2014, etc.), led to compensatory expressions of father hunger, highlighting the symbolic and psychic importance of this archetype. However, as *Away We Go* shows, Tacey argues 'archetypes are always in danger of being deprived of their Shadow' (1997, p. 60). Conventional and mainstream Hollywood cinema either denied the patriarchal power that the American father represented, or overstated this agency, effectively shutting out the power of the feminine. The father archetype was also either effectively deprived of its Shadow, or worse, was all Shadow. Adding to this recognition of the dangers of unbalanced depictions of archetypes often leading to stereotypes, Tacey further states that 'social stereotypes do not emerge out of thin air; they represent an amalgam of nurture and nature, culture and psyche, time and eternity . . . ideology has archetypal foundations that are ignored at our peril' (ibid, p. 194). American cinema's recognition of the American paternal Shadow and cultural complex, and the resulting redemptive journey of the American father, is one indicator that culturally speaking, we are beginning to accept and recognise the American father as a pluralistic, and consequently more balanced, masculine presence. Father hunger effectively is indicative of a motion towards cultural individuation. As Tacey muses about the ongoing gender and cultural debates:

> [H]ow to liberate without also destroying, how to make free without also creating horror and devastation? This is the big internal and external problem of our culture, and until we have come up with answers we cannot claim to be a post-patriarchal world.
> 
> (ibid, pp. 71–72)

This resonates in accord with Monick's point that 'unless masculinity is differentiated from patriarchy, both will go down the drain together' (1987, p. 9). Culturally, it is crucial that the paternal needs to be differentiated from the patriarchal; a caring masculinity should not be the same as a controlling masculinity. For a succinct final summary of where we are at in terms of culture and cultural products that contain paternal energy, we can refer to an earlier cultural and analytical commentary by the post-Jungian writer Andrew Samuels, who is quoted at length on this issue:

> A wheel has turned full circle, for the father was the key parent in the early days of psychoanalysis – the tyrannical, castrating, oedipal father. Then we got hooked – validly and necessarily – on the mother; now we're coming back to the father. He is still often the prohibitive father but also, increasingly, the positive father; the facilitating, empathic, mirroring father who aids imagination, creativity, and psychic health generally. . . . In a way this is puzzling because, just as psychological thinking touches the image of the positive father, so a great deal of cultural and social criticism has at last caught up

with the image of the negative father: patriarchy, a phallocentric culture, male violence, male sexual abuse of children, male chauvinism. Perhaps depth psychologists, not for the first time, are engaged in something subversive. At the moment when the image of the father in the social world and his authority therein are under as exclusively negative, we, in our limited ways as analysts, are struggling to preserve a balance.

(1989, p. 67)

This recognition of the need for a balanced and nuanced cultural paternal journey, and a journey that the American father appears to be on, is increasingly reflected in cultural texts such as film. Perhaps, arguably, it is long overdue.

## Notes

1 'This is why we are able to have unconscious affective relationships with images – they mean something to us and can move us in ways that the rational and conscious part of our minds is unable to comprehend' (Bassil-Morozow and Hockley, 2017, p. 72).
2 'It is this common archetypal base that that allows us to empathise with each other. It is also this base that ensures a film's popularity and commercial success, for it makes a narrative understandable to a wide range of people all around the world (Bassil-Morozow and Hockley, 2017, p. 22).
3 These are usually independent, low-budget drama or comedy productions with little action, self-consciously naturalistic performances and lengthy, emotionally inflected dialogic exchanges. Directors include Lynn Shelton, Mark Duplass, Joe Swanberg and Andrew Bujalski.

# Filmography

## Primary titles

*A Bronx Tale* (1993) [Film] Directed by Robert De Niro. USA: Price Entertainment/ TriBeCa Productions.
*American Beauty* (1999) [Film] Directed by Sam Mendes. USA: Jinks/Cohen Company.
*Away We Go* (2009) [Film] Directed by Sam Mendes. USA: Big Beach/Neal Street Productions.
*Boogie Nights* (1997) [Film] Directed by Paul Thomas Anderson. USA: Lawrence Gordon Productions/Ghoulardi Film Company.
*Catch Me If You Can* (2002) [Film] Directed by Steven Spielberg. USA: Amblin Entertainment.
*Fight Club* (1999) [Film] Directed by David Fincher. USA: Fox 2000 Pictures/Regency Enterprises.
*Frozen River* (2008) [Film] Directed by Courtney Hunt. USA: Sony Pictures Classics.
*Happiness* (1998) [Film] Directed by Todd Solondz. USA: Killer Films.
*Hard Eight* (1996) [Film] Directed by Paul Thomas Anderson. USA: Rysher Entertainment.
*Jarhead* (2005) [Film] Directed by Sam Mendes. USA: Red Wagon Entertainment/Neal Street Productions.
*Magnolia* (1999) [Film] Directed by Paul Thomas Anderson. USA: Ghoulardi Film Company/JoAnne Sellar Productions.
*Revolutionary Road* (2008) [Film] Directed by Sam Mendes. USA/UK: BBC Films/Neal Street Productions.
*Road to Perdition* (2002) [Film] Directed by Sam Mendes. USA: The Zanuck Company.
*The Master* (2012) [Film] Directed by Paul Thomas Anderson. USA: JoAnne Sellar Productions/Ghoulardi Film Company/Annapurna Pictures.
*The Pursuit of Happyness* (2006) [Film] Directed by Gabriele Muccino. USA: Relativity Media/Overbrook Entertainment/Escape Artists.
*There Will Be Blood* (2007) [Film] Directed by Paul Thomas Anderson. USA: Ghoulardi Film Company.
*Winter's Bone* (2010) [Film] Directed by Debra Granik. USA: Anonymous Content/Roadside Attractions.

## Secondary titles

*A Good Day to Die Hard* (2013) [Film] Directed by John Moore. USA: Giant Pictures, TSG Entertainment and Temple Hill Entertainment.
*About a Boy* (2002) [Film] Directed by Chris Weitz and Paul Weitz. USA: Studio Canal,/ TriBeCa Productions/Working Title Films.

## Filmography

*Absolutely Fabulous* (1992–2012) [TV] Created by Jennifer Saunders. UK: BBC.
*Affliction* (1997) [Film] Directed by Paul Schrader. USA: Kingsgate Films/Largo Entertainment.
*Apocalypse Now* (1979) [Film] Directed by Francis Ford Coppola. USA: United Artists and Omni Zoetrope.
*Baby Boom* (1987) [Film] Directed by Charles Shyer. USA: United Artists.
*Breaking Bad* (2008–2013) [TV] Created by Vince Gilligan. USA: AMC.
*Broken Blossoms* (1919) [Film] Directed by D.W. Griffith. USA: United Artists.
*Courage Under Fire* (1996) [Film] Directed by Edward Zwick. USA: Davis Entertainment.
*Die Hard* (1988) [Film] Directed by John McTiernan. USA: Gordon Company / Silver Pictures / 20th Century Fox.
*Die Hard 2* (1990) [Film] Directed by Renny Harlin. USA: Gordon Company / Silver Pictures / 20th Century Fox.
*Die Hard with a Vengeance* (1995) [Film] Directed by John McTiernan. USA: Cinergi Pictures.
*Die Hard 4.0* (2007) [Film] Directed by Len Wiseman. USA: Cheyenne Enterprises, Dune Entertainment and Ingenious Film Partners.
*Executive Suite* (1954) [Film] Directed by Robert Wise. USA: Metro-Goldwyn-Mayer.
*Fargo* (2014–2020) [TV] Created by Noah Hawley. USA: MGM Television.
*First Blood* (1982) [Film] Directed by Ted Kotcheff. USA: Anabasis N.V./Elcajo Productions.
*Full Metal Jacket* (1987) [Film] Directed by Stanley Kubrick. USA/UK: Natant and Harrier Films.
*Live From Baghdad* (2002) [Film] Directed by Mick Jackson. USA: HBO.
*Mayans M.C.* (2018–2020) [TV] Created by Kurt Sutter and Elgin James. USA: 20th Century Television.
*Missing In Action* (1984) [Film] Directed by Joseph Zito. USA: The Cannon Group Inc.
*Platoon* (1986) [Film] Directed by Oliver Stone. USA: Hemdale Film Corporation.
*Pulp Fiction* (1994) [Film] Directed by Quentin Tarantino. USA: Miramax.
*Rebel Without a Cause* (1955) [Film] Directed by Nicholas Ray. USA: Warner Bros.
*Rushmore* (1999) [Film] Directed by Wes Anderson. USA: Touchstone Pictures.
*Song of Ceylon* (1934) [Film] Directed by Basil Wright. UK: Ceylon Tea Propaganda Board / General Post Office.
*Sons of Anarchy* (2008–2014) [TV] Created by Kurt Sutter. USA: 20th Century Television.
*Star Wars* (1977) [Film] Directed by George Lucas. USA: Lucasfilm Ltd.
*Terminator 2: Judgment Day* (1991) [Film] Directed by James Cameron. USA: Columbia Pictures.
*The Darjeeling Limited* (2007) [Film] Directed by Wes Anderson. USA: Fox Searchlight Pictures.
*The Great Gatsby* (2013) [Film] Directed by Baz Luhrmann. USA/Australia: Village Roadshow Pictures/A&E Television/Bazmark Productions/Red Wagon Entertainment.
*The Great Santini* (1979) [Film] Directed by Lewis John Carlino. USA: Bing Crosby Productions.
*The Ice Storm* (1997) [Film] Directed by Ang Lee. USA: Fox Searchlight, Good Machine, Canal + and Image International.
*The Life Aquatic with Steve Zissou* (2004) [Film] Directed by Wes Anderson. USA: Touchstone Pictures.
*The Man in the Gray Flannel Suit* (1956) [Film] Directed by Nunnally Johnson. USA 20th Century Fox.

*The Royal Tenenbaums* (2001) [Film] Directed by Wes Anderson. USA: Touchstone Pictures.
*The Sopranos* (1999–2007) [TV] Created by David Chase. USA: HBO.
*Three Kings* (1999) [Film] Directed by David O. Russell. USA: Village Roadshow Pictures/Atlas Entertainment.
*Wall Street* (1987) [Film] Directed by Oliver Stone. USA: American Entertainment Partners/Amercent Films.

# Bibliography

## Works cited

Arnold, G.B. (2013) *Projecting the end of the American Dream: Hollywood's Visions of U.S. Decline*. Santa Barbara: Prager Publishing.
Arthur, E. (2004) Where Lester Burnham Falls Down: Exposing the Façade of Victimhood in American Beauty. *Men and Masculinities*, 7(127), pp. 127–143.
Baker, B. (2006) *Masculinity in Fiction and Film: Representing Men in Popular Genres*. London: Bloomsbury.
Baker, B. (2016) *Contemporary Masculinities in Fiction, Film and Television*. London: Bloomsbury.
Bassil-Morozow, H. (2010) *Tim Burton: the Monster and the Crowd, a Post-Jungian Perspective*. London: Routledge.
Bassil-Morozow, H. (2011) *The Trickster in Contemporary Film*. London: Routledge.
Bassil-Morozow, H. (2014) Tim Burton at 50: The Hero's Mid-life Crisis. *International Journal of Jungian Studies*, 6(2), pp. 143–150.
Bassil-Morozow, H. (2015) Analytical Psychology and Cinema. *The Journal of Analytical Psychology*, 60(1), pp. 132–136.
Bassil-Morozow, H., and Hockley, L. (2017) *Jungian Film Studies: The Essential Guide*. London: Routledge.
Baumlin, J.S., Baumlin, T.F., and Jensen, G.H. (2004) *Post-Jungian Criticism: Theory and Practice*. Albany: State University of New York Press.
Beck, B. (2003) Between Their Loved Homes: The Road to Perdition, Sunshine State, and Homeland Security. *Multicultural Perspectives*, 5(2), pp. 24–27.
Benshoff, H.M., and Griffin, S. (2003) *America on Film: Representing Race, Class, Gender, and Sexuality at the Movies*. Oxford: Wiley-Blackwell.
Beynon, J. (2002) *Masculinities and Culture: Issues in Cultural and Media Studies*. Maidenhead: Open University Press.
Biddulph, S. (1995) *Manhood: An Action Plan for Changing Men's Lives*. 2nd edition. Lane Cove: Finch Publishing.
Biddulph, S. (1997) *Raising Boys*. London: Thorsons.
Biddulph, S. (2013) *Raising Girls: Helping Your Daughter to Grow Up Wise, Warm and Strong*. London: Harper Thorsons.
Bingham, D. (1994) *Acting Male: Masculinities in the Films of James Stewart, Jack Nicholson and Clint Eastwood*. New Brunswick, NJ: Rutgers University Press.
Bini, A. (2015) *Male Anxiety and Psychopathology in Film: Comedy Italian Style*. London: Palgrave Macmillan.

## Bibliography

Biskind, P. (1983) *Seeing is Believing: Or How Hollywood Taught Us to Stop Worrying and Love the 50s*. London: Bloomsbury.
Blankenhorn, D. (1995) *Fatherless America: Confronting Our Most Urgent Social Problem*. New York: Harper Collins.
Bly, R. (1990) *Iron John: Men and Masculinity*. 2nd edition. London: Rider.
Bly, R. (1996) *The Sibling Society*. New York: Addison-Wesley.
Bly, R. (1998) *The Maiden King: The Reunion of Masculine and Feminine*. New York: Henry Holt and Company.
Bordwell, D. (1985) *Narration and the Fiction Film*. Madison: University of Wisconsin Press.
Bordwell, D. (1989) The Case for Cognitivism. *Iris*, 9, pp. 11–40.
Bordwell, D., and Carroll, N. (eds.) (1996) *Post-Theory: Reconstructing Film Studies*. Madison: University of Wisconsin Press.
Bruzzi, S. (2005) *Bringing Up Daddy: Fatherhood and Masculinity in Post-war Hollywood*. London: British Film Institute Publishing.
Bruzzi, S. (2013) *Men's Cinema: Masculinity and Mise-En-Scene in Hollywood*. Edinburgh: Edinburgh University Press.
Buckland, W. (2000) *The Cognitive Semiotics of Film*. Cambridge: Cambridge University Press.
Burgess, A. (1997) *Fatherhood Reclaimed: The Making of the Modern Father*. London: Vermilion.
Burrill, D.A. (2014) *The Other Guy: Media Masculinity Within the Margins*. Oxford and New York: Peter Lang Publishing.
Butler, J. (1990) *Gender Trouble: Feminism and the Subversion of Identity*. London: Routledge.
Butler, J. (2004) *Undoing Gender*. London: Routledge.
Campbell, J. (1949, 1993) *The Hero With a Thousand Faces*. London: Fontana Press.
Carmago, S. (2002) Mind the Gap. *Journal of Media and Culture*, 5(5), pp. 1–3.
Cavalli, T. (2013) The Lost Cause. *Jung Journal*, 7(4), pp. 55–59.
Chachere, R. (2003) *American Beauty: Opus I – Jungian Reflections on Literary and Film Classics*. Lafayette: Cypremort Point Press.
Chapman, R., and Rutherford, J. (1987) *Male Order: Unwrapping Masculinity*. London: Lawrence & Wishart.
Charles, L.H. (1951) Drama in First-Naming Ceremonies. *Journal of American Folklore*, 64(251), pp. 11–35.
Charles, M. (2013) On the Conservatism of Post-Jungian Criticism: Competing Concepts of the Symbol in Freud, Jung and Walter Benjamin. *International Journal of Jungian Studies*, 5(2), pp. 120–139.
Charles, M., and Townsend, K. (2011) Full Metal Jarhead: Shifting the Horizon of Expectation. *The Journal of Popular Culture*, 44(5), pp. 915–933.
Chevalier, J., and Gheerbrant, A. (1994) *The Penguin Book of Symbols*. 2nd edition. London: Penguin.
Chopra-Gant, M. (2005) *Hollywood Genres and Postwar America: Masculinity, Family and Nation in Popular Movies and Film Noir*. London and New York: I.B. Tauris.
Clare, A. (2000) *On Men* London: Chatto and Windus.
Clatterbaugh, K. (1997, 1998) *Contemporary Perspectives on Masculinity: Men, Women and Politics in U.S. Society*. Boulder: Westview Press.
Cohan, S. (1997) *Masked Men: Masculinity and Movies in the Fifties*. Bloomington: Indiana University Press.

## Bibliography

Cohan, S., and Hark, I.R. (1993) *Screening the Male: Exploring Masculinities in Hollywood Cinema*. London: Routledge.

Cohen, P. (1972) Subcultural Conflict and Working-Class Community. Working Papers in Cultural Studies, 2 (Spring). CCCS, University of Birmingham.

Colman, W. (2017) Soul in the World: Symbolic Culture as the Medium for Psyche. *Journal of Analytical Psychology*, 62(1), pp. 32–49.

Combe, K., and Boyle, B. (2013) *Masculinity and Monstrosity in Contemporary Hollywood Films*. London: Palgrave Macmillan.

Connell, R.W. (1987, 1991) *Gender and Power: Society, the Person and Sexual Politics*. Cambridge: Polity Press.

Connell, R.W. (1995, 2005) *Masculinities*. Cambridge: Polity Press.

Coon, David R. (2014) *Look Closer: Suburban Narrative and American Values in Film and Television*. New Brunswick: Rutgers University Press.

Cooper, J.C. (1978) *An Illustrated Encyclopaedia of Traditional Symbols*. London: Thames & Hudson.

Corneau, G. (1991) *Absent Fathers, Lost Sons: The Search for Masculine Identity*. Boulder: Shambhala Publications.

Cromb, B. (2007) War Films Without War: The Gulf War at the Movies. *Cinephile*, 3(1), pp. 33–41.

Currie, G. (1995) *Image and Mind: Film, Philosophy and Cognitive Science*. Cambridge: Cambridge University Press.

D'Alisera, J. (1998) Born in the USA: Naming Ceremonies of Infants Among Sierra Leoneans Living in the American Capital. *Anthropology Today*, 14(1), pp. 16–18.

Davies, J., and Smith, C.R. (1998) *Gender, Ethnicity and Sexuality in Contemporary American Film*. Keele: Keele University Press.

Dermott, E. (2008) *Intimate Fatherhood: A Sociological Analysis*. London: Routledge.

Di Lauro, A., and Rabkin, G. (1976) *Dirty Movies: An Illustrated History of the Stag Movie: 1915–1970*. New York: Chelsea House.

Dix, A. (2008) *Beginning Film Studies*. Manchester: Manchester University Press.

Douglas, S.J., and Michaels, M.W. (2004) *The Mommy Myth: The Idealization of Motherhood and How IT Has Undermined Women*. New York: Free Press.

Duncan, A.M. (2015) *Gambling with the Myth of the American Dream*. London: Routledge.

Ehrenreich, B. (2001) *Nickel and Dimed: On (Not) Getting By in America*. New York City: Henry Holt and Company.

Ellis, J. (1982) *Visible Fictions: Cinema: Television: Video*. 2nd edition. London: Routledge.

Faludi, S. (1991) *Backlash: The Undeclared War Against Women*. London: Vintage.

Faludi, S. (2000) *Stiffed: The Betrayal of Modern Man*. London: Vintage.

Farrell, W. (1974) *The Liberated Man*. New York: Random House.

Farrell, W. (1988) *Why Men Are The Way They Are: The Male-Female Dynamic*. New York: McGraw-Hill Publishing.

Farrell, W. (1993) *The Myth of Male Power: Why Men are the Disposable Sex*. New York: Berkeley Books.

Farrell, W. (2001) *Father and Child Reunion: How to Bring the Dads We Need to the Children We Love*. New York: Jeremy P. Tarcher.

Featherstone, B. (2009) *Contemporary Fathering: Theory, Policy and Practice*. London: Policy Press.

Fisher, W.R. (1973) Reaffirmation and Subversion of the American Dream. *Quarterly Journal of Speech*, 59, pp. 160–167.

Fontana, D. (1993) *The Secret Language of Symbols: A Visual Key to Symbols and Their Meanings.* London: Piatkus Books.

Fouz-Hernandez, S. (2009) *Mysterious Skin: Male Bodies in Contemporary Cinema.* London and New York: I B Tauris.

Fradley, M. (2013) *Boys in Trouble? White Masculinity and Paranoia in Contemporary Hollywood Cinema.* Saarbrucken: Scholars Press.

Fredericksen, D. (1979) Jung/Sign/Symbol/Film. In: Hauke, C., and Alister, I. (eds.) *Jung and Film: Post-Jungian Takes on the Moving Image.* Hove: Brunner-Routledge, pp. 17–56.

Fredericksen, D. (2014) Fellini's 8½ and Jung: Narcissism and Creativity in Midlife. *International Journal of Jungian Studies,* 6(2), pp. 133–142.

Freud, S. (1927, 2012) *The Future of an Illusion.* Peterborough, Ontario: Broadview Press.

Freud, S. (1930, 2002) *Civilisation and its Discontents.* London: Penguin Publishing.

Gardner, L. (2015) Post-Jungian Criticism: Theory and Practice; Rhetoric and Kairos: Essays in History, Theory, and Praxis. *International Journal of Jungian Studies,* 7(3), pp. 256–262.

Gavanas, A. (2004) *Fatherhood Politics in the United States: Masculinity, Sexuality, Race, and Marriage.* Champaign: University of Illinois Press.

Gelder, K., and Thornton, S. (2005) *The Subcultures Reader.* 2nd edition. Abingdon and New York: Routledge.

Gerstner, D. (2006) *Manly Arts: Masculinity and Nation in Early American Cinema.* Durham: Duke University Press.

Gilbey, R. (2009) The Revolution That Wasn't. *New Statesman,* 2nd February, p. 47.

Gilmore, D.D. (1991) *Manhood in the Making: Cultural Concepts of Masculinity.* Yale: Yale University Press.

Gold, Stephen N. (2004) Fight Club: A Depiction of Contemporary Society as Dissociogenic. *Journal of Trauma and Dissociation,* 5(2), pp. 13–34.

Goldberg, H. (1974, 1990) *The Hazards of Being Male: Surviving the Myth of Male Privilege.* London: Penguin Publishing.

Goldberg, H. (1991) *What Men Really Want.* New York: Penguin.

Goldberg, H. (2007) *What Men Still Don't Know About Women, Relationships and Love.* Fort Lee: Barricade Books.

Goscilo, H., and Hashamova, Y. (2010) *Cinepaternity: Fathers and Sons in Soviet and Post-Soviet Film.* Bloomington: Indiana University Press.

Goss, B.M. (2002) 'Things Like This Don't Just Happen': Ideology and Paul Thomas Anderson's *Hard Eight, Boogie Nights* and *Magnolia. Journal of Communication Inquiry,* 26(171), pp. 171–192.

Grant, B.K. (2010) *Shadows of Doubt: Negotiations of Masculinity in American Genre Films.* Detroit: Wayne State University Press.

Greven, D. (2013) *Psycho-sexual: Male Desire in Hitchcock, De Palma, Scorsese, and Friedkin.* Austin: University of Texas Press.

Greven, D. (2017) *Ghost Faces: Hollywood and Post-Millennial Masculinity.* Albany: State University of New York Press.

Grodal, T. (1999) *Moving Pictures: A New Theory of Film Genres, Feelings, and Cognition.* Cary, NC: Oxford University Press.

Grodal, T. (2009) *Embodied Visions: Evolution, Emotion, Culture, and Film.* Cary, NC: Oxford University Press.

Gronstad, A. (2008) *Transfigurations: Violence, Death and Masculinity in American Cinema.* Amsterdam: Amsterdam University Press.

Gunn, J., and Frentz, T. (2010) Fighting for Father: *Fight Club* as Cinematic Psychosis. *Western Journal of Communication,* 74(3), pp. 269–291.
Gutmann, D. (1997) Rake's Progress. *Newsweek,* 11th September, New York City.
Halberstam, J. (2005) *In a Queer Time and Place: Transgender Bodies, Subcultural Lives.* Albany: New York University Press.
Hall, M. (2005) *Teaching Men and Film.* London: British Film Institute.
Hall, S., and Jefferson, T. (eds.) (1976) *Resistance through Rituals: Youth Subcultures in Post-war Britain.* 8th edition. London: Routledge.
Hamad, H. (2014) *Postfeminism and Paternity in Contemporary U.S. Film: Framing Fatherhood.* Abingdon: Routledge.
Harwood, S. (1997) *Family Fictions: Representations of the Family in 1980s Hollywood Cinema.* London: Palgrave Macmillan.
Hauke, C. (2000) *Jung and the Postmodern: The Interpretation of Realities.* London: Brunner-Routledge.
Hauke, C. (2005) *Human Being Human: Culture and the Soul.* Abingdon: Routledge.
Hauke, C. (2014) *Visible Mind: Movies, Modernity and the Unconscious.* Hove: Routledge.
Hauke, C., and Alister, I. (2001) *Jung and Film: Post-Jungian Takes on the Moving Image.* Hove: Brunner-Routledge.
Hauke, C., and Hockley, L. (2011) *Jung and Film II: The Return – Further Post-Jungian Takes on the Moving Image.* Hove: Routledge.
Hemmings, C. (2017) *Be A Man: How Macho Culture Damages Us and How To Stop It.* London: Biteback Publishing.
Henderson, J. (1984) *Cultural Attitudes in Psychological Perspective.* Toronto: Inner City Books.
Henderson, J. (2000) Jungian Analysis: An Elder's Perspective. *Psychological Perspectives: A Quarterly Journal of Jungian Thought,* 41(1), pp. 10–21.
Herzog, J.M. (1980) Sleep Disturbance and Father Hunger in 18-to-28-month-old Boys. In: Solnit et al. (eds.) *Psychoanalytic Study of the Child,* 35, pp. 223–230.
Herzog, J.M. (1983) *Father Hunger: Explorations with Adults and Children.* 2nd edition. London: Routledge.
Heyraud, J.K. (2000a) American Beauty. *Psychological Perspectives: A Quarterly Journal of Jungian Thought,* 40(1), pp. 144–148.
Heyraud, J.K. (2000b) Magnolia. *Psychological Perspectives: A Quarterly Journal of Jungian Thought,* 41(1), pp. 143–147.
Heyraud, J.K. (2008) There Will be Blood. *Psychological Perspectives: A Quarterly Journal of Jungian Thought,* 51(1), pp. 179–180.
Hobson, B. (2002) *Making Men into Fathers: Men, Masculinities and the Social Politics of Fatherhood.* Cambridge: Cambridge University Press.
Hockley, L. (2001) *Cinematic Projections: The Analytical Psychology of C.G Jung and Film Theory.* Luton: University of Luton Press.
Hockley, L. (2007) *Frames of Mind: A Post-Jungian Look at Cinema, Television and Technology.* Bristol: Intellect Books.
Hockley, L. (2013) *Somatic Cinema: The Relationship between Body and Screen – a Jungian Perspective.* London: Routledge.
Hockley, L. (2015) Jungian Screen Studies: 'Everything is Awesome?' *International Journal of Jungian Studies,* 7(1), pp. 55–66.
Hockley, L. (ed.) (2018) *The Routledge International Handbook of Jungian Film Studies.* London: Routledge.

Hoggart, R. (1957) *The Uses of Literacy: Aspects of Working Class Life*. London: Penguin Books.
Holmlund, C. (2001) *Impossible Bodies: Femininity and Masculinity at the Movies*. London: Routledge.
Homans, P. (1979, 1995) *Jung in Context: Modernity and the Making of a Psychology*. London and Chicago: University of Chicago Press.
Horrocks, R. (1994) *Masculinity in Crisis: Myths, Fantasies and Realities*. London: Palgrave Macmillan.
Iaccino, J. (1994) *Psychological Reflections on Cinematic Terror: Jungian Archetypes in Horror Films*. Westport: Greenwood Press.
Iaccino, J. (1998) *Jungian Reflections Within the Cinema: A Psychological Analysis of Sci-Fi and Fantasy Archetypes*. Westport: Praeger.
Iocco, Melissa. (2007) Addicted to Affliction: Masculinity and Perversity in *Crash* and *Fight Club*. Gothic Studies, 9(1), pp. 46–56.
Izod, J. (2000) Active Imagination and the Analysis of Film. *Journal of Analytical Psychology*, 45, pp. 267–285.
Izod, J. (2001) *Myth, Mind and the Screen: Understanding the Heroes of Our Time*. Cambridge: Cambridge University Press.
Izod, J. (2006) *Screen, Culture, Psyche: A Post-Jungian Approach to Working With the Audience*. Hove: Routledge.
Janssen, D.F. (2007) Male Initiation: Imagining Ritual Necessity. *Journal of Men, Masculinities and Spirituality*, 1(3), pp. 215–234.
Jenks, C. (2005) *Subcultures: The Fragmentation of the Social*. Thousand Oaks: SAGE Publications.
Joosten, E. (2011) Digital Ghosts: The Lingering Presence of Vietnam in Films of Modern Warfare. *Kino: The Western Undergraduate Journal of Film Studies*, 2(1), pp. 1–7.
Jung, C.G. (1933, 2001) *Modern Man in Search of a Soul*. Abingdon: Routledge.
Jung, C.G. (1940) 'The psychology of the child archetype'. *The Collected Works of C.G. Jung*, Vol 9i, Princeton, NJ: Princeton University Press.
Jung, C.G. (1954) *Collected Works 17: Development of Personality*. London: Routledge and Kegan Paul.
Jung, C.G. (1964) *Man and His Symbols*. London: Aldus Books.
Jung, C.G. (1966) *Collected Works 15: Spirit in Man, Art and Literature*. London: Routledge and Kegan Paul.
Jung, C.G. (1967) *Collected Works 7: Two Essays on Analytical Psychology*. London: Routledge and Kegan Paul.
Jung, C.G. (1969) *Collected Works 8: Structure and Dynamics of the Psyche*. London: Routledge and Kegan Paul.
Jung, C.G. (1970) *Collected Works 10: Civilisation in Transition*. London: Routledge and Kegan Paul.
Jung, C.G. (1989) *Aspects of the Masculine*. London: Routledge.
Jung, C.G. (2009) *The Red Book*. Zurich: Philemon Foundation & W.W. Norton & Co.
Jung, C.G. (2014) *Analytical Psychology*. London: Routledge.
Karlyn, K.R. (2004) 'Too Close for Comfort': *American Beauty* and the Incest Motif. *Cinema Journal*, 44(1), pp. 69–93.
Keen, S. (1991) *Fire in the Belly: On Being a Man*. New York: Bantam Books.
Kimmel, M.S. (ed.) (1995) *The Politics of Manhood: Profeminist Men Respond to the Mythopoetic Men's Movement (and the Mythopoetic Leaders Answer)*. Philadelphia: Temple University Press.

Kimmel, M.S. (2000) *The Gendered Society*. Oxford: Oxford University Press.
Kimmel, M.S. (2009) *Guyland: The Perilous World Where Boys Become Men*. New York: HarperTorch Publishing.
Kimmel, M.S. (2015) *Angry White Men: American Masculinity at the End of an Era*. New York: Nation Books.
King, G. (2002) *New Hollywood Cinema: An Introduction*. London: I B Tauris.
King, G. (2005) *American Independent Cinema*. London: I B Tauris.
King, G. (2009) *Indiewood, USA: Where Hollywood Meets Independent Cinema*. London: I B Tauris.
Kirkham, P., and Thumim, J. (eds.) (1993) *You Tarzan: Masculinity, Movies and Men*. London: Lawrence & Wishart.
Konow, D. (2000) PTA Meeting: An Interview with Paul Thomas Anderson. *Creative Screenwriting*, 7(1), p. 48.
Kord, S., and Krimmer, E. (2011) *Contemporary Hollywood Masculinities: Gender, Genre, and Politics*. New York: Palgrave Macmillan.
Kryzwinska, T. (2006) *Sex and the Cinema*. New York City: Wallflower Press.
Lee, J. (1991) *At My Father's Wedding: Reclaiming Our True Masculinity*. London: Piatkus Books.
Lehman, P. (1998) *Boogie Nights*: Will the Real Dirk Diggler Please Stand up? *Jump Cut: A Review of Contemporary Media*, 42, pp. 32–38.
Lehman, P. (2001) *Masculinities: Bodies, Movies and Culture*. London: BFI/Routledge.
Lehman, P. (2007) *Running Scared: Masculinity and the Representation of the Male Body*. Detroit: Wayne State University Press.
Leonard, G. (2010) Tears of Joy: Hollywood Melodrama, Ecstasy, and Restoring Meta-Narratives of Transcendence in Modernity. *University of Toronto Quarterly*, 79(2), pp. 819–837.
Levinson, J. (2012) *The American Success Myth on Film*. Basingstoke: Palgrave Macmillan.
Lizardo, O. (2007) *Fight Club*, or the Cultural Contradictions of Late Capitalism. *Journal for Cultural Research*, 11(3), pp. 221–243
Lupton, D., and Barclay, L. (1997) *Constructing Fatherhood: Discourses and Experiences*. London: Sage Publications.
Mac an Ghaill, M. (1994) *Making of Men: Masculinities, Sexualities and Schooling*. London: Open University Press.
Magnuson, E. (2007) *Changing Men, Transforming Culture: Inside the Men's Movement*. Boulder: Paradigm Publishers.
Maine, M. (2004) *Father Hunger: Fathers, Daughters and the Pursuit of Thinness*. Carlsbad: Gurze Books.
McQuillan, D.B., and McQuillan, M. (2008) There Will Be Blood. *Journal of Feminist Family Therapy*, 20(3), pp. 271–273.
Merleau-Ponty, M. (1945, 2013) *Phenomenology of Perception*. London: Routledge.
Merleau-Ponty, M. (1964) *Sense and Non-Sense*. Evanston: Northwestern University Press.
Mitchell, J. (1974) *Psychoanalysis and Feminism: A Radical Reassessment of Psychoanalysis*. New York: Basic Books.
Mitscherlich, A. (1974) *Society Without the Father: A Contribution to Social Psychology*. Lanham, MD: Jason Aronson.
Modleski, T. (1991) *Feminism Without Women: Culture and Criticism in a "Postfeminist" Age*. London and New York: Routledge.
Moir, A., and Moir, B. (1998) *Why Men Don't Iron: The Real Science of Gender Studies*. London: HarperCollins.

Monick, E.A. (1987) *Phallos: Sacred Image of the Masculine*. Toronto: Inner City Books.
Moore, R., and Gillette, D. (1990) *King Warrior Magician Lover: Rediscovering the Archetypes of the Mature Masculine*. New York: Harper Collins.
Moore, R., and Gillette, D. (1992) *The King Within: Accessing the King in the Male Psyche*. New York: William Morrow and Company.
Morag, R. (2009) *Defeated Masculinity: Post-Traumatic Cinema in the Aftermath of War*. Oxford: Peter Lang Publishing.
Mulvey, L. (1975, 1989) *Visual and Other Pleasures*. London: Palgrave Macmillan.
Narloch, J. (2008) *Facets of the American Dream and American Nightmare in Film*. Duisberg-Essen: GRIN Publishing.
Neale, S. (1983) 'Masculinity as Spectacle' *Screen*, Volume 24, Issue 6, Nov-Dec 1983, Pages 2–17.
Neale, S. (1993) Masculinity as Spectacle. In: Kirkham, P., and Thumim, J. (eds.) *You Tarzan: Masculinity, Movies and Men*. London: Lawrence & Wishart, pp. 9–20.
Noll, R. (1994) *The Jung Cult: Origins of a Charismatic Movement*. Princeton: Princeton University Press.
Noll, R. (1997) *The Aryan Christ: The Secret Life of Carl Jung*. New York: Random House.
O'Rawe, C. (2014) *Stars and Masculinities in Contemporary Italian Cinema*. London: Palgrave Macmillan.
Ortner, S.B. (2013) *Not Hollywood: Independent Film at the Twilight of the American Dream*. Durham: Duke University Press.
Osteen, M. (2012) *Nightmare Alley: Film Noir and the American Dream*. Baltimore: Johns Hopkins University Press.
O'Toole, L. (1998) *Pornocopia: Porn, Sex, Technology and Desire*. London: Serpent's Tail.
Oxoby, M. (2002) Road to Perdition. Film & History. *An Interdisciplinary Journal of Film and Television Studies*, 32(2), pp. 110–112.
Peberdy, D. (2011) *Masculinity and Film Performance: Male Angst in Contemporary American Cinema*. Basingstoke: Palgrave Macmillan.
Perry, G. (2016) *The Descent of Man*. London: Penguin Publishing.
Pfeil, F. (1995) *White Guys: Studies in Postmodern Domination and Difference*. London: Verso.
Pittman, F. (1994) *Man Enough: Fathers, Sons and the Search for Masculinity*. New York: TarcherPerigee.
Pomerance, M. (2001) *Ladies and Gentlemen, Boys and Girls: Gender in Film at the End of the Twentieth Century*. New York: State University of New York Press.
Pomerance, M., and Gateward, F. (eds.) (2005) *Where the Boys Are: Cinemas of Masculinity and Youth*. Detroit: Wayne State.
Potash, J.S. (2015) Archetypal Aesthetics: Viewing Art through States of Consciousness. *International Journal of Jungian Studies*, 7(2), pp. 139–153.
Powrie, P. (1997) *French Cinema in the 1980s: Nostalgia and the Crisis in Masculinity*. Oxford: OUP.
Powrie, P., Davies, A., and Babington, B. (2004) *The Trouble with Men: Masculinities in European and Hollywood Cinema*. London: Wallflower Press.
Rehling, N. (2009) *Extra-Ordinary Men: White Heterosexual Masculinity in Contemporary Popular Cinema*. Plymouth: Lexington Books.
Reiter, G. (2008) *Fathers and Sons in Cinema*. Jefferson: McFarland and Company.
Richardson, C. (2010) The Empty Self, or How I Learned to Stop Worrying and Love the Blonde. *European Journal of American Culture*, 29(1), pp. 5–17.
Rigoletto, Sergio. (2014) *Masculinity and Italian Cinema: Sexual Politics, Social Conflict and Male Crisis in the 1970s*. Edinburgh: Edinburgh University Press.

Robinson, S. (2000) *Marked Men: White Masculinity in Crisis*. New York: Columbia University Press.
Ronnberg, A., and Martin, K. (2010) *The Book of Symbols: Reflections on Archetypal Images*. Cologne: Taschen.
Rosen, M. (1973) *Popcorn Venus: Women, Movies and the American Dream*. New York: Avon Publishing.
Rowland, S. (ed.) (2008) *Psyche and the Arts: Jungian Approaches to Music, Architecture, Literature, Painting and Film*. Abingdon: Routledge.
Rowland, S. (2013) *American Soul: A Cultural Narrative* by Schenk, R. *International Journal of Jungian Studies*, 5(3), pp. 264–267.
Rushing, J.H., and Frentz, T.S. (1989) The Frankenstein Myth in Contemporary Cinema. *Critical Studies in Mass Communications*, 6(1), pp. 61–80.
Samuels, A. (1985a) *Jung and the Post-Jungians*. London: Routledge and Keegan Paul.
Samuels, A. (1985b) *The Father: Contemporary Jungian Perspectives*. New York: New York University Press.
Samuels, A. (1989) *The Plural Psyche: Personality, Morality and the Father*. London: Routledge.
Samuels, A. (1993) *The Political Psyche*. London: Routledge.
Samuels, A., Shorter, B., and Plaut, F. (1986) *A Critical Dictionary of Jungian Analysis*. London: Routledge.
Sands, Z. (2017) *Film Comedy and the American Dream*. London: Routledge.
Schwalbe, M. (1996) *Unlocking the Iron Cage: Men's Movement, Gender Politics and American Culture*. Oxford: Oxford University Press.
Schwartz, S.E. (2009) Puella's Shadow. *International Journal of Jungian Studies*, 1(2), pp. 111–122.
Segal, L. (1990) *Slow Motion: Changing Masculinities, Changing Men*. 3rd edition. London: Virago.
Seidler, V.J. (1989) *Rediscovering Masculinity: Reason, Language and Sexuality*. London: Routledge.
Seidler, V.J. (1997) *Man Enough: Embodying Masculinities*. London: Sage Publications.
Seidler, V.J. (2005) *Transforming Masculinities*. London: Routledge.
Shapiro, H. (2003) *Shooting Stars: Drugs, Hollywood and the Movies*. London: Serpent's Tail.
Shary, T. (ed.) (2013) *Millennial Masculinity: Men in Contemporary American Cinema*. Detroit: Wayne State University Press.
Shaviro, S. (1993) *Cinematic Body: Theory Out of Bounds*. Minneapolis: University of Minnesota Press.
Shaviro, S. (2010) *Post Cinematic Affect*. Ropley, Hants: Zero Books.
Shwalb, D.W., Shwalb, B.J., and Lamb, M.E. (2012) *Fathers in Cultural Context*. London: Routledge.
Singer, T., and Kimbles, S.L. (2004) *The Cultural Complex: Contemporary Perspectives on Psyche and Society*. Hove: Routledge.
Singh, G. (2009) *Film After Jung: Post-Jungian Approaches to Film Theory*. Hove: Routledge.
Singh, G. (2014) *Feeling Film: Affect and Authenticity in Popular Cinema*. Hove: Routledge.
Smith, T.R. (1992) *Walking Swiftly: Writings and Images on the Occasion of Robert Bly's 65th Birthday*. St Paul: Ally Press.
Sobchack, V. (2004) *Carnal Thoughts: Embodiment and Moving Image Culture*. Oakland: University of California Press.
Sperb, J. (2013) *Blossoms & Blood: Postmodern Media Culture and the Films of Paul Thomas Anderson*. Austin: University of Texas Press.

Stacey, J. (1994) *Star-Gazing: Hollywood Cinema and Female Spectatorship*. Abingdon: Routledge.
Stam, R. (2000) *Film Theory: An Introduction*. Oxford: Blackwell Publishing.
Stevens, A. (1990a) *Archetype: A Natural History of the Self*. London: Routledge.
Stevens, A. (1990b) *On Jung*. London: Routledge.
Stevens, A. (1994) *Jung: A Very Short Introduction*. Oxford: Oxford University Press.
Stevens, A. (1998) *Ariadne's Clue: A Guide to the Symbols of Humankind*. Princeton, NJ: Princeton University Press.
Storr, A. (1983) *The Essential Jung: Selected Writings*. London: Fontana Press.
Strauss, N. (2005) *The Game*. London: Canongate Books.
Sullivan, M. (1996) The Analytic Initiation: The Effect of the Archetype of Initiation on the Personal Unconscious. *Journal of Analytical Psychology*, 41, pp. 509–527.
Ta, Lynn, M. (2006) Hurt So Good: *Fight Club*, Masculine Violence, and the Crisis of Capitalism. *Journal of American Culture*, 29(3), pp. 265–277.
Tacey, D. (1997) *Remaking Men: Jung, Spirituality and Social Change*. London: Routledge.
Tacey, D. (2006) *How To Read Jung*. London: Granta.
Tasker, Y. (1993) *Spectacular Bodies: Gender, Genre and the Action Cinema*. London: Routledge.
Thomas, D. (1993) *Not Guilty: In Defence of the Modern Man*. London: Weidenfeld and Nicolson.
Tincknell, E. (2005) *Mediating the Family: Gender, Culture and Representation*. London: Hodder Arnold.
Trice, A.D., and Holland, S.A. (2001) *Heroes, Antiheroes and Dolts: Portrayals of Masculinity in American Popular Films 1921–1999*. Jefferson: McFarland & Company Inc.
Urwin, J. (2017) *Man Up: Surviving Modern Masculinity*. London: Icon Books.
Van Leeuwen, M.S., McCloughry, R., and Storkey, E. (2003) *Fathers and Sons: The Search for a New Masculinity*. Downers Grove: Inter-Varsity Press.
Waddell, T. (2006) *Mis/takes: Archetype, Myth and Identity in Screen Fiction*. London: Routledge.
Walsh, F. (2010) *Male Trouble: Masculinity and the Performance of Crisis*. London: Palgrave Macmillan.
Waxman, S. (2005) *Rebels on the Backlot: Six Maverick Directors and How They Conquered the Hollywood Studio System*. New York: HarperEntertainment.
Webb, R. (2017) *How Not To Be a Boy*. London: Canongate.
Williams, L. (1999) *Hard Core: Power, Pleasure, and the "Frenzy of the Visible"*. Berkeley. University of California Press.
Williams, R. (1961) *The Long Revolution*. London: Chatto and Windus.
Williamson, M. (2004) The Importance of Fathers in Relation to their Daughters' Psychosexual Development. *Psychodynamic Practice*, 10(2), pp. 207–219.
Winn, J.E. (2007) *The American Dream and Contemporary Hollywood Cinema*. New York: Continuum.
Winnicott, D.W. (1973) *The Child, The Family and the Outside World*. London: Penguin Books.
Yates, C. (2007) *Masculine Jealousy and Contemporary Cinema*. London: Palgrave Macmillan.
Zipes, J. (1979, 2002) *Breaking the Magic Spell: Radical Theories of Folk & Fairy Tales*. Lexington: University Press Kentucky.

# Index

Note: Page numbers followed by 'n' indicate a note.

*About A Boy* 149–50
absent father 15, 57, 80, 143; generational betrayal 81–4; lost rural father 86–9
abusive father 80, 146
adequate parenting 45, 46
adjectival masculinities 22
affect 27, 33
*Affliction* 47
alcohol 144
Alger, Horatio 55
Alister, I. 40, 49, 52, 94
*American Beauty* 7, 47, 56, 57, 61–5, 75, 76, 79, 100, 103, 107–8, 109, 111, 114, 115–25, 133, 145–6, 150, 152n7
American culture 5, 51, 53–7, 128, 145
American Dream 4, 5, 43, 49, 50, 54, 55, 59, 71, 82, 90, 145, 147; and cinema 59; and cultural complex 57; cultural myth of 99; dangers of 100; elements of success and failure with regard to 56; and gambling 65; geographical and social locations 85; as multi-generational immigrant dream 95–6; myths 55, 59, 99; as parental ambitions 157; and paternal theme 56; self-invention aspect of 147; short-circuiting 56–7; shortcuts to achieving 131; and social mobility 97; and spiritual awareness 60; success myth 59, 102; and survival 85
American father *see* father(s)/father-figure
*American Success Myth on Film, The* 59
Anderson, Paul Thomas 1, 46, 47, 48, 64, 66, 70, 72–3, 88, 89, 90, 94, 95, 103, 125, 127, 128, 129, 130, 131, 132, 133, 139, 141, 142, 147, 148, 151, 152n16
Anderson, Wes 2, 46

anima 40, 41, 64, 103, 111–14, 117–21, 150
animus 40, 41, 103, 111, 112, 114
*Apocalypse Now* 134
archetypal dark father behaviour 72
archetypal images 32, 33, 36, 37, 39, 42, 44
archetypal journey 77
archetypal masculine 41, 90
archetype(s) 32, 36, 158; of the child 48; classical Jungian school definitions 38–9; concept of 37–40; contrasexuality 41; and cultural complexes 53; and the daughter 111–14; discernibility 39; energies of 41–2; evolutionary and universal 37; of father 40–2; forms of 44; function of 40; misuse of the term 37; of the shadow 49–50; and stereotypes 113, 158; structures of 45; unconscious 37; undefinable 37
*Ariadne's Clue* 74
Arnold, G.B. 55
Arthur, E. 124
Ashes/ashes 140–1
*Aspects of the Masculine* 40
*At My Father's Wedding* 131
audience, archetypal affective response of 33
*Away We Go* 153, 156–9, 157

Babington, B. 11
*Baby Boom* 55
balanced father 156–9
Ball, Alan 108, 109, 117, 120
baptism 70–1
Barclay, L. 23
Bassil-Morozow, H. 3, 4, 29, 31, 32, 36, 49, 52, 58n1, 60–1, 70, 94, 101, 104, 105, 113, 114, 118–19, 153

Baudrillard, J. 134, 152n14
Baumlin, J.S. 32, 33
*Be a Man* 25
Beck, B. 67
Beebe, John 34
belief system 30
Beynon, J. 11, 21, 22
Biddulph, S. 19, 46, 47, 78, 80, 86, 105, 131, 135, 140
biological father 151n3
blood symbolism 123
Bly, Robert 4, 6n1, 11, 12, 13, 15, 17–18, 20, 24, 25n5, 26n6, 41, 42, 47, 80, 86, 99, 105, 117, 130, 135, 136, 140, 152n9, 152n17
*Boogie Nights* 1, 46, 47, 56, 65, 88, 89–95, 125–30, 151, 152n11
Bordwell, D. 27
*Breaking Bad* 155
*Bringing Up Daddy: Fatherhood and Masculinity in Post-War Hollywood* 7, 11
*Broken Blossoms* 7
*Bronx Tale, A* 89, 95–100, 153, 154
Brooke, Roger 39
Broyles, William, Jnr 134
Bruzzi, Stella 1, 7, 8, 11, 12, 14, 16, 18, 46, 47, 54, 75, 78, 89, 100, 107, 108, 109, 119, 128, 142, 144, 145, 151, 153, 157
Buckland, W. 27
Burgess, A. 23
Butler, Judith 9, 13

Campbell, Joseph 67
Carmago, S. 132, 139, 143
*Catch Me If You Can* 5, 56, 146–7
Chachere, Richard 108, 116, 117, 118
Chapman, R. 23
Charles, M. 5, 31, 101n6
chauvinism 71, 159
Chevalier, J. 48, 91, 140
Child/child: anima and the inadequate paternal 115–25; archetype of 48, 101, 102, 103, 125, 132, 149, 150; body of 132; as a catalyst for father hunger 149; development, psychologically potentialised 44; and erotic paternal 110–11; exploitation 125–38; futurity 103; male and female children within American cinema 150–1; rebellious child 145–9; wounded child 139–45
Chopra-Gant, M. 13
Clare, A. 19

classical Jungian school 38, 39
Clatterbaugh, Kenneth 22–3
Clinton, Bill 80
cognitive theory 3, 27–8
cognitivism 27–8, 35
Cohen, P. 8
collective unconscious 39, 52
Collins, Max Allan 66
Colman, W. 31
community, Shadow or negative side of 98, 99
complex, definition of 52
Connell, R.W. 2, 9, 20, 22, 54, 149
conscious gender performance 13
consumerism 81
contrasexual archetypes 41, 113
Coon, David 61, 96, 98, 99
Cooper, J.C. 48, 74, 91, 119, 141
Corneau, G. 19
*Courage Under Fire* 134
culture 22, 50; cultural complexes 50, 53, 62, 64, 79, 95, 151, 154, 158; cultural individuation 154; cultural initiation 83; cultural myths 151; cultural psychic buffer zone 51; cultural shifts 51; cultural unconscious 13, 33, 50–2, 50–4, 52–4, 62, 64, 77, 79–80
Currie, G. 27

D'Alisera, J. 101n6
dark father figure 47, 89
dark psychic resonance 83
daughter(s) 150; and archetypes 111–14; body of 115; and father, developmental relationship between 103; and the father's body 106–9; and paternal 'otherness' 104–6; potential 75; psychological pluralism 110; puberty 108; relationship with the mother 105; and syzygy 113, 114
Davies, J. 11
Davis, Oliver 32
deadbeat dads 80
*Deep Throat* 101n5
Dermott, E. 23
*Descent of Man, The* 25
*Die Hard* series 9
dis-initiation 22, 83, 133, 135, 137, 149
Dix, A. 8, 22
dogma 30
doorway symbolism 122–3
drug 73, 84, 94–5, 126–7, 129, 144
Duncan, A. M. 55

## Index

Edinger, Edward 35
Electra complex 128, 152n10
Eliade, Mircea 135
Ellis, J. 8
emotional hunger 76
equal opportunities 85
*Eros* 86, 123
erotic paternal 110–11
erotic playback 74, 110, 111, 122, 150
*Executive Suite* 78
exploited child: in *Boogie Nights* 125–30; in *Jarhead* 133–8; in *Magnolia* 130–3
*Extra-Ordinary Men* 12

Faludi, Susan 11, 24
familial conflicts 88
*Fargo* 5
Farrell, Warren 17, 63
father-energy 105
fatherhood 2, 10–12, 149, 157; definition of 14; external pressures 23; and gender 41; gender perspectives on 30; as performance 12–14; and potential redemption 48
father hunger 1, 2, 6n1, 11, 14–19, 57, 59, 60, 75–7, 80, 82, 89–90, 111, 114, 115, 128, 129, 139, 142, 146–50, 155, 157, 158; as an archetypal need 42–6; cause and effect of 46–7; collective level 42; and crisis in masculinity 46; of daughter 108–9; of daughters 104; fathering 48; for feminine 106; and gender imagery 103; and guilt 66; impact on American film 42; individual level 42; and masculine development 101; non-recognition of 130; from point view of father 64–6; as a psychological response 43; and shadow patriarchy 70–2; surrogate fathers 86; and violence 66
*Father Hunger* 108
*Fathers and Sons in Cinema* 11, 80
father(s)/father-figure 1, 4, 7, 13, 43, 53, 54, 55, 59, 158; abusive father 80, 146; ambivalent nature of 78; archetype of 24, 38, 40–2; binary-role masculine privileges 78; body of, and daughters 106–9; child's identification with 44; cultural complex 54; cultural shadow 54; dark father 70–2; and daughters 103; and daughter's psyche 73; desires 107–8; erotic presence, for the daughter 115; and fatherhood within film 10–12;

within the family 23; figure of 23; as figure of power 68; and gender 46; heterosocial role 79; individuation 44; lack of presence of 17; location of 96; and *Logos* 70; masculine figure 2; masculinity 54; and masculinity 46–8; mythologisation of 42; as a national symbol 15–16; negative father complex 72–5; Otherness of 105; portraying as being sexual or sexualised 128; position within the psyche 47; positive father 158; presence by their absence 57; presence of 145, 150; role in film, confusion about 16; roles of 43, 54; and self/Self 47; social position of 23; in social structure 10; societally approved role 79; as the *sole* source of masculinity 47; son's conflict with 14; space in terms of home and workplace 62; symbolic portfolio 57; transcendence of 16; wound 19
father-widower 15
Featherstone, B. 23
female psyche 5, 105–6
feminine/femininity 8, 157; acting as father 85; analyses of 113
feminism 19, 23
Ferenczi, Sandor 27
Fifties Man 18
*Fight Club* 57, 80, 81–4, 100, 153
filmolinguistic theory 27
Fincher, David 80, 81
fire 97
*First Blood* 134
Fisher, W.R. 55
Flying Dutchman quest 45
Fontana, D. 70
Fouz-Hernandez, S. 10
Fradley, M. 10
*Frankenstein Myth, The* 157
Fredericksen, Don 35, 36, 58n6, 61, 129, 142, 154
Frentz, T.S. 82, 83, 157
Freud, Sigmund 16, 28, 44, 67, 152n1
Freudian unconscious 39
Freudian view of symbols 30
frogs 74, 75, 150–1
*Frozen River* 41, 86–9, 100, 153
*Full Metal Jacket* 134, 135

*Game, The* 152n16
Gardner, L. 31

Gavanas, A. 23
gender: construction 14; discourses 2, 7; essentialism 8; issues 4; journey 104–5; performances 9, 13, 17, 114; pluralism 2; roles 17, 46, 47, 114; studies 17; syzygy 41, 113, 114, 157; as unconscious and conscious performance 13
Gerstner, D. 11
Gheerbrant, A. 48, 91, 140
Gilbey, Ryan 80
Gillette, D. 19, 117
Gilmore, David 21
Goddard, Jean-Luc 34
Goldberg, Herb 17, 79
Golden Age of Porn 90, 101n5
good enough parents 45, 105, 115, 156
Goss, B.M. 65, 87, 127
Granik, Debra 84
*Great Gatsby, The* 147
*Great Santini, The* 142
Greenfield, Barbara 41
grey color 76, 80
Griffiths, D.W. 7
Gronstad, A. 81
group consciousness 50
*Guardian Weekend* 24
Gunn, J. 82, 83
guns, as paternal symbol 57

Halberstam, J. 88
Hamad, H. 12, 14, 15, 67, 71
*Happiness* 47, 56, 102, 144–5, 145, 151
*Hard Eight* 56, 64–6, 72, 88, 89
Hark, I.R. 8
Harwood, S. 10
Hauke, C. 4, 31, 32, 39, 40, 49, 52, 94, 114
hegemonic masculinities 2, 20, 22, 54
Hemmings, Chris 25
*Heroes, Anti-heroes and Dolts* 11
Herzog, James 6n1, 17, 43, 106, 111
heteronormative American society 64
heterosocial society 76
Heyraud, J.K. 70, 71, 72, 76, 117
Hobson, B. 23, 24
Hockley, L. 3, 4, 29, 31, 32, 33–4, 36, 39, 40, 42–3, 44, 45, 49, 51, 52, 60–1, 70, 94, 103, 104, 105, 113, 114, 118–19, 153
Holland, S.A. 11
Holmes, John 101n4
Holmlund, C. 10
Homans, P. 31
*How Not to Be a Boy* 25
hypermasculinity 139, 141

*Ice Storm, The* 143–4
identity theft 147
image, importance of 31–4
*Independent on Sunday* 24
Indiewood 2, 5, 125, 130
individual psyche 13, 24, 30, 33, 39, 50, 113
individuation 29, 30, 42, 43–4, 58n5, 103, 105, 118, 157
initiation 22, 137, 148; archetypal process of 134; cultural initiation 83; dis-initiation 22, 83, 133, 135, 137, 149; mis-initiation 22, 133, 135, 149; rite of passage of 21; and wound 135–6
innate individuative journey 150
intermediate psychic zone 50
*Iron John* 12, 17, 19, 26n5, 26n6, 47, 140, 152n9
Izod, J. 34, 38–9, 41, 50–1, 100, 113, 154

Janssen, D.F. 138
*Jarhead* 47, 57, 133–8, 148
Jeffords, Susan 10–11
Jeffries, Ross 152n16
*Johnny Wadd* series 101n4
Joosten, E. 134
Jung, Carl 21, 29, 30, 31, 36, 43, 67, 99, 106, 113, 118, 157; archetypes 37; on archetypes 111–12; definition of archetype 37; definition of psychological and visionary art 30, 100, 156; definition of shadow 49, 94; definition of archetypal image 34; emphasis on the image 32; on gender archetypes 40; on importance of image 31; on individuation 43; on psychological images 44; symbolic approach 4, 60–1; on unknowable 35
Jungian concepts 28–31

Karlyn, K.R. 71, 124
Keen, S. 19, 86
Kimbles, S.L. 53, 54
Kimmel, M.S. 22
King, G. 64, 91, 124, 152n5, 152n7
Kirkham, P. 8, 9, 10, 12
Konow, D. 88
Kord, S. 7, 10, 15–16, 46
Krimmer, E. 7, 10, 15–16, 46

Lacan, Jacques 28, 99
lakes 69
late-capital culture 51

# Index

Lee, Ang 143
Lee, J. 19
Lee, John 131
Lehman, Peter 10, 11, 95, 136
Lennihan, Lydia 50
Levinson, J. 59, 63
*Life Aquatic, The* 46
*Live from Baghdad* 134
Logos 86, 99, 106, 112, 148
Lupton, D. 23

*Magnolia* 46, 47, 56–7, 66, 70, 72–5, 88, 100, 103, 111, 114, 125, 130–3, 133, 139–43, 150, 151
*Maiden King, The: The Reunion of Masculine and Feminine* 25n5, 41
Maine, Margo 108–9, 115, 151n4
male anxiety and the body, transposition of 9
male body, cinematic representations of 10
male mother 133, 136–7, 138
male movements 25n2
maleness 126
male psyche 5, 15, 105–6
male sexuality 126
male victimhood 12
*Manhood* 79
*Man in the Gray Flannel Suit, The* 78
*Manly Arts* 11
*Man Up* 25
Martin, K. 69, 71, 74, 76, 84, 90, 93, 121, 122, 129, 132, 140–1
masculine/masculinities 2, 66, 75; aspects of national cinema 10; as becoming 23; caring masculinity 158; and cinema 7–10; of civil rights, feminism and gay liberation 18; and conflict with father 14; as a continuum 47; crisis in 2–3, 10, 18, 25n4, 46, 83; as cultural performances 8; demarcation of 9; depictions of 9; erotic potential of 111; families and anxieties around 10; and father-daughter relationship 104; and father-figure 46–8; as a gender continuum 11; gender perspectives on 30; individuative masculine 157; journey of the father-son relationships 100; later developmental stage of 86; masculine continuum 2, 41, 86, 100, 104, 139, 149; masculine cultural complex 54; masculine dividends 149; masculine gender discourses, future of 20; performance theories

9, 12–14; pluralisation of 154; plurality 8, 9; political approach to 22–5; presence 148; problematisation 128; psychological approach to 21; representations 10; and social sciences 21–2; sociological approach to 22–5; space 138; transfer of worldly knowledge 65; and varieties of masculinity, distinction between 23
*Masculinities and Culture* 22
*Masculinity and Film Performance* 12
*Masculinity: Bodies, Movies, Culture* 11
masquerade and dramaturgical performance 13
*Master, The* 22, 47, 147–9
matriarchy 148
*Mayans M.C.* 155
McCartney, Bill 24
McQuillan, D. B 71
McQuillan, M. 71
meaning-space 154
Medhurst, Andy 11
media, on fatherhood and fathers 24–5
*Me Jane* 8
men: expected role of 21; as nurturers 21; role of 24; as victims 19
Mendes, Sam 47, 109, 115, 117, 119, 120, 121, 134, 136, 137, 138, 152n7, 156
*Men's Cinema* 12
middle classes 85
mid-life crisis 108–9, 116
*Millennial Masculinity* 12
mis-initiation 22, 133, 135, 149
*Missing in Action* 134
missing paternal *see* absent father
Mitchell, Juliet 124
Mitscherlich, Alexander 11, 80, 105
*Modern Man in Search of a Soul* 30
Modleski, T. 157
Monick, E.A. 91, 158
Moore, R. 19, 117
mother(s) 128; identity 44; male mother 133, 136–7, 138; rejection of 15
Mulvey, L. 7, 28
mytho-poetic (spiritual) men's movement 2, 4, 17–18, 41, 46, 86, 87, 136

naming ceremonies 101n6
narcissism 141
Narloch, J. 55
narratives 27
Neale, Steve 8
negative masculinities 154–5

neoliberal economies 85
normative American societal expectations 64
nuclear family 83, 88, 128, 144
numinosity 64, 81

objective psyche 50
*Observer Magazine* 24
Oedipus complex 28, 128, 129, 152n1
older men, as masculine mentors 86
oppressed cultural identities 53
Ortner, S.B. 55, 82, 85
Osteen, M. 55
Oxoby, M. 67

parents 45, 47; archetype 44; parental emotional poverty 143; parental 'hole' in the psyche 105; parental hunger 45
paternal 2–3, 16, 25n1, 41, 47, 64, 65, 81, 102; absence of 15; and American Dream 56; lack of 80; as *logos* 68
paternal conflict 14–15, 16, 29
paternal control 145
paternal discourses 23
paternal frustration 109
paternal gender roles 41
paternal incestuous desires 108
paternal performative, plurality of 153
paternal phallus 148
paternal pimp 131
paternal post-feminism 67
paternal presence 106, 137
paternal relationships 11
paternal shadow 103
paternal symbols 154
paternal wisdom 145
patriarchal dividends 2, 20
patriarchy 7–8, 24, 25
Peberdy, D. 2, 9, 12, 13, 15, 16, 18, 46, 140, 142
performance of masculinity 142
performative paternal 12–14
Perry, Grayson 25
Peter Pan 101n3
phallus 89, 90–3
Pittman, F. 19
*Platoon* 134
political, and masculinity 22–5
political (pro-feminist) men's movement 4
*Political Psyche, The* 41, 106, 110
Pomerance, M. 9
popular culture 24–5
porn industry, shadow aspects of 94, 95
pornography 93

positive father 158
*Postfeminism and Paternity in Contemporary U.S. Film: Framing Fatherhood* 12
post-feminist fatherhood 67
post-Jungian concepts and approach 3–4, 5, 21, 28–31, 61; *see also* signs and symbols
post-Jungian sensitivities 153–6
post-war paternal 1–6
Potash, J.S. 31
Powrie, P. 11
primordial images 34
pro-feminist men's movement 4
Promise Keepers 24
psyche 4, 5, 24, 28, 43, 44, 49, 68, 124, 157; analytical models of 29; anima and animus's existence within 41; and archetypal images 33; of daughter 104; daughter's psyche 73; father's position within 47; female psyche 5, 105–6; and image 32; individual psyche 13, 24, 30, 33, 39, 50, 113; male psyche 5, 15, 105–6; objective psyche 50; parental 'hole' in 105; and symbolism 30
psychic darkness 100
psychic distortion 45
psychic energy, and archetype 39
psychic journey 102, 119
psychic resonance 33, 34, 36
psychic Self-actualisation 44
psychoanalysis 27–8
psychoanalytical gender biases 113
psychological art 30, 100, 156
psychological pluralism 110
psychological wholeness 114
psychology 27, 28–31
puer aeternas, or flying boy/eternal youth 101n3
*Pulp Fiction* 50
*Pursuit of Happyness, The* 55–6, 102, 145

rain 121
reactive masculinity 46
rebellious child 145–9
*Rebel Without a Cause* 1
rebirth 70–1
reconciliation 100
redeemed father 150; by rebellion 61–4; redemption of criminal father 66–9; redemption of replacement father 64–6
reductive fallacy 35
Rehling, Nicola 12, 18, 46
Reiter, Gershon 11, 80, 105, 151n1
*Remaking Men* 20

re-naming 92
reverse alchemy 61
*Revolutionary Road* 56, 62, 63, 64, 75–80, 100, 146
Richardson, C. 76, 78
right-wing policies 24
rite of passage of initiation 21
*Road to Perdition* 16, 47, 57, 66–9, 67, 92, 100, 102, 121, 125, 154
Ronnberg, A. 69, 71, 74, 76, 84, 90, 93, 121, 122, 129, 132, 140–1
Rosen, M. 55
roses 119–20, 121
Rowland, Susan 4, 31, 114
*Royal Tenenbaums, The* 2, 46
rule of the father (*logos*) 99, 101n2, 112
rural working-class, absent father 86–9
Rushing, J.H. 157
Rutherford, J. 23

sacrifice, act of 69
Samuels, Andrew 18, 20, 25n1, 25n2, 33, 38, 40, 41, 46, 47, 49, 50, 52, 86, 94, 106–7, 109, 110, 111, 150, 151n1, 151n3, 158
Sands, Z. 55
Savage Man 152n17
Schwalbe, M. 19
Schwartz, S.E. 73
*Screening the Male: Exploring Masculinities in Hollywood Cinema* 8, 10
'seduction community' seminars 152n16
Seidler, V.J. 19
self/Self 43, 44; archetypal energies of 42; journey of 58n4
semiotics 27–8, 34–7, 61, 68, 132
senex 77, 87, 88, 89, 95, 127, 142
sexualised father 151
Shadow/shadow 57, 66, 68, 82, 87, 94, 126, 130, 157; American patriarchy 70–2; archetypal aspect of 68; archetype of 49–50; aspects of the symbolic rose 123; shadow father 42, 47; shadow mother 128; side of a community 98; side of patriarchal social structures 137; side of the American Dream 143, 155; side of the rose 120; surrogate fathers 87
Shary, Timothy 12
Shwalb, D.W. 19
*Sibling Society, The* 25n6
signs and symbols 34–7, 129
Singer, T. 53, 54
Singh, Greg 8, 33, 35–6, 39, 41, 51, 93, 112, 113–14

social mobility 97
social sciences, and masculinity 21–2
societal gender norms 2
society, and masculinity 22–5
socio-political men's movement 19–20
Solondz, Todd 102
*Song of Ceylon* 36
*Sons of Anarchy* 5, 155
*Sopranos, The* 5
soul search 109
soul unconsciousness 62
*Spanish Gardener, The* 11
*Spectacular Bodies* 9
Spielberg, Steven 146, 147
spiritual awakenings 50
spiritual seeking 81
Stacey, J. 8
stage acting and screen acting, differentiates between 34
Stam, R. 27, 28
*Star Wars* 32
Steinem, Gloria 17
stereotypes 113, 158
Stevens, Anthony 6n1, 14, 38, 39, 44, 45, 70, 74, 80, 86, 91, 120, 122, 141
*Stiffed* 11, 24
Storr, Anthony 111
Strauss, Neil 152n16
subaltern masculinities 54
subcultures 88
substitute or surrogate father 44
suburbia 61, 75, 76, 144
*succeed* 32
successful art 33
successful films 36
success myth 59, 102
*Sunday Times* 24
surrogate father 68, 86–9: clash of fathers 95–100; dangers 87; guilt of 89; as pimp 89–95; Shadow aspects 87
surrogate parental role 64–6
surrogate paternal darkness 89
symbols/symbolism 30, 31, 50, 60–1, 68, 69, 70, 74, 154; cultural and natural, differences between 51; symbolic signifier systems 51
syzygy 41, 113, 114, 157

Tacey, David 4–5, 18, 19, 20, 25n2, 41, 47, 77, 86, 87, 98, 109, 118, 119, 124, 127, 128, 129, 130, 137, 140, 142, 152n17, 155, 158
Tasker, Y. 9

*Temenos* 152n6
*Terminator 2* 10
*There Will Be Blood* 5, 47, 48, 56, 70–2, 71, 100
Thornton, Sarah 88
*Three Kings, The* 134
Thumim, J. 8, 9, 10, 12
*Times, The* 24
Tincknell, E. 10
Trice, A.D. 11
Trickster 44, 49, 65, 81, 83, 101n1
*Trouble with Men, The* 11

unconscious 68
unconscious gender performance 13
underground spaces 68
universal father 4, 43, 54
unknown 61
unredeemed father 150; dark tones 70–2; incestuous father 72–5; trapped by obstacles 75–80
urine 132
Urwin, Jack 25

Van Leeuwen, M.S. 19
*Visible Fictions* 8
visionary and psychological binary 30–1

visionary art 30, 100, 156
von Franz, Marie Louise 101n3

Waddell, Terrie 29, 38
*Wall Street* 56, 146
Walsh, F. 10
war, effects on men and masculinities 133–8
water 121
Waxman, S. 152n5
Webb, Robert 25
Western (British and American) masculinity 21
*What Do Children Know?* 114
white-collar worker 78
Wild Man 12, 18, 140, 152n17
Winn, J.E. 55
Winnicott, D.W. 45, 115, 156
*Winter's Bone* 41, 57, 85, 86–9, 100, 153
workplace, real power or agency within 62–3
wounds: and initiation 135–6; psychic and physical 136; wounded child 139–45
Wright, Basil 36

*You Tarzan* 8, 11

Zipes, J. 25n3